Marketing without Wires

Targeting Promotions and Advertising to Mobile Device Users

Kim M. Bayne

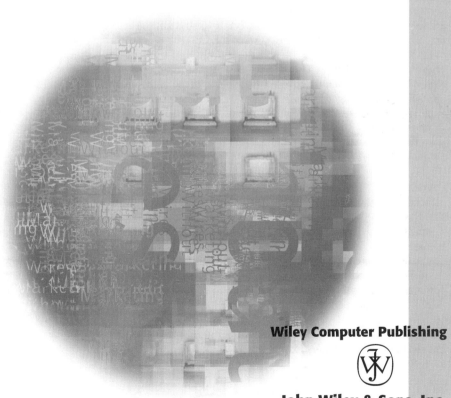

Wiley Computer Publishing

John Wiley & Sons, Inc.

Publisher: Robert Ipsen
Editor: Carol A. Long
Managing Editor: Pamela Hanley
Assistant Editor: Adaobi Obi
Associate New Media Editor: Brian Snapp
Text Design & Composition: D&G Limited, LLC

Designations used by companies to distinguish their products are often claimed as trademarks. In all instances where John Wiley & Sons, Inc., is aware of a claim, the product names appear in initial capital or ALL CAPITAL LETTERS. Readers, however, should contact the appropriate companies for more complete information regarding trademarks and registration.

This book is printed on acid-free paper. ∞

This publication is designed to provide accurate and authoritative information in regard to the subject matter covered. It is sold with the understanding that the publisher is not engaged in professional services. If professional advice or other expert assistance is required, the services of a competent professional person should be sought.

Library of Congress Cataloging-in-Publication Data:

JK

Bayne, Kim M.
  Marketing without wires : targeting promotions and advertising to mobile device users / Kim Bayne.
     p. cm.
Includes index.
  ISBN 0-471-129607 (pbk : alk. paper)
  1. Internet marketing. 2. Telemarketing. 3. Internet advertising. 4. Personal communication service systems. I. Title.
  HF5415.1265 .B394 2002
  658.8'4—dc21   2001008245

Printed in the United States of America.
10 9 8 7 6 5 4 3 2 1

CONTENTS

This book is dedicated to family and friends, but first and foremost, I dedicate it to:

Bruce Davis Bayne, my better half. Thanks for being Mr. Mom.

Kaitlyn Ruth Bayne, who will always be my "Baby Girl."

ACKNOWLEDGMENTS

My thanks go to the following people without whom I would not have started this book. Whenever I needed inspiration or needed to bounce ideas around, these folks have always been open to my e-mails and telephone calls:

Jim Sterne, who continues to amaze me with his insights and supports my new projects enthusiastically

Dan Janal, who once revealed to me that his personal trainer uses a Palm

Kristin Zhivago, who continues to think of me from time to time regarding the world of high-tech marketing communications

M. H. "Mac" McIntosh, speaker, trainer, and consultant, who is still the foremost expert in sales leads management

My thanks go to the following people without whom I would not have finished this book:

Carol A. Long, Executive Acquisitions Editor, John Wiley & Sons, Wiley Computer Publishing, who gently but firmly prodded me along, reminding me that the market was waiting

Adaobi Obi Tulton, Assistant Developmental Editor, John Wiley & Sons, Wiley Computer Publishing, who put up with dozens of e-mails from me regarding content updates and caption revisions

Additional thanks go to:

Pamela Hanley, Assistant Managing Editor, John Wiley & Sons, Wiley Computer Publishing

Erica Weinstein, Editorial Assistant, John Wiley & Sons, Wiley Computer Publishing

I'm reminded of author Jim Sterne's presentation at Internet World, titled "Fifty Ways to Leave Your Message," an obvious play on Paul Simon's song title "Fifty Ways to Leave your Lover." Since then, I've had some time to brainstorm my own version of the song, geared toward mobile handheld devices.

Fifty Ways to Leave Your Desktop

By Kim M. Bayne

"The problem is all inside your Palm," she said to me

"Going mobile's easy if you take it logically

I'd like to help you in your quest for wire-free

There must be fifty ways to leave your desktop."

She said, "It's really not my habit to intrude

Furthermore I hope my message won't be lost or misconstrued

I use SMS, at the risk of being rude

There must be fifty ways to leave your desktop.

Fifty ways to leave your desktop."

Just unplug the back, Jack

Access a new plan, Stan

Download a ring tone, Joan

Do it wirelessly

Email on the bus, Gus

You don't need to install much

Just learn graffiti, Lee

And get yourself free.

Buy a new cell, Mel

Send a quick page, Sage

Play a few games, James

Do it wirelessly

Beam a few files, Giles

Buy some batteries for the miles

Just drop off the key, Lee

And get yourself free.

And get yourself free.

Kim M. Bayne is an internationally recognized writer and former marketing executive specializing in Internet and wireless marketing communications. With a masters degree in computer resources management and more than a decade of practical, hands-on marcom experience with both corporations and agencies, she successfully bridges the gap between the creative and technical sides of high-tech marketing communications. Bayne is the author of the highly acclaimed book *The Internet Marketing Plan*, which reached No. 1 in February 1999 on Amazon.com's Best Seller List for Web Marketing. From December 1997 to May 2000, Bayne hosted the syndicated weekly public radio talk show "The Cyber Media Show with Kim Bayne," an hour-long look at Internet use, marketing strategies, and tactics.

Bayne has written breaking news, trends analysis, opinion columns, case studies, profile features, and product reviews for trade publications such as Advertising Age, American Demographics' Marketing Tools, Business Marketing, CMP Media's Planet IT Mobile Computing TechCenter, Digitrends.net, *eBusiness Advisor* magazine, *M-CommerceTimes*, and *Publish* magazine. As an expert source in digital enterprise marketing, Bayne has been interviewed and/or featured by Advertising Age, Business Marketing, CNBC TV's "The Money Wheel," Interactive Age, Marketing Computers, PR News, Sales & Marketing Management, United Airlines' *Hemispheres* and *The Washington Post*. She is a top-rated speaker at Internet conferences and seminars around the world on topics like "Using Traditional Media to Brand Web Sites," "Building Online Strategic Alliances," and "Developing A Successful Internet Marketing Plan."

CHAPTER 1

The Wireless Revolution

"You say you want a revolution. Well, you know, we all want to change the world."

*Sung by a little-known boy band called **The Beatles**, in the song "Revolution"*

I t's almost irreverent—wireless marketing, that is. The thought that a business would even consider putting advertising on a person's mobile device smacks of bad manners, right? That's probably what many veteran users thought when the Internet went commercial in the past decade and the first banner ad appeared. But with a little ingenuity and lots of respect for the user, wireless marketing can and will succeed. At the very least, the invasion of the handheld is certainly a revolution that marketers can't ignore.

What can be said of a communications vehicle that keeps people connected no matter where they go? What can be said of a media that enables us to peek into the lives of others when we least expect it? The events of September 11, 2001 taught us that mobile devices are an essential part of people's lives. Rescue workers might have never been able to communicate with fire and rescue personnel at the scene had it not been for mobile telephones. And sad but true, we might never have shared the final thoughts and moments of the lives of true American heroes. Mobile devices have changed the world.

Businesses now recognize the impact that wireless devices have on many people's daily lives. From calling a loved one to ask that dinner be kept warm to improving company communications, mobile devices are here to stay. Companies worldwide are just now tapping into the customer service potential that is inherent in mobile devices. And, in spite of the increasing availability of productivity solutions for the mobile user, the best is yet to come. Meanwhile, what is it about the wireless Web that confounds us?

What Is the Wireless Web?

The term "wireless Web" isn't the best moniker for the now-growing library of mobile-friendly content, but it's a start. Before I picked up my first wireless device, I was misinformed. Like many users, I believed that I could pull in any Web site and read any page. Oh well. Wireless it is, but the Web it isn't—at least, not yet.

In truth, there are two wireless worlds of content out there, maybe more. I'll explain. My Web site at www.kimbayne.com works well for the average wired Web visitor. It's a simple site designed to present "just the facts, ma'am." I'm a writer, and it adds no value to the user's experience if I add tons of glittery effects. You won't come to my site to win a million bucks in a hot new sweepstakes, so having an animated monkey jump all over the site would be like putting up a Web banner that says, "Kick me." To claim that my site's elementary design would not be available to the typical mobile telephone user would be absurd, so I've told myself. But you guessed it already. First, there is no typical mobile user. There are many different wireless devices on the market today and just as many reasons to use them. Second, most wired sites are not for wireless user consumption. And third, my site has frames and that's another story altogether. Now, imagine that.

For me, adding wireless to my promotional mix started with calling my current Web hosting service and inquiring about when its servers would support wireless content. I was ready to start programming in *Wireless Markup Language* (WML), if need be. Making that call was a total waste of time. Not only did the customer service representative not know the upgrade schedule, but he kept insisting that there was something wrong with my Internet-ready telephone and I should be able to see any site. Yeah, right. Thank you very much (click!).

Wait! It gets even crazier. Bear with me. Here comes my rant. You see, I managed to add my content to a *Wireless Access Protocol* (WAP) site hosting service, but I couldn't look at the site using the limited browser on my wireless PDA. A colleague in Japan couldn't see my WAP site with his mobile telephone. If you were logged on to the Internet on your desktop PC and tried to access the site with Netscape Navigator, you were up the creek without a paddle. And I'm just getting started.

In my enthusiasm for mobile media, I put together a simple Palm application that Pocket PC owners could *not* take advantage of. There's nothing like deliberately ignoring a growing portion of the mobile user base. Then, I had this conversation with the folks at my wireless carrier about adding a second line and telephone to my monthly service plan. I had an extra phone and hated having it sit on the shelf and gather dust. Well, it's still a paperweight. The carrier informed me that the phone wasn't manufactured to work with its service. (Aargh!)

So, where the heck is the Web in the wireless Web? It sounds more like a maze to me. I'm hoping that someday the industry will make the connected world a seamless experience for all users, whether tethered or untethered. Until then, the wireless Web should be renamed *segregated systems of inaccessible content and incompatible technology*. Yeah, I know. That isn't very catchy.

The Hype and the Promise

According to a report from The Boston Consulting Group, one in four users of wireless devices stops using mobile commerce, or m-commerce (another term for mobile e-commerce), applications after the first few attempts. Your mission, if you choose to accept it, is not an impossible one. You must learn to understand what interests mobile users, how to encourage their interests, and how to serve their needs.

Are You Ready for Wireless Marketing?

The concept of wireless enterprise marketing is two-fold. First, outfit your marketing staff with mobile devices. Second, add mobile devices to your marketing communications mix. In essence, you are deploying selected elements of your business presence to the mobile user base, which coincidentally also includes you and your company employees.

One great thing about mobile devices is how they appeal to both personal and professional users. If your company advertises, promotes, or otherwise markets products and services, you are ready for wireless marketing. If your company serves any type of user on the Web, you're a future mastermind of wireless marketing. If your company markets to any type of user through any other media, you are, too.

We haven't even scratched the surface on what wireless enterprise marketing could entail. Wireless marketing involves reaching and serving customers. It involves developing relationships with them. It could involve asking users to take a leap of faith and make a purchase wirelessly. Your definition of and involvement in wireless marketing is up to you. I hope that you'll contact me after your wireless marketing program is underway to share your insights and successes. I'd love to include your case study in an issue of my e-mail newsletter *Marketing Wirelessly* or in a future edition of this book.

Reasons to Market to Mobile Devices

If the Internet has taught us anything, it's that developing marketing acumen is an ever-evolving experience. How do mobile devices fit into this picture? Here are some thoughts. By 2004, the wireless market will be 29 million users strong in the United States, according to IDC. M-commerce transactions have the potential to generate $20.8 billion in the United States alone. In Europe, this number could reach $37.6 billion that same year. Europe's potential could be close to 47 million users with mobile commerce on their minds. How do you take advantage of this attractive future? If a competitive environment doesn't interest you, I don't know what will. Users expect to find timely and critical information wirelessly to make easier and quicker decisions. Your absence from the wireless arena will not make their hearts grow fonder.

The Wired Internet: Is It Dying a Slow Death?

A few industry analysts have suggested that the wired Internet is dying a slow death. It's too soon to predict how the impact of wireless will eat away at the health of the wired Web. I'd venture to say that the decline in Web advertising revenue over the past few years has been more a product of the economy and the dot-bomb fallout than the birth of a new media. Many online business failures could be attributed to a lack of Internet business savvy on the part of many would-be e-commerce millionaires.

I say that the wired Internet is far from dead and buried. The absence of full-featured computing power affects my willingness to stay on the wireless side for long periods. Not only that, but thousands of new domain names, for forthcoming wired Web sites, continue to be registered each week. New online businesses debut on the Web each day. For example, I know a small business retailer who recently launched a new e-commerce site. He's found a few product niches, and in three short months he is doing more than $9,000 in sales per month. He's good at applying what he knows about retail product sales and he has well-established supply chain connections. He places advertising strategically throughout the Web and in other media, and it's working for him. His recent venture is a latecomer to the world of e-commerce, but he's making a decent go of it for a small business. Say that the wired Internet is dead when you talk to him, and he'll scratch his head in amazement at your assumptions.

The Future of Wireless Marketing

I wish that I had a crystal ball. I'd bet on the lottery. In the absence of a crystal ball, I can only call 'em as I see 'em. I judge the future of the wireless Web by a few simple, real-world indicators. At a recent industry trade show, more mobile device manufacturers and solutions providers were exhibiting than ever before. More attendees were carrying mobile devices.

Every major telephone company is on board with wireless technology and products in some way or another. Television, print, and radio advertising, touting the convenience of mobile devices, appears daily. Appliance and transportation manufacturers are adding wireless features and functions to their products. More people are buying into the wireless world every day. It's a whole new economy, and it's moving fast. I can't ignore it. It won't go away. The customers are here. You're here reading this book. We see a future that is not bound by wires or bulky devices. We see the future of communications and commerce. If this scenario isn't proof of the future of wireless, I'm not sure what is.

Overview of the Book

This book aims to educate the reader—that's you—with an *overview* of wireless enterprise marketing and related projects. I'll tell you something up front. If you want a technical education, pick up a different book. I don't pretend to be an electrical engineer, and I don't think like one, either. Don't expect a long, tedious explanation of the history of analog telephones or well-researched diagrams detailing how mobile systems transmit data. That's not my strong suit. I will speak to you from the mindset of a former marketing communicator, however. I'm someone who has a well-rounded background with hands-on experience in using traditional, Web, and wireless media. And I actually enjoy it! All in all, I hope *you* enjoy reading this book. My writing can be a bit quirky, and I love telling stories. So, take a good look at the case studies throughout. These early-adopters are great role models for your wireless marketing plans.

This book gives you what you need to develop approaches to delivering wireless content that mobile consumers want and need. You'll discover how to evaluate and select the best implementation options and to research and create a well-executed wireless marketing program. You will learn about best practices for creating a comprehensive, wireless marketing agenda, cutting-edge case studies of early adopters who are currently setting the trends for wireless marketing, and expert tactics for linking offline and online programs for a comprehensive, integrated marketing presence.

Who Should Read This Book?

This book guides business and marketing professionals in understanding the needs of mobile device users. It leads project managers to create actionable, strategic, and tactical programs for wireless marketing success. Ideal readers for this book include the following:

- Beginning e-marketers who need help in conceptualizing how wireless enterprise marketing fits into the big picture

- Experienced Internet marketers who are ready to add wireless devices to their marketing mix

- Other business professionals who are looking for insights into building a wireless marketing program

I assume that you have some exposure to marketing already; otherwise, you won't understand basic concepts like advertising placement. If you have in-depth knowledge of Internet marketing, you might wish to skim the chapters in this book and focus on the case studies. Those who have detailed experience in measuring results and determining *return on investment* (ROI) can probably skip that chapter, because you get it already. If you have no first-hand knowledge about mobile handheld devices or Internet marketing at all, I recommend that you give this book a thorough reading. Finally, subscribe to my newsletter *Marketing Wirelessly* for an ongoing education into wireless marketing. E-mail subscribe@marketingwirelessly.com to be added to the subscriber database.

About This Book

The chapters in this book represent different functional areas in a marketing communications plan. Your plan might have more or fewer areas to consider. Often, I'll reference *information technology* (IT) activities as though they were an intimate part of the marketing communications process. When dealing with a technology that *is* the media, you can't avoid going over to the geek side. Personally, that's what makes the Internet and wireless marketing so compelling for me. Now, here is a brief overview of this book's chapters.

Chapter 1–The Wireless Revolution

Oh, hey, that's this chapter. I don't have to tell you about it. You're already reading it.

Chapter 2–Understanding the Wireless World

This chapter is an overview of wireless with simple definitions. I know that you want to get on with it, so I touch upon how certain wireless elements have an impact on your marketing. Anyway, while writing this chapter, I started to yawn when I realized that I couldn't bear the thought of explaining different cellular networks to anyone.

Chapter 3–Unplugging Marketing Communications Strategies

Put on your thinking cap. It's time to strategize. Will you go wireless alone? Who will be your partner? What is the focus of your wireless marketing initiative? This chapter gets you started by posing questions that only you can answer.

Chapter 4–Chartering Your Wireless Marketing Team

This chapter helps you decide who is going to play on your team. It's like the children's game of Red Rover, isn't it? To humble those playground bullies, ask them to take the quiz titled "What's Your Wireless Marketing IQ?"

Chapter 5–Building the Wireless Brand

Yes, a mobile device can have an effect on your branding activities. But mobile branding can get sticky because technology tends to get in the way. This chapter looks at branding through the mobile user's eyes. Plus, I throw in a few (gasp!) technical tips on how to fix minor mobile branding glitches.

Chapter 6–Advertising without Wires

The mobile user has certain expectations, and your advertising should fulfill them. This chapter will highlight current wireless advertisers and how they are reaching the mobile audience. By the way, don't dump your traditional and Web advertising just yet. You're going to need it.

Chapter 7–Delivering Content to Wireless Devices

This chapter challenges naysayers who claim that there isn't anything good on the wireless Web. Got something to say? Share it with the mobile user. Oh yeah, don't flip to these pages to find out how to code in WML. I didn't write about that. But you will get some good ideas on what type of content users want.

Chapter 8–Untethering Public Relations and Publicity

This chapter is my favorite. In another life, I was personally responsible for high-tech media relations and garnering as much ink as possible. This chapter contains some cool case studies of *public relations* (PR) practitioners at their best. It was exciting to see wireless marketers put things into action that I'd always dreamed about.

Chapter 9–Enabling Mobile Commerce Sales and Finance

Have you ever thought about the mobile point-of-sale? Is there such a beast? This chapter will define it for you. Plus, you'll find out that mobile sales applications aren't just for the customer. Your sales staff will like them, too.

Chapter 10–Mobilizing Customer Service

If you're thinking about applying current customer service practices to mobile customer service, this chapter will tell what works and what doesn't. And you might want to rethink that e-mail response system you're using.

Chapter 11–Measuring Wireless Marketing Results

Just because you can measure something, should you? This chapter will talk about the current possibilities. This chapter is a review of typical measurement activities, rephrased in wireless marketing terms.

Chapter 12—Budgeting for a Wireless Future

This chapter is the final wrap-up for all of the other budget line items I've touched upon throughout the book. This chapter is best read after you've completed the rest of the book. Then and only then will you have a good concept of what pulling together a wireless marketing program involves.

Tools You Will Need

In order to perform certain tasks as a wireless marketer, it would be a good idea to own a device or two. I provide lots of screen shots, so if you don't have a certain device handy, don't worry—you'll still be able to figure out what I mean.

If you have a mobile telephone but haven't enabled its Internet service yet, here's your justification. Looking for an excuse to buy a *personal digital assistant* (PDA) or two-way pager? This book is that excuse. Mobile devices are personal so I won't make any brand recommendations. You'll notice by my examples in the book where most of my experience lies, but that could change tomorrow as we all discover new wireless toys. I'm about as fickle as the technology I write about. Don't let that color your thinking if you choose a different device or two. The practical marketing examples still apply.

What's on the Web Site

The complementary Web site addresses for this book are www.marketingwithoutwires.com and www.marketingwirelessly.com. You'll find content related to this book in the form of newsletters and article links.

And So . . .

This book will help you get a handle on the latest and greatest star of the marketing world: mobile devices. The examples throughout will make it easier for you to integrate mobile devices and their users into your daily marketing activities. I hope you will enjoy reading about wireless marketing as much as I enjoy writing about it. As your programs develop, please drop me a line. I want to know about them. Just e-mail author@kimbayne.com. TTFN (ta ta for now)!

CHAPTER 2

Understanding the Wireless World

"Don't know much about history. Don't know much biology. Don't know much about science books. Don't know much about the French I took."

From the song "What a Wonderful World" as sung by Herman's Hermits, Otis Redding, Sam & Dave, James Taylor, Art Garfunkel, and several others

I f you don't know much about wireless devices, don't worry. You're not alone. While thousands of geeks attend technology trade shows each year to preview the latest bleeding-edge products, the rest of the buying population is still managing to get by without them. During a recent parent-teacher conference, I took out my Palm handheld and a portable folding keyboard to make some notes. The conversation quickly turned to my gadgets, and before I knew it we weren't talking about class assignments or the curriculum anymore. Suddenly, the teachers were distracted and engaged in looking at my cool toys. Of course, that didn't mean that they actually wanted them. They were just fascinated. Yes, the school had wired computers in every classroom, so Web access wasn't the attraction. It was these scaled-down doodads that piqued their interest (for a while, anyway). So, I shared. It made me realize that new technology is such a big part of my life that I've lost track of whether it is for everybody else. But I have hope.

Wireless devices are like the Internet was a decade ago. Back then, the average businessperson might have used computers but might not have been exposed to the Internet yet. Once a person heard about the Internet, it might have been a while before he or she logged on. Soon, that person was sending e-mail every day at work and eventually got to surf the Web. Finally, he or she signed up for an *America Online* (AOL) account for his or her home computer, and the rest is history. Widespread acceptance of new technology is often a gradual thing among the general populace. This situation compares quite nicely to what's happening now with mobile devices.

The main difference between Internet and wireless access is the devices. Mobile telephones are more prevalent than computers in many parts of the world. Many people consider it essential to have a mobile phone so that the kids can reach them after band practice. They don't consider it essential to pack a PDA in a pocket or purse (at least, not yet). In that regard, wireless telephone carriers score a few extra points. Now that they have squeezed Internet features into most new mobile telephones, your friends and relatives can't help but get their first taste of the wireless Web. And the rest will be history.

About This Chapter

This chapter is an overview of wireless. For the novice, I'll provide a bare bones definition of mobile devices along with their potential for functionality. In a few cases, I'll make you think about how this information applies to your marketing. You might not have thought in terms of how the media (wireless) affects the marketing (advertising, for example), but believe me, you will.

A Wireless Primer

It never ends, does it? You've learned about cookies, advertising banners, and secure e-commerce servers. Now, you need to come up to speed on wireless. Well, here's some help, divided into small chunks of digestible matter.

What Is a Mobile Device?

For the purposes of this book, I've defined a mobile device within the confines of computing and telecommunications. Mobile devices are electronic gadgets that are owned and operated by both personal and professional users. Mobile devices are by definition portable, which translates to freedom for the user. This freedom creates different marketing opportunities for companies that employ business-to-consumer, business-to-business, or both types of channels. That's simple enough, isn't it?

There are three main types of mobile devices discussed in this book: Internet-ready telephones, PDAs, and pagers.

Internet-ready telephones. These days, most mobile or cellular telephone handsets—illustrated by Figure 2.1—are enabled to receive data from the

Figure 2.1 The Ericsson R600 mobile phone has enhanced messaging features, and the background light can link to one's personal contacts list for identifying callers. (© Copyright 2001-2003 Sony Ericsson Mobile Communications. All rights reserved.)

Internet, either through e-mail or through a resident mini-browser used to view wireless-ready Web sites. Data entry through mobile telephones can be annoying at first, but users get used to it eventually.

As a side note, your wireless marketing plan should address more than just the Web-related features of mobile telephones. Consider voice-specific programs as well, and I don't mean incoming telemarketing, either. Over the next couple of years, voice-activated menu-driven telephone services will blossom, creating yet another way for you to serve the mobile customer.

PDAs. PDAs were first launched to help make users' lives easier, hence the name "personal digital assistants." Resident functions include applications like a date book or calendar, address book, to do lists, and memo or notepads. PDAs are pocket- or palm-size devices (Figure 2.2) that can sometimes be made wireless through the addition of modems. Many newer PDAs come with internal modems, which really does make life easier. Data entry on PDAs can also be annoying, but it is not nearly as bad as the thumb-entry method used by telephone users. Users enter data by using a pen stylus and handwriting recognition software or by tapping a miniature

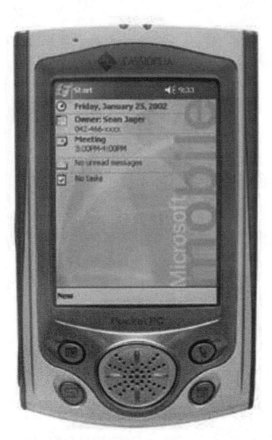

Figure 2.2 The Casio Cassiopeia E-200 Pocket PC offers users expandability and optional wireless Internet connectivity. (Used with permission of Casio. Casio is a registered trademark of Casio Computer Co., Ltd., Tokyo, Japan.)

on-screen keypad. Users can also attach an external full-size keyboard or type on a built-in mini-keyboard (Figure 2.3), depending on the make and model of the mobile handheld device.

Most PDAs resemble smaller versions of devices first seen on the classic science fiction TV show *Star Trek*. In just about every episode, Captain James Tiberius Kirk would sign off on duty rosters and other reports on an electronic clipboard of sorts. *Star Trek: The Next Generation* showed us smaller versions of the device that became a prototype for most palmtop devices in use today. Looking back, it appears that the 1960s TV show might have inspired Microsoft designers to create the Tablet PC.

Pagers. Pagers, formerly known as *beepers*, used to be these ugly gray or black devices that hung on a user's belt buckle, making an awful beep-beep-beep racket. Someone, like your boss, would dial a telephone number and

Figure 2.3 Cirque's Pocket Keyboard provides an alternative method of data entry to the PDA user.

enter his telephone number to alert your device plus everyone else in the room. Eventually, pagers toned it down with vibrating functions. That inspired me to call my own pager so I could use it to massage my neck and shoulders for a few seconds. (Just kidding!) Personally, I was glad when we were first able to send e-mail to someone's device rather than stop to pick up the telephone. These days, pagers run the gamut from tiny matchbook-sized toys in neon orange that only receive text-based data to the more complex personal computing devices with color screens and mini-keyboards (Figure 2.4).

Sure, there are more than three types of mobile devices. High-end *global positioning systems* (GPS) are one example. But these other contraptions don't play a vital role in the average enterprise's marketing communications. Chances are that your advertising and promotional initiatives won't target customers while they're engaged in using other gizmos.

In this book, I'll waffle back and forth between different device types while talking about marketing strategies and tactics. I'll reference mobile Internet-ready telephones occasionally. But most of the time, I'll fixate on PDAs because they offer more functionality to the average device owner. In fact, this book contains an overabundance of Palm references because the majority of PDA users *were* Palm users when I wrote this book.

Figure 2.4 The Motorola Accompli personal communicator offers a combination of features, including Internet access, a QWERTY keyboard, and a 256-color screen. (© Motorola, Inc.)

Device Functionality

The mobile device world is multifaceted. Single-purpose gadgets have evolved into multi-purpose ones. Manufacturers are going the way of convergence, creating all-in-one telephones that function as PDAs. There are also PDAs that function as telephones. Everyone wants to make a device that is the definitive entry point to the wireless Web (see Figure 2.5).

When it comes to actually accessing the Web, Internet-ready telephone subscribers often rely on tiered menus of content as decided upon by each wireless carrier. Such menus are not an issue with PDA users, who can pretty much pick and choose what's available on their device. Software, such as Web clipping applications that grab Web pages, are prevalent in the PDA world, as shown in Figure 2.6. Several portal Web sites exist for users who want to download new applications for free or for a fee.

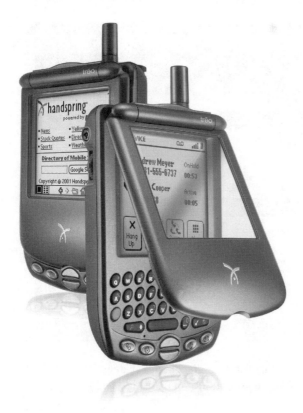

Figure 2.5 The Handspring Trèo—Is it a telephone, a personal organizer, or a wireless PDA? (Courtesy of Handspring, Inc.)

Getting Information onto Mobile Devices

Depending on your marketing objectives, you'll be concerned with reaching device users who grab data in one of two ways:

1. **Wireless access.** With a modem, the device makes a wireless connection to the Internet via a network.

2. **Synchronization.** Without a modem, the device compares and matches data with a computer by using a cradle or a cable, as seen in Figure 2.7.

One other way to get data onto a mobile device is by beaming. For example, users can aim the infrared (IR) ports of their PDAs at each other to exchange applications and other files. This function might not apply much to the big marketing picture, but you should be aware of it nonetheless. At some point, you will invent some pretty creative reasons for beaming data to another device

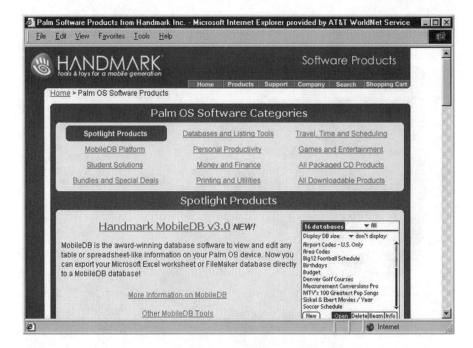

Figure 2.6 Handmark, Inc., highlights several different categories of available software for Palm OS® users. (© 2002 Handmark, Inc. All rights reserved.)

user. At the very least, you could always share that freeware version of solitaire if a meeting drags on too long.

Static versus Dynamic Mobile Content

Here's what I've decided about mobile device content. You've got your static mobile content and your dynamic mobile content.

Static content. This content is dead and unchanging. What's there is there. The only update that a user will ever see is in the next version of the hardware or software. PDA users have a bit more freedom to download and install new stuff, which is why I'm so partial to these devices. But there's no guarantee that the user will do it. With services like AvantGo or Vindigo, the user has the computer do all the work, which works better than reminding users to update manually. The systems synchronize the latest content while connected to the Internet so that the user doesn't have to perform this task. Once you've invited the user to add a link to your content to his AvantGo account, the rest is a matter of daily habit (at least, we hope). Right before a business trip, I make sure that I synchronize PDA content via the Internet. The content doesn't get updated again until three to five days later, which means that your company could be out of luck if you have something to say

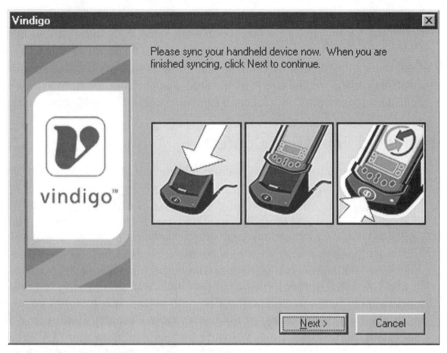

Figure 2.7 The installation screen on Vindigo shows the user how to install its travel-related application onto a PDA. (© Vindigo)

to me between now and then. Take your best shot before I become unreachable for a few days. Anyway, examples of static content might be clipped pages from a Web site, a database, or a help file.

Dynamic content. This content is alive and ever-changing. The user can update it immediately, even on a minute-by-minute basis. A mobile device user with wireless access can pull in the latest information in a few seconds. If I'm constantly surfing the wireless Web, to use an inaccurate phrase, you can reach me a lot sooner than if I clip data once a week. If your content has a time-sensitive aspect, like news, you have a better chance of reaching me when I'm on the road. Examples of dynamic content might be news briefs, weather updates, and stock prices.

These types of content aren't totally exclusive of each other. But you'll want to think about *changing* versus *unchanging* content so you can make strategic decisions about their makeup and delivery.

Impact on Marketing

Why should marketers care about the frequency of content updates? You won't always have the opportunity to update content or applications once they're installed on or received by someone's device. By recognizing that users might not come back to get your latest software version or file, you can make more strategic decisions about what will reside within an application versus what the user must clip from the Web. By becoming aware of the delay in delivering information to certain users, you might also be able to time your marketing messages to coincide with a user's typical content acquisition schedule.

The Handheld Popularity Contest

When you first think of a mobile handheld device like a PDA, which one comes to mind? Palm? Visor? Pocket PC? Something completely different? I hope I'm not offending anyone by initiating a discussion of handheld preferences. It's like asking someone if he or she prefers IBM to Macintosh. I lost count of the office politics and arguments that broke out, and continue to break out, over that religious debate.

But let's go back to that question of handheld popularity. There's no use giving you any solid numbers on current PDA unit shipments. It would be an exercise in futility. Palm is at the top of the list for now. Compaq, Handspring, HP, RIM, and Casio follow behind Palm in varied order. And then there's Microsoft. Yes, the Pocket PC could leapfrog over all other handheld devices in the next few years. If it does, plenty of content in this book will need revision along with most of the screen shots. I'll worry about that when it happens.

Growth in the handheld market has had its ups and downs of late. The dribbling economy has created revenue woes for technology companies trying to stay afloat (sales down). The September 11 tragedy reminded many of us how important it is to stay in touch. That fact alone has encouraged individuals to purchase more mobile telephones for emergency and other reasons (sales up). Delays in product shipments and other U.S. mail issues have caused corporate buyers to put purchasing plans on hold (sales down). Trade show management has increased conference hall security, asking attendees to leave laptops at the hotel. As a result, many business travelers have switched their on-the-road computing to handheld devices (sales up). Proprietary operating systems have made it difficult for longtime handheld users to migrate to other devices (sales down). Product development plans of various companies have swayed investors from one company to another (sales up and down). There are a million reasons why the mobile handheld market is so manic.

Impact on Marketing

Why should marketers care about device popularity? By tracking handheld sales trends, you might be able to anticipate certain changes in your customer base a year or even five years from now. Below are a few points to address as you formulate strategies for targeting mobile device users. Consider how your recognition of these issues will affect your marketing tactics in such disciplines as advertising, collateral, PR, and so on.

Which device platforms are your current customers using, and which devices are they likely to use in the future? (Warning: These factors might influence advertising creative and collateral development.)

To which devices will you target your promotional messages? (Warning: This factor might influence advertising creative, ad server network selection, and perhaps public relations.)

Who can handle the delivery of your ad message to multiple wireless platforms and users? (Warning: This factor might influence advertising creative, ad placement, and ad server network selection.)

Do you need to publish marketing material or deploy a wireless site for more than one platform? (Warning: This factor might influence collateral creative, copywriting, and literature distribution.)

If you create something for PDA users, how soon will you need to recreate it for other handheld users? (Warning: This factor might influence collateral development and distribution.)

You might still want some solid numbers about handheld sales to plug into your wireless marketing plan. In that case, go to the Web, make a few telephone calls, pick up a trade journal, and get the latest information. FYI, Gartner, Dataquest, and Jupiter Media Metrics are a few technology firms whose past reports have tracked the leader in the handheld sales race. Check back with industry trend watchers frequently as you develop your wireless marketing plan.

Research firms aren't the only people who can provide insights into where you should concentrate your marketing efforts. Check out who has developed strategic partnerships with the various handheld manufacturers. Is Palm your focus? The Palm operating system is the foundation for products from several companies including Acer, Franklin Covey, HandEra, Handspring, IBM, Kyocera, Samsung, Sony, and Symbol Technologies, according to a November 8, 2001 news release by Palm, Inc. Platform licensees also include AlphaSmart, Garmin, and Nokia. During your market research, visit mobile portal sites like Handango.com to count the number of applications for each platform. That by itself should highlight some industry momentum to support your decision-making.

PDAs and The Mobile Office

Now that I've focused primarily on PDAs, let's talk about software. Just what can a PDA do?

PDAs just don't have the same computing power as desktop and laptop computers just yet, so available applications aren't as full featured. But PDAs can get close enough for mobile office work.

Most of the basic needs of a PDA user are included with the product. Device manufacturers throw in a few extra goodies just to sweeten the deal and to get the software acquisition ball rolling. Once the user tires of the basic stuff, he or she ventures out to the Web to gather more. Available applications usually fall into one of several categories, including business and professional, personal productivity, and entertainment.

PDA applications offer varying degrees of functionality. Business applications like Quickoffice by Cutting Edge Software combine three applications into one package, enabling the mobile user to complete word processing, spreadsheet, and charting duties, as captured in Figure 2.8. Other applications are limited to single-function, such as iMessenger, which enables only e-mail sending and receiving. Many documents offer data synchronization with sister applications that reside on a computer. Some PDA applications offer the user the ability to merge or input data into widely used software like Microsoft Word or Excel. Applications can include password keepers, event reminders, calculator upgrades, language translation, currency conversion, and sales management tools. Reference tools like dictionaries, telephone directories, and guidebooks make up a big portion of the PDA market as well.

Dualing Standards

The biggest problem anyone will encounter when trying to reach mobile device users is the rule of multiples. There are multiple operating systems, multiple

 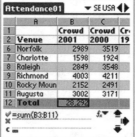 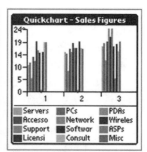

Figure 2.8 Palm OS® users can use Quickoffice to compose a mid-year report, track attendance at recent trade shows, or graph m-commerce sales figures.

networks, multiple protocols, multiple standards, and multiple languages with which to fight over the wireless space.

A WAP on the Side of the Head

Wireless Access Protocol (WAP) is one of the industry specifications for wireless applications used by networks that deliver them. Around 1997, WAP standards were published when a bunch of wireless carriers like Nokia, Motorola, and Ericcson got together. In the United States, WAP has gotten a lot of visibility because most mobile telephone users are familiar with viewing WAP sites. In other countries, like Japan, WAP is not so hot, which means that the jury is still out on the best way to make wireless access work.

This is a marketing book and not a technical treatise on wireless technology, so there won't be any nitty-gritty explanation of this protocol or that protocol or this network or that network. Just be aware that not all devices can view all wireless data, because competing standards exist.

It's not like the wired Web at all. On the Web, you can view a Web page coded in *Hypertext Markup Language* (HTML) regardless of which browser you open. Sure, there are a few formatting glitches once in a while because there are so many revisions of HTML in use today, but for the most part, if a user is logged onto an *Internet service provider* (ISP), he or she can easily view Web pages anywhere in the world. But normal Web pages can't be read by mobile telephones because the phone and its network can't handle it. What happens when I try to look at my wired site on a telephone? See Figure 2.9.

Impact on Marketing

This situation means that your global marketing plan won't be global if you can't find a way to deliver material to multiple users. Some wireless service providers have solved that problem for marketers. You'll meet a few of them in this book.

Summary: Top Five Expert Tips

1. Your budget or other resources might not be able to court every mobile user right now. There are different devices and different networks, so you might need to prioritize your target mobile audiences.

2. Differences in how often a user updates mobile content can affect your marketing communications timing and content choices. Plan accordingly.

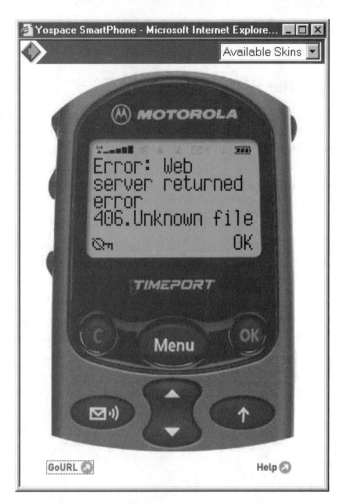

Figure 2.9 Using a Web-based telephone emulator, the user tries to access www.kimbayne.com. No luck. (Telephone image © Motorola, Inc. SmartPhone Emulator © 1999–2001 Yospace Holdings Ltd. Used with permission.)

3. Don't sweat over the technology. Just be aware that competing standards exist, creating another step in the content delivery and marketing process.

4. Reaching mobile device users involves the marketer's willingness to scale down features and content to the essentials. Low-bandwidth issues make it hard for users to pull in everything you want them to see.

5. Mobile devices were designed to make users' lives easier. Your marketing communications plans should address the unique needs of this mobile, on-the-go user. Don't reinvent the Web. Mobile users aren't interested.

CHAPTER 3

Unplugging Marketing Communications Strategies

"If I could turn back time, if I could find a way, I'd take back those words that have hurt you and you'd stay."

As sung by Oscar-winning actress and pop music diva *Cher*

When my daughter was very little, we had an agreement. Whenever she did something inappropriate, such as cutting in line or interrupting, she would automatically get one "rewind" which was her opportunity to make it right. I would pretend that the incident never occurred, and we would replay the last few minutes but with a better outcome. As Kaitlyn gets older, she's learning her requests to turn back time won't be granted as often. This lesson has become very meaningful since she entered middle school. Kaitlyn has to approach her tasks more strategically and plan accordingly. She has to look ahead and decide what her goals will be for each project. She must find ways to meet her goals in a professional, efficient manner and execute accordingly. As a result, we're all a lot happier with her report cards these days.

In business, the customer doesn't always give companies a second chance, and market losers pay the consequences. Are you happy with your Internet marketing report card? If you could turn back time on your e-business programs, what would you do differently? Would you take a novel approach to customer service or content offerings so that online users would return more often and actually stay? And how would this action affect your long-term plans to increase sales revenue and market share? Well, as much as you'd like to turn back time on your marketing mistakes, you can only move forward. Fortunately, mobile handheld devices have provided you with another opportunity to do so. You now have a new and different reason for forging useful marketing strategies. It's called wireless.

About This Chapter

This chapter will ask you tons of questions about your mobile marketing strategy. I can't answer a single one of them for you. The purpose of this chapter is to get you thinking about what it will take to succeed in wireless marketing. Actually, the real purpose of this chapter is to get you thinking about what it will take for *your company* to succeed. Your results might differ from your competitor. Keep the questions in this chapter in the back of your mind as you read through this book.

What Strategy?

Army generals will tell you that strategy is a science and an art that involves engaging all the resources you have at your disposal to accomplish certain objectives, a definition confirmed by the Encyclopædia Britannica. Well, marketing might be an art, but it sure isn't a true science. That's why so many marketing people say one thing (strategy) then do something else (tactics).

Whenever a new media emerges, someone's first crack at "strategy" always includes reusing preexisting marketing material and adapting it, rather then creating something new or better. I'm happy to see that industry players join me in questioning this single-minded approach.

"M-business isn't about squeezing a watered-down version of your Web site onto a smaller device; it's about building a personalized solution that adds value to your customers and your business," summarizes a Netmorf.com ad placed in the December 7, 2000 issue of *The Industry Standard's Wireless News*. Don't say that I didn't warn you. Repurposing by itself isn't the best approach to mobile marketing. So, what is?

In a report entitled "Mobile Wireless Internet Briefing: A Guide To The Marketplace, Technologies & Solutions," by the Intermarket Group LP, two main points provide insight into formulating a workable wireless marketing strategy:

Wireless is part of the overall e-business strategy. Mobile programs must center on retaining current customers by enhancing communication and customer service, according to the report.

Wireless means connected from anywhere, anytime. Assume that customers and staff will want to get in touch with your company more easily through whatever tool is available—telephone, e-mail, or wireless.

The report goes on to emphasize that mobile strategies that focus on specific targets have a better chance of succeeding than those that try to focus on the global marketplace. Finally, applications should leverage the unique characteristics of mobile devices.

Just to set the tone, here are some other ideas to think about while deciding on your approach to mobile strategy.

Goals and objectives. What is the purpose of your mobile marketing campaign? Do you have an objective in sight that's attainable and measurable?

Target market. Who are your wireless customers? Are they the same people who visit you on the Web? How do they compare to the customers who shop your catalog or your retail store? Will your current customers be interested in visiting you wirelessly?

Buying habits. Why do customers visit or buy from companies like yours? Is it branding? Is it value? How much do features play a role in why your customers buy?

Market research. What does your research tell you about what your mobile users want and need? Are you even in a position to ask yet?

Mobile offerings. How can you tailor your offerings to apply to the mobile marketplace? Do you need to create new products and services that fit the mobile space?

Implementation. Who can help you execute a mobile marketing program, or at the very least, share in some of the responsibilities? Is your staff big enough, savvy enough, or dedicated enough to do what it takes? If not, how helpful will your advertising or PR agency be in this quest?

Partner opportunities. Who would be a good partner(s) to help you achieve your mobile marketing goals? Do you offer something unique that can attract thousands of users? How can you convey this value to a wireless carrier or network?

The marketing mix. And finally, how will the wireless channel fit into your overall marketing communications program? How does mobile marketing complement your business model?

These are the questions that you'll ask yourself repeatedly as you read this book, as you discuss your plans with your colleagues, and after you've already launched your wireless marketing presence.

Do You Have a Mobile Mission?

The decision to go wireless shouldn't be taken lightly. Sure, you can dabble in applications and ideas, but a real purpose would be nice. While that thought is assaulting your marketing psyche, take a moment to snicker at these obtuse possibilities offered laughingly by the Web site Flounder's Mission Statement Generator:

- It is our job to authoritatively facilitate highly efficient strategic theme areas and continue to proactively communicate diverse meta-services so that we may endeavor to completely customize competitive materials with 100% on-time delivery.

- Our first priority is to continually build interoperable services to allow us to seamlessly integrate an expanded array of strategic theme areas in order to intrinsically leverage other's economically sound core competencies to set us apart from the competition.

- Our mission is to globally develop unique potentialities in order that we may assertively maintain competitive paradigms because that is what the customer expects.

- We have committed to dramatically communicate just in time testing procedures in order to credibly re-invent alternative supply chains for 100% customer satisfaction.

- We strive to credibly administrate unique value while continuing to competently re-invent orthogonal potentialities in order to solve business problems.

- We envision to holistically engineer parallel initiatives so that we may collaboratively utilize scalable alignments to stay competitive in tomorrow's world.

Did any of these statements make sense to you? Me neither. Here are a few down-to-earth reasons to reposition your products and services within the wireless media channel:

Improve customer relationship management.

Encourage more customer feedback.

Perform data collection anywhere.

Gain more control over inventory management.

Expedite order processing and tracking.

Improve project management.

Enable sales force automation.

Like most professionals, you don't have time to create indecipherable statements about your wireless marketing initiative. Let's get down to business.

Identify Your Wireless Niche

The research firm Strategy Analytics predicted that sales of wireless handheld sets would reach $440 million by the end of 2001. For a more recent view, Cahners In-Stat Group said the total number of world telephone subscribers would be about 91 million by 2005. No matter who has the best numbers or insights, you must admit: you can't possibly reach and serve everybody. So, who's it going to be?

Define the target audience for your mobile presence. Make your definition very precise. Make your description apply only to your company's products and services. Does your target definition resemble any of these statements?

- Adult female drivers older than 25 years of age interested buying a new automobile
- Consumers who enjoy shopping
- Male and female business professionals, ages 27 to 35, with household incomes of $100,000 or more
- Members of the local community
- People on the go
- Property managers responsible for interior decorating
- Tourists and residents of Wyoming seeking a wholesome family summer activity
- Video, film, and audio professionals in need of ongoing education and training

Not all of these statements will be useful in formulating a decent marketing strategy. Which of these definitions have the best chance of helping an enterprise marketer formulate a strong plan? Which have the least chance? Take a moment to mentally rank these audience definitions in order.

While doing research for this book, I lost track of how many marketing executives gave me a vague portrait of their wireless market segment. Phrases such as "Buyers interested in high-quality products" sounded silly to me. I wondered how many buyers were interested in low-quality products and how soon I could launch a business to serve this indiscriminate body of customers.

If you're vague about your mobile customers' identity and lifestyle, you might never understand their buying habits. The more nebulous your audience definition, the harder it will be to meet its needs. The next time someone reveals a marketing strategy that includes nearly everybody, recognize it for what it is—untargeted and unquantifiable.

Will a mass-marketing approach work in an unplugged world? Early indicators say no. Market segmentation is essential to mobile marketing success. Without market segmentation, mobile marketing outcomes can't be predicted or planned. But once you identify your user, you can focus on why your user buys and how to encourage him or her to do so.

Mercedes-Benz and Windwire

Unveiling a car called the C-Coupe in the United States meant that Mercedes-Benz would need to add a new media touch to its advertising campaign. Traditionally, its main audience was age 27 to late 30s with a household income of more than $100,000. These buyers were professionals, both male and female. Mercedes-Benz knew that it had to generate the right sales leads.

From a practical standpoint, wherever the targeted car buyer turned, he saw the C-Coupe. Mercedes-Benz chose the right Internet and TV properties for the launch. Still, it knew that part of its target market was on the wireless Web, and it had to reach this population somehow. It chose wireless advertising network WindWire to hand-pick the right wireless sites. WindWire afforded Mercedes-Benz one more avenue to achieve the comprehensive coverage that the C-Coupe needed. Marketing executives felt that associating the C-Coupe with a progressive and innovative medium like wireless would enhance the car's branding.

The targeted platforms were Internet-ready telephones (as seen in Figure 3.1) and PDAs owned by users who accessed channels like Sporting News. The full wireless marketing blitz included a sweepstakes to win a C-Coupe and/or a way for interested users to "get the scoop on the new C-Coupe." The campaign's goal was fairly straightforward. The company simply wanted buyers to come to dealer showrooms for a test drive, as encouraged in Figure 3.2.

What was so special about this wireless campaign? David Wilson and Billy Purser at WindWire clued me in.

Targeted demographics. Mercedes-Benz needed to reach a "mover and shaker" audience. Wireless meets that demand, and specific wireless content properties also met that demand.

Good creativity. The ads had "nice copy." On PDAs, the image displayed well, as seen in Figure 3.3, and the layout enabled the user to identify with the Mercedes logo.

Ease of response. The wireless ad made it easy for users to respond. When courting mobile users, marketers must rely on a less-complex interface because there's no mouse and keyboard for interaction. Interaction has to be based on a one-click operation without a lot of data entry.

Good offer. Coupled with a sweepstakes, the offer attracted qualified interest. Asked whether sweepstakes was a good promotional vehicle for mobile marketing, Wilson replied, "I don't think there's anything about wireless that makes sweepstakes more or less important."

Novelty. The automobile was a brand new product, generating interest on its own.

Uncluttered medium. When Internet users see an ad on the wired Web, it takes up a small part of the screen or is accompanied by six or seven other ads. After a while, the user ignores these ads. But even if a user is interested in the message, it can be hard to focus attention. When a viewer is watching TV or listening to the radio, the media typically dominates that space. In print, the reader is turning pages. He or she will typically see a full-page ad for a Mercedes and then move on. But on mobile devices, the user sees the ad, it gets his or her attention, and the customer is less distracted. There is a greater chance that he or she will interact with a wireless ad, which gives it a big advantage over the same ad placed on the wired Web.

How did this mobile advertising campaign fare? Results started coming in, and they were better than expected. The targeted placements did an excellent job in terms of performance and generating leads. Started in late June 2001, the wireless ad campaign had already achieved a 4 percent response rate to its test drive offer by October and it hadn't even run its course. Preliminary tallies point to a 4.5 percent response rate. According to WindWire, that's four to five times better than typical response rates on the wired Web.

Figure 3.1 Mobile travelers on ConvertIt.com had an opportunity to click through to get more information on the new Mercedes-Benz. (Mercedes ad © Copyright 2001–2002 DaimlerChrysler AG. Wireless site © 2000–2002 ConvertIt.com, Inc. All rights reserved. Screen capture courtesy of WindWire, Inc.)

Figure 3.2 Just enter your zip code and Mercedes-Benz will locate the nearest dealer. (Mercedes ad © Copyright 2001–2002 DaimlerChrysler AG. Screen capture courtesy of WindWire, Inc.)

Figure 3.3 Mobile users can win a C-Class Sports Coupe or other prizes. (Mercedes ad © Copyright 2001–2002 DaimlerChrysler AG. Screen capture courtesy of WindWire, Inc.)

Analyze Purchase Behavior

In October 2001, NPD INTELECT Market Tracking reported that sales of PDAs grew by 11.9 percent in August 2001. Palm had a 51.2 percent of the market share, having lost ground due to aggressive pricing and product development strategies of Handspring and Sony. Market conditions had worsened. Sales were down from a 207.5 percent increase tallied for August 2000.

In the study, the top five reasons for purchasing one PDA over another were as follows (see Table 3.1):

"This reaffirms advertising efforts by manufacturers to focus on brand when touting their products," concluded Stephen Baker, senior hardware analyst for NPD INTELECT. The Aberdeen Group predicts that the PDA market could be worth $6.6 billion by 2005. Combine these two reports, and you have a fairly significant market to target with brand-oriented marketing.

But just who is buying these devices? NPD INTELECT's survey highlighted that 70 percent of PDA buyers are male, ages 25 to 54, and most of them bought their devices because they had faith in the brand. That age span covers quite a bit of the population. How well can this data be applied to a marketing campaign for Pocket PC software, handheld accessories, or even your offerings? I think you need a few more pieces of data before you proceed.

Conduct Custom Primary Research

Some companies do an excellent job of keeping track of, analyzing, and understanding users' needs. They conduct their own regular focus groups and usability studies. They gather useful data through telephone interviews, Internet

Table 3.1 Top Five Reasons for Purchasing One PDA over Another, as Reported by NPD INTELECT Market Tracking

REASON	PERCENTAGE OF BUYERS
It's a brand that I trust.	31%
It has the latest technology.	19.5%
The product had the features that I wanted.	12.9%
It was recommended by a friend or relative.	10.3%
The brand is a good value for the money.	10%

Source: NPD Online Research and NPD TechWorld[SM], October 2001.

surveys, and online focus groups with their customers. These companies even apply these reports to ongoing product development.

Now, if the idea of gathering your own primary research bothers you, you can easily grab someone else's data to help you justify your wireless presence if you have the budget. A word of warning—at best, most industry-wide reports give you a broad overview of the market with a few paltry insights that might be specific to your company. If you're lucky, you can massage these insights to sound like they fit your business model. Generic industry research is just a start. After that, you really have to know your own users.

Once you've identified your mobile users, it's time to tap into their hands-on expertise and ask for their help. A little compensation wouldn't hurt, either. I hear that's what Yahoo! does in order to maintain its competitive edge—it pays users for their time. I'll bet such primary research is a lot more valuable than someone's one-size-fits-all research strategy, and it's certainly a lot more personalized.

CoolSavings Asks My Opinion

One day I logged into my account at CoolSavings.com to print some coupons for grocery shopping. I had been invited to complete a wireless survey directly related to CoolSavings' future plans for marketing in the mobile space. For those of you who don't know this Web coupon provider, CoolSavings works with advertisers such as NetGrocer, Barnes and Noble, Kmart, and Chuck E. Cheese.

Let's think about why this company would be a good prospect for mobile marketing:

- Advertisers look to CoolSavings as a way to drive qualified traffic. Coupons, free samples, rebates, and other discount offers cut through the mishmash of self-serving brand messages.

- CoolSavings has established relationships with both brick-and-mortar and online companies. The site has good market visibility.

- Every person who receives material from CoolSavings has already indicated that he or she is interested. The program is entirely opt-in.

- Because CoolSavings only provides personalized offers, it understands one-to-one marketing. That's a big step toward understanding one-to-one marketing to mobile device users.

Anyway, about that survey . . . it asked me 32 questions. Yes, that was quite a lot, but I'm the type of person who would go through and answer them all just to gain some insight into a company's marketing.

CoolSavings revealed that it was planning to launch a program to offer coupons and related offers to registered (spelled "opt-in") members who owned Internet-ready telephones, PDAs, and text pagers. The survey was an attempt to gather data on what the Web site's user might want. I was motivated to answer the questions because I had already developed a relationship with this site. The survey first asked me if I owned a mobile device. Answering "no" jumped the user ahead to question #20, where CoolSavings inquired about future purchase plans. For members who were untethered (that is, owned mobile devices), questions covered device capabilities, usage, and mobile content preferences. Presumably, CoolSavings was going to aggregate the answers to these questions and apply them accordingly. As of this writing, CoolSavings' mobile marketing program had not yet begun, but I can tell you one thing: if this company continues to offers savings like the ones I've found on its wired Web site, I'll be one of the first users to sign up. It sure beats cutting out coupons.

It's the Eleventh Hour: Do You Know Where Your Partners Are?

Taking a look at all the traffic in the telecommunications industry, you'd think that wireless telephone carriers and device manufacturers had it made. That rationale could place the enterprise marketer at the side of the road, so to speak, but hey—I don't mind hitching a ride from there. Do you?

Contemplate what might be driving the adoption of mobile handheld devices. To me, it doesn't look like the answer is hardware. The average person doesn't really care much about buying any of these gadgets until he or she has some type of real-world applicability to his or her business or personal life. That would mean that services, content, and applications are pushing the adoption of wireless devices, not hardware.

AT&T knows what I'm talking about. Their marketing strategy includes adding plenty of services, which in turn keeps the customer satisfied. Last year, I received an e-mail from AT&T Wireless about the #121 service that's included in my calling plan. The e-mail solicitation read as follows:

```
AT&T Wireless #121 service makes getting the information you want easier
than ever before. And the service is so simple to use. Just dial #121
from your wireless phone, follow the voice menu and select the news you
want to know about all with the sound of your voice. You can even set up
your own personalized "Favorites" menu, so you can access the content
you want with ease.
```

More than 15 million AT&T Wireless subscribers can surf the Internet wirelessly through voice commands. At least, that's what the June 12, 2001 news release from Tellme Networks said. Voice application provider Tellme worked with AT&T to provide customers with "one-to-one information on demand." The service offers Internet-based content like driving directions, movie listings, stock quotes, news updates, and weather. I can even schedule a wake-up call to my cell phone if I so choose, but when would I need to? Every hotel I've ever stayed in has had a free wake-up call service. Perhaps this feature would be good the next time I go camping.

Meanwhile, back to my reasons for mentioning the #121 service. First, I want you to know that AT&T and similar wireless carriers would not be able to offer such services without strategic partnerships with companies like Tellme, a consumer voice portal provider. Tellme is an Internet and voice technologies specialist with infrastructure in place that partners like AT&T can tap into. Second, the call to #121 might be free, but the time is not. A quick call to customer service confirmed that minutes were being charged against my monthly plan. What's AT&T's marketing strategy? Obviously, if I like the #121 service I'll use it a lot, but I'll have to upgrade to more minutes.

How does this scenario affect your marketing strategy? I'll spell it out for you.

1. Wireless carriers want to generate more revenue.

2. Subscribers want more useful services and content, especially those that can be personalized.

3. If your company can offer such value, your strategic plan should include partnering with a wireless telephone carrier in some manner.

The same strategy holds true for mobile computing networks. If your mobile computing application has helpful features, great content, and a real-time connection that eats up subscriber minutes, some type of partnership might make sense to wireless ISPs like OmniSky, GoAmerica, or Palm.Net.

Here is a word of advice. Remember that report I mentioned earlier? In it, The Intermarket Group advises checking out a partner's finances before signing on. You want your partner to be around to help complete your mission. Too many dot-coms have gone bust, and wireless is a new, untried channel for marketers. Be careful out there.

Choose the Right Mix of Media

What's your current mix of marketing media, and how will mobile devices fit into your future marketing campaigns? How can you use wireless marketing to enhance an already successful television advertising campaign? Decide how you will apply mobile media methods to print, broadcast, online, and other marketing methods. There are plenty of examples to draw on throughout this book.

Currently, wireless advertising is an experiment for many enterprise marketers, which means that it's hard to tell what results will come of it. But like most media, wireless marketing implementation is not an all-or-nothing proposition. Wireless media are multifaceted. You might need to massage wireless media to fit your needs before adding it to your ongoing marketing plan, but add it you will.

SkyGo and MTV's Video Music Awards

In preparation for the 2001 Video Music Awards, music channel MTV decided to launch a wireless advertising campaign to reach Generation Wireless, the coveted 15- to 29-year-old market. According to a Harris Interactive survey completed in 2000, 42 percent of respondents in this age group own a mobile phone or other wireless device. 46 percent of those surveyed use their devices at least three times per week. Viewers of the "Video Music Awards" and youthful mobile device owners have a lot in common, which is why MTV thought it would complement their marketing strategy to add wireless advertising to the mix.

MTV worked with wireless advertising pioneer SkyGo in designing contextual ads that would appeal to potential viewers of the TV awards program. The mobile advertisements were part of a bigger promotional campaign that included online, print, and broadcast placements in advance of the September 6, 2001 event. Daren Tsui, co-founder and president of SkyGo, outlined an integrated marketing campaign run across multiple carriers and multiple publishers. SkyGo arranged to serve the ads to audiences through several wireless networks including AT&T, OmniSky, Palm, and Sprint.

The ad campaign appeared among specific content that was relevant to its audience. For example, PDA users on OmniSky who were reading RollingStone.com would see an ad promoting the event. In general, entertainment properties were selected (including Real Cities), as shown in Figure 3.4. Once the user clicked the link, the next screen, seen in Figure 3.5, would appear—then a roster of celebrities was revealed, as shown in Figure 3.6. In some cases, ads displayed a link to enable PDA users to add the item to their date books.

Most mobile marketing campaigns like this one will support other media placements rather than go solo. Tsui calls wireless devices "remote controls for other media."

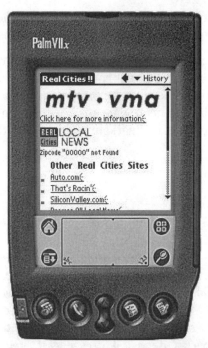

Figure 3.4 I saw the VMA ad on my Palm™ VIIx handheld when I browsed content in Real Cities. And yes, I do watch MTV. (Source: SkyGo. VMA ad © MTV Networks. MTV and related marks are trademarks of MTV Networks. All rights reserved.)

Figure 3.5 Generation Wireless icon Jamie Foxx was slated to host the VMA awards show. (Source: SkyGo. VMA ad © MTV Networks. MTV and related marks are trademarks of MTV Networks. All rights reserved.)

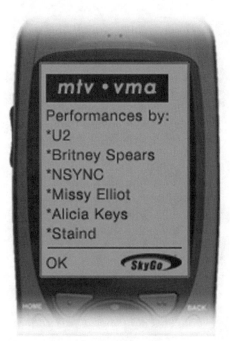

Figure 3.6 Some of my favorite stars were to appear at the 2001 MTV VMA Awards, as seen on an Internet-ready telephone. (Source: SkyGo. VMA ad © MTV Networks. MTV and related marks are trademarks of MTV Networks. All rights reserved.)

Summary: Top Five Expert Tips

1. Understand your wireless niche. Precise audience definitions work best in a one-to-one marketing channel.

2. Find out why current customers buy from you, and translate these points to better serve mobile users.

3. Nothing replaces real customer feedback. Your users will tell you if you're hitting the mark.

4. Look for a partner to broaden your market reach. Your content or services might be just what the user ordered.

5. Mobile handheld devices complement everything else you are doing.

CHAPTER 4

Chartering Your Wireless Marketing Team

"Voulez-vous coucher avec moi ce soir?"

From the song "Lady Marmalade," as sung by R&B soul sister Patti LaBelle

Every time I think about people who are planning to do business together, I'm reminded of the scheming character Alexis Carrington Colby in the 1980s' ABC TV prime time soap opera *Dynasty*. As played by actress Joan Collins, Alexis always had a flair for the outrageous. She once asked a foreign businessman about the possibility of getting into bed with her. His eyes lit up until she explained that she meant partnering in the business sense, rather than the carnal one. She was such an over-the-top person that it would have never occurred to her to take time to develop a decent relationship, which is where I'm going with this discussion.

In the near future, you will become intimately involved with the wireless channel. As marketing team leader, you will be responsible for defining objectives and prioritizing projects. You will build a team, and you will have certain expectations. That's why it's important to choose the right people for that team. Besides assigning various duties to those already on your list of in-house professionals, you'll look to agencies, vendors, and other service providers for outside help. It's important that each person understands his or her responsibilities and handles them to the best of his or her abilities. Also, it's equally important that team members complement each other—in skills, in work ethics, and in personality. No matter who comprises this close-knit crew, one thing's certain—you'll be in bed together for a long time.

About This Chapter

In the course of assembling your mobile marketing corps, you'll meet a few job candidates, evaluate a handful of businesses, and browse through a few hundred Web sites looking for the right service providers. This chapter will provide you with a few thoughts on putting the best people on your wireless marketing team. Consider this topic only an introduction.

Most marketing departments haven't yet caught up with the specialty of wireless enterprise marketing, so sample job descriptions are hard to come by. In this chapter, you will find a section titled "What's Your Wireless Marketing IQ?" You might want to apply this section to your evaluation of marketing employees and potential agencies. The challenges are segmented by functional marketing area. They'll give you a good idea of where certain people stand with regard to understanding wireless marketing concepts.

Finally, just for fun, I'll point you to some resources for learning how to communicate with your staff in abbreviated wireless text. You might need that information someday when you're trying to send a short message to the wireless pager that your PR coordinator brought to a major trade show.

The Needs Assessment

I'm probably putting the cart before the horse. You might not even know whom you need to hire until you finish this book and decide on the elements of your plan. Put a bookmark right here, and I'll see you later after you've digested the remaining pages. On the other hand, if you want to get this chapter over with now, feel free to proceed.

So, who will help you plan and execute a comprehensive wireless marketing plan? Putting together a wireless marketing task force or team involves looking at three things: using in-house personnel, using professional services firms, and using a combination of the other two. Presumably, you'll want to evaluate all the possibilities.

Evaluate In-House Staff

I'm assuming that you want to tap into in-house talent first, so I've provided you with a brief checklist of what to look for.

Skill Sets

- What types of marketing and technical skills are you looking for?
- Does anyone on your staff have them?
- Can anyone on your staff acquire them to a proficient level within a reasonable time?

Personality

- Will this staff person work well with outside vendors and agencies?
- If so, could he or she be a point person or liaison?
- If not, is there a better role for him or her?

Interest and Availability

- How much time is this person able to put into your wireless marketing project?
- Is this person interested in learning about wireless products and services to the extent that it applies to your marketing plans?

Flexibility

- Will this person be willing to find ways to understand what it takes to meet the mobile user's unique needs?
- Does he or she have the capability to pick up new skills in the wireless arena, such as using a handheld device (low skill level) or building an application (higher skill level)?
- How devoted is this person to the cause of wireless marketing, and would he or she be willing to change jobs?

Talent

- How fast can he or she learn wireless-related skills?
- Has he or she demonstrated an ability to grasp new concepts in the past?
- To what level can this person acquire these skills—basic, intermediate, or advanced?
- Will that meet your immediate marketing communications project needs?

What's Your Job Title?

Whenever marketing develops a new specialty, new job titles ultimately emerge. Back in 1994, we began to see traditional job descriptions like marketing communications manager, public relations director, and trade show administrator—quietly enhanced with a short line or two about the Internet. By the late 1990s, it wasn't unusual to find business cards sporting the titles Internet marketing manager and director of e-business strategies. A few free-thinkers believe that job titles don't mean anything and conveniently refuse to provide them to anyone who asks. But whether you call a member of your new team unplugged marketing guru, movable digital feast director, or wireless advertising sprite, your corporate marketing culture will be defined by how members of your team complement each other, not what's on each person's business card.

If this project is your first in wireless marketing, perhaps you don't know what skills are needed yet. So, take a look at the following examples from companies that are recruiting to fill positions with a wireless twist. See anything that you like?

Marketing Staff Job Descriptions

I visited a number of job search sites, like the Career Builder Network, HotJobs.com, Headhunter.net, BrassRing.com, and Monster.com, to check out the hiring trends of enterprises moving into the wireless space. Nothing unusual appeared in the types of openings posted, but I did notice that the keywords *wireless* and *mobile* were creeping into the picture. Here are a few examples:

Job Title: Vice President—Strategic Marketing Responsibilities

Company: Loews Cineplex Entertainment, New York, NY

Duties:

- Secure new strategic partners.
- Develop additional ancillary revenue streams and direct all business development.
- Develop, design, and implement profitable in-theatre programs.
- Manage national partnerships and strategic alliances in major categories, including credit card, automotive, beverage, wireless, and music.

Job Title: Marketing Manager/Director Designate

Company: TMP Melville Craig

Duties:

- Oversee and drive all corporate marketing activity.
- Support regional activities and be responsible for the strategic positioning of the brand, products, and services.

Qualifications:

- Minimum of five years in marketing or product management gained within the high-tech marketplace, preferably mobile enterprise applications.

Job Title: Product Manager

Company: Applied Data Systems, Inc.

Duties:

- Responsible for managing the existing products, defining strategic product direction, creating and maintaining the product road map, pricing, competitive analysis, product positioning, and promotion activities.
- Work with engineering to transform market requirements and business goals into new features, products, and revenue.
- Support the field with on-site and corporate visits and sales tools.
- Collaborate with marketing communications and public relations to deliver the product message to the press through industry analysts and at trade shows.
- Wireless, Factory Automation/Process Control, and Multimedia expertise is highly desirable.

Common Themes

Overall, there were some common themes among most generic marketing-related job openings, regardless of the position:

- Ability to explain technical concepts to end users in a clear and friendly manner
- Highly motivated self-starter
- Possesses a keen attention to detail
- Proven oral and written communications skills

- Willing to learn about new products and technologies
- Team player
- Works well under pressure, such as meeting multiple deadlines
- Able to leap tall buildings in a single bound

Look! Up in the sky! Sorry, I got carried away.

How Will You Find The Right People?

If your in-house resources are a bit scanty, you will want to start the outside review process. Other than beating the bushes with a stick, here are some simple ways to find candidates for your wireless marketing team or even for gathering a list of agency recommendations.

Advertise in all the typical places. I hope you have a big budget for this one.

Ask your current employees. Somebody here knows somebody out there, I'm sure of it.

Give a colleague a call. Say, who did that PDA application for you? Who's handling your wireless hosting?

Read e-mail lists. The best places to find out which outside vendors to avoid are the advertising and marketing discussion groups on the Internet. I've read the best scathing reviews on such lists.

Start a viral recruitment campaign. Let your pals know that you've got an opening. The word will get around quickly.

Job fairs. You can cover a lot of ground in one or two days.

Organizations. For starters, talk to members of the American Marketing Association, the Business Marketing Association, and the Public Relations Society of America.

Read the marketing trade journals. Keep track of which agencies won which accounts. You might find a candidate for handling your wireless advertising campaign.

Use the Web, Luke. Do a search with the keyword wireless and look for links to developer, agency resources, and job sites.

Work with an executive recruiter. There are more details about that option right in this chapter.

If you live in Britain, you can narrow down your search for qualified candidates rather quickly. Imagine posting a notice for a job opening on a WAP job site? There'd be little question that the candidate had wireless skills if he or she replied through a wireless-only job site. Pictured in Figure 4.1, JustPeople.com

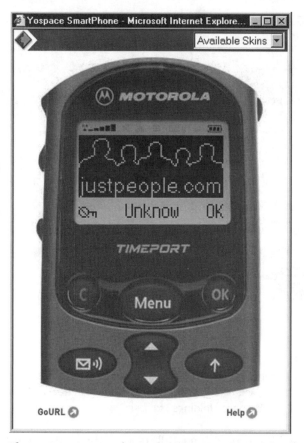

Figure 4.1 Justpeople.com's Hiring Manager section can help you locate candidates for your wireless marketing search. (Telephone image © Motorola, Inc. WAP site © Justpeople, Limited. All rights reserved. SmartPhone Emulator © 1999-2001 Yospace Holdings Ltd. Used with permission.)

is a mobile site for recruiting people with skills in accounting, banking, engineering, government, and entertainment.

Other wireless sites include the following:

- TopJobs at wap.topjobs.net
- Phone-a-Job at wap.phoneajob.com
- Contract Warehouse Recruitment Agency at wap.cwjob.com (see Figure 4.2)

As a side note, remember to use your wired site to notify Web site visitors that your own job openings are available wirelessly, if that's the case. Post an informative banner on your wired pages or add a scrolling message to the bottom of the browser window, as done in Figure 4.3. Users of the email submission form at Contract Warehouse get the message again after sending a message to the online recruitment firm (see Figure 4.4). Obviously, these Internet- and wireless-savvy recruitment specialists left no stone unturned. If you're not recruiting

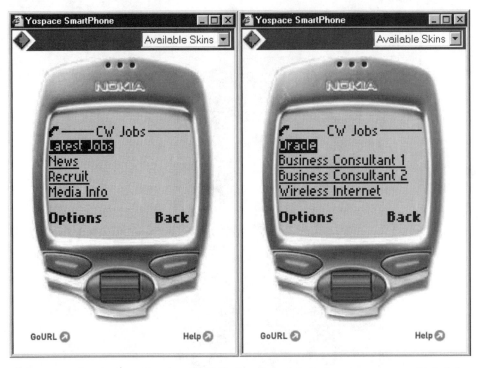

Figure 4.2 The Contract Warehouse WAP site allows job seekers to access multiple job listings anytime and anywhere. (WAP site © Contract Warehouse Limited 2002. Smart-Phone Emulator © 1999–2001 Yospace Holdings Ltd. Used with permission.)

anyone right now, these little promotional tidbits are a free and easy way to get the word out about your wireless presence. There'll be more on that in later chapters.

What's Your Wireless Marketing IQ?

From my own observations, enterprises that are looking to hire staff for various wireless marketing projects should look for individuals who can express basic wireless insights into one or more marketing specialties noted as follows. But if that's not possible, at the very least an otherwise qualified candidate should exhibit a willingness to explore wireless topics further.

The following list could be used as a quick quiz to see how much your current staff truly understands marketing wirelessly. You might even want to use it to evaluate agencies that claim to be experts in the field. Meanwhile, take a look at each functional area to see how much you really know. No, I won't grade you— but I do expect you to be able to add more items to the list after you finish reading this book and as your wireless marketing team grows.

Figure 4.3 Visitors to Contract Warehouse's wired site are told that job openings can be accessed on a mobile device. (Web site © Contract Warehouse Limited 2002.)

Advertising

- Name three types of wireless advertisements.
- Explain how wireless advertising can be used to support other forms of advertising.
- Identify how wireless advertising specifications differ from Web advertising.

Brand Marketing

- Address the limitations of branding products and services via wireless handheld devices.
- Identify a few wireless branding opportunities for existing products and services.
- Name ways to combine traditional and Internet branding tactics to support wireless branding initiatives.

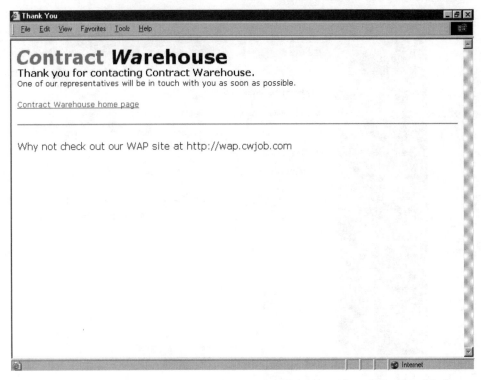

Figure 4.4 After sending a message to the company, the user is reminded to visit the WAP site at wap.cwjob.com. (Web site © Contract Warehouse Limited 2002.)

Content Management

- Compare and contrast product information as it might appear in print, Web, and wireless form.
- Discuss the specific demands of publishing content to the wireless user.
- Suggest several ways to make marketing and technical content readily available to interested wireless device users.

Direct Marketing

- Explain how the user perceives his or her mobile device and how that relates to direct marketing boundaries.
- Examine privacy concerns of the wireless user and clarify how they differ from the Internet, if at all.
- Outline typical methods for appealing to wireless users by using traditional direct mail and e-mail.

Event Marketing

- Name simple ways to incorporate wireless devices into trade show environments to improve the exhibit experience for attendees.

- Brainstorm about how wireless devices could be used to improve show logistics and exhibit management.

- Recommend ways to use wireless devices to improve off-site communications among event managers and staff.

Marketing Research

- Demonstrate how to use both Internet and wireless resources to keep track of relevant trends, competitors, products, and services.

- Interpret the significance of selected industry statistics and surveys as they relate to your company's wireless marketing plans.

- Name some effective ways to survey current customers regarding their future wireless marketing preferences.

Internet Marketing

- Provide a brief overview of how Web-based marketing differs from wireless marketing.

- Offer some tips for encouraging Web-based visitors to access new wireless tools and services, such as Web clipping applications or wireless sites.

- Voice your opinion on wireless marketing's role in the overall e-business picture.

Product Marketing

- Define the wireless user's basic needs requirements.

- Suggest a few out-of-the-box ideas for wireless extensions of a currently successful product line.

- Compose a few product-positioning statements that could appeal to wireless audiences.

Public Relations

- Invent some ways in which wireless tools can be used to assist spokespeople and executives on a media tour.

- Name some restrictions on communicating with journalists who own wireless handheld devices.

- Suggest ideas for providing wireless access to news and press kits to media contacts.

How did you do? Did you expect this section to end with the answers? Sorry, but there are no answers—at least, not in this chapter, anyway. Correct answers aside, the best candidate is one who isn't afraid to tackle the preceding marketing communications challenges. Got an in-house person who looks like a close fit right now? Give her a copy of this book, and I'll bet she will be able to offer some good insights the next time you meet.

Executive Recruiters

Judith Cushman, president of retained executive search firm Judith Cushman & Associates, says that there will be an ongoing positive need for marketing staffing and support for the entire wireless marketing initiative. If done correctly, she predicts that hiring for mobile marketing programs will be vital to how the sector grows. Based in Issaquah, Washington, Cushman's firm specializes in filling PR, corporate communications, marketing communications, and *investor relations* (IR) positions throughout the United States. She's been watching the hiring trends for quite a while now. We chatted at length about what it takes to hire people for the coming wireless marketing revolution.

A Recruiter's Thoughts

Ask Judith Cushman, and she'll tell you that the enterprise has to find people who understand the needs of mobile users without being overwhelmed by the technology. A retained search firm earns its dollars by the value it brings to the process. There are many firms that claim value because they can take a list of job openings and fill it quickly, as though they're going through the aisles of a grocery store and pulling cans off the shelves. By contrast, a good executive search firm will understand the need to step in and evaluate a company's needs. Put this information in the context of a realistic market perspective, and everyone will accomplish the right hiring objectives.

"Marketing vice-presidents always feel that you have to know the territory," she said. And while vice-presidents are always asking for a candidate that knows 'the space,' a VP or two may have the view that his company is 'God's gift to the marketplace,'" quips Cushman.

So, what should you look for when hiring for a wireless marketing project? Obviously, the best person for the job has to understand marketing messages, branding, and the audience.

"The last thing they need to understand is the technology," says Cushman. But not everyone agrees. Recent searches in job sites produced key phrases like "knowledge of the wireless communication a must."

"Marketing VPs sometimes have blinders on about that," says Cushman. At this point, not many people are experienced in hiring staff for an enterprise marketing team that will handle wireless media. Cushman recommends looking for someone who has dealt with similar marketing issues—adapting marketing activities to a new technology. One example would include looking for a candidate who has developed effective consumer-oriented advertising messages based around other technology like the Internet.

There are challenges in not only hiring the right people but in working with executive recruiters as well. A good search person will go "toe-to-toe" with the hiring manager to see who is truly the best person, not to mention who the company can attract and actually afford. Remember, your competition is lined up and "you're fighting with four to five other companies for the same people," says Cushman. You have to be realistic about whether your company's position is an attractive one.

Realistic Compensation

Fortune 500 salaries and movement in the recruiting space might have a bearing on what could be termed a realistic compensation level for wireless marketing team members. Unfortunately, some companies approach hiring as though most people would come begging to work there. That might be true in a few unique cases, but regardless, "There are no bargains for excellent people," Cushman adds. A good executive search firm will help a company address these issues.

What's Your Fall-Back Position?

In an ideal world, we would all be able to fill all job openings with the best possible candidate. But that's not real life. Consider making an "investment hire." This person has all the right marketing skills but needs to come up to speed on the industry. Cushman has observed that many young companies ask for a "plug-and-play" person. If everyone has that approach, everyone is competing in the same tiny little space for the same terrific employees. In truth, the right person could be working in another area but might only need two months or fewer to come up to speed on the uniqueness of the media. Still, many companies think that two months is too long. They want to jump on the bandwagon now and get the project off the ground (so much for realistic time frames).

Nothing Happens Overnight

Cushman sees many managers who approach hiring with a project mentality, as in devoting a week or two to recruitment. In doing so, they think that results are forthcoming soon. Most executive search firms know from experience that the search process takes longer, particularly in a new space.

"While they're busy pursuing the person who meets every requirement, the company could have invested the time in people who would have come up to speed by now," says Cushman.

What About Job Sites?

When job search and career Web sites first emerged, thousands of people logged on. Job seekers, companies, and recruiters alike believed that all their job needs would be solved through a handful of screens and clicks. Recruitment firms, like Judith Cushman and Associates, tried them with different clients only to find that responses to job postings were a waste of time. Leads were either "totally inappropriate or unqualified," says Cushman, adding that if a company were filling a commodity position, these sites might be helpful to a degree. But many human resource people and recruiters say that job sites can be imprecise tools, mostly because online job seekers can be undiscriminating, applying to every possible and remotely relevant opening. It's very time consuming to deal with applicants who use a shotgun approach to job applications. In that regard, the odds that you'll find the candidate you're seeking can be very slim.

Agencies: The Experts

Looking for tips on hiring and working with outside agencies? I spoke at length with Lisa Hendrickson, president of LCH Communications in Port Washington, New York. She has these comments to share regarding working with PR firms.

"I would look for someone who understands the wireless space and someone who has the hands-on experience for a particular technology," says Hendrickson. Hendrickson feels that the client should hire a PR professional who not only understands the media but has a strong rapport with reporters who cover the wireless space. The PR agency should be able to showcase how users are actually using the technology to communicate its benefits. And even if an agency doesn't have direct experience with promoting your specific products and services, a PR practitioner who understands technology would quickly learn how to talk to the right press.

And what about the agency liaison? You know, the person in-house who is the interface between agency executives and upper management?

"You need a well-organized person in-house who can be a conduit to the agency," observes Hendrickson, adding that the client-agency relationship is more like a partnership. According to Hendrickson, the PR agency's role is to identify PR program objectives, determine messages, and target these messages accordingly. Like any public relations campaign, the agency has to be able to identify and target the right people.

Tips for Hiring an Outside Firm

Whether you're hiring an outside advertising, marketing, or public relations firm, most professionals will tell you that it's important to evaluate an agency's experience, client references, and media contacts. But how important is it to hire an agency with wireless experience? Here are Lisa Hendrickson's tips:

1. Look for relevant experience that transfers to your place in the wireless segment.
2. Ask for the agency's record of successful deliverables for other clients.
3. Evaluate whether or not the agency has a basic understanding of your technology, even if it hasn't worked with your exact product.
4. Recognize that this early in the game, it might not be possible for an agency to have experience in the wireless enterprise space.

Finding Outside Technical Help

I went to www.elance.com and entered the keyword *wireless*. I was presented with a skimpy list of just 24 service providers. Granted, this field is new. For what it's worth, here are some services that you might consider, along with what it might cost for each:

- Enterprise & Wireless Application Development—$100 per hour
- Wireless Solutions for PDAs and Other Handhelds—$25 per hour
- Application Development for Voice, Mobile, and Wireless Computing—$75 per hour

- Wireless Internet Applications—$25 per hour
- Java, Microsoft, PDA, and Wireless Applications—$100 per hour

Sure, there's some overlap in what services are called. By the way, are these rates representative of the entire wireless development industry? The answer is, probably not. I'm sure that it'll change drastically in the next year or two, just like fees for designing Web sites have gone up and down.

As you can see, there's quite a range of rates listed—and they come from both independent software developers and development firms. Just so you know what types of service specialties might exist for your wireless marketing project, here are a few areas you'll want to look into:

- Wireless application development
- Wireless database design and development
- Wireless enterprise development
- Wireless hosting services
- Wireless Web design and programming
- Wireless system administration

One resource that narrows down the contractor search is MobileCoders.com, a site that strives to bring "experienced mobile software developers together with custom handheld software projects." In other words, if your company is interested in making its product literature or services wireless users, this site could be a good place to stop. As seen in Figure 4.5, you can search here for developers who can handle Palm OS and Pocket PC projects, request a project proposal, read testimonials, and catch up on handheld news. Again, rates are all over the map, but I'm sure that you know the *request for quote* (RFQ) drill already.

Now, if hiring all these individual folks seems a bit daunting, don't worry. I have a list of solutions providers in the back of this book. A turnkey solution could be the best choice for you.

Get into Bed with Wireless

One of the best pieces of advice I've ever heard with regard to building a marketing team for a new technology was as follows: get intimate with the wireless culture, and the rest of this stuff will start falling in place. Subscribe to newsletters. Read newsgroups. Attend conferences. Understand what the wireless user is thinking so that you can organize a group of employees and vendors who are right for the job. Please don't rely exclusively on a marketing book or two. Immerse yourself in the wireless world, not just because you'll do a better job

Figure 4.5 MobileCoders.com offers hundreds of developer profiles and an opportunity for you to post your project, too. (© 2001 MobileCoders.com)

of executing your wireless marketing campaign but also because wireless is the wave of the future.

Please Unplug Me, Let Me Go

By the way, because you're educating your in-house people anyway, let me make a suggestion. Unplug them. Wouldn't it be great if every member of your marketing team had access to the tools plus the following wireless educational opportunities throughout the year?

- Attendance at industry events to hold and play with the latest handheld devices

- Ongoing hands-on training sessions in a variety of handheld applications

- Introductions to new mobile marketing tools, such as wireless PR software, as soon as they emerge

- Departmental practice of using various forms of wireless communications between team members

Japanese and Scandinavian school children use mobile devices for homework, class tests, and note taking. Have I shamed you yet? At the very least, each member of your marketing team should have his or her own mobile handheld device. Put it in the budget.

Fear of Texting

As long as you're developing a corporate culture that accepts—er, embraces—mobile media, you might as well have fun using it. Once you form your wireless marketing team, use mobile devices to stay in touch often. You can't communicate with team members via e-mail, *Simple Mail Service* (SMS), or wireless chat unless you know the lingo. After all, it's not a good idea to appear old-fashioned while managing a dynamic crew. Here's some beginning help:

ABBREVIATION	MEANING
AFAIK	As far as I know
ASAP	As soon as possible
B	Be
BCNU	Be seeing you
BRB	Be right back
BTDT	Been there, done that

Had enough for now? Okay, here is a list of sites that can help you overcome your fear of using SMS text messaging. Come back to this page when you're ready.

- AskOxford.com—E-mail, SMS, and online chat at www.askoxford.com/betterwriting/emoticons/
- BBC Online—The Joy of Text at www.bbc.co.uk/joyoftext/facts/abbreviations.shtml
- Cellular South—E-mail-to-Go at www.cellularsouth.com/email-to-go/glossary.html
- Talking Students—SMS Text Messaging Guide at www.talkingstudents.co.uk/smsguide.asp
- WAP.com—SMS shortcuts at www.wap.com/share/osas/cache/artid400340.html

Summary: Top Five Expert Tips

1. Put your in-house marketing staff at the top of the list for your wireless marketing team. They already have the basic skills, and wireless knowledge could be the icing on the skills cake.

2. Hire individuals who can either express basic wireless insights into one or more marketing specialties or who are open to learning more.

3. Fees for outside technical development vary greatly, so take your time to get several competitive bids before farming out that project.

4. Use wireless tools. There's no better way for your people to understand the wireless culture than to have hands-on, real-world experience. If your agency folks aren't wireless yet, ask them why.

5. Look at hiring and contracting out as an ongoing need. Your wireless marketing program will grow over time.

Building the Wireless Brand

"Say my name, say my name. If no one is around you, say baby I love you."

As sung by best-selling female R&B group Destiny's Child in their hit song "Say My Name"

It sure would be nice to have such devoted attention from customers. If mobile users are going to say anyone's name, why shouldn't it be yours? In fact, that's the whole point about branding: Whenever someone thinks about products and services, they should think about you first. With any luck, the mobile user has blinders on and acts like no one else exists but your company. And, if no one else in your industry is around, you could have the customer's undivided attention for quite a while.

Unfortunately, mobile branding will soon follow the paths of other media, the Internet being the most recent and obvious example. At first, you might be the only company in your industry cutting the plug for online users. You could gain a huge market share because you were the first to market wirelessly. Everything will be cool until the mobile user hears someone else's voice in the background. Like the best-selling song by divas Beyoncè Knowles, Kelly Rowland, and Michelle Williams, the writing's on the wall with regard to mobile brands and their customer relationships. This opportunity is your chance to get it right and dig your heels in.

Why should you be concerned about branding within the mobile environment? Think about why you're reading this book. You want to do a good job of marketing wirelessly. Maybe you're in a particular profession because you like it. It makes you feel good. In fact, it makes you feel so good, you want to convey that good feeling to others. Others, who happen to be your customers, need help in understanding why you feel so good. You want to involve the user in your experience. You want the user to feel the same fun, sexy excitement. Are you warming up yet to the branding mindset?

About This Chapter

If you've wondered how a mobile device affects traditional branding activities, this chapter will tell you. You'll read an overview of mobile branding concepts and constraints, like the walled garden, name recognition, and logo use. This chapter will also help you understand not only mobile's impact on branding but also your strategic and tactical choices.

What does your mobile branding need most to succeed? This chapter will give you a few examples, complete with real-world case studies. Plus, you'll find tips on leveraging your brand's uniqueness for the mobile space and ideas for making your mobile presence the center of a user's attention.

What's It All About, Branding?

All you middle-aged folks on the left side of the room can sing this paragraph title to the tune of Burt Bacharch and Hal David's song "Alfie." See? I'm an intergenerational goofball (grin). Now for a few basic reminders about what branding implies for the user.

Branding means a trademark that stands for something. Branding means that something special is forthcoming whenever the customer buys and/or uses the brand. Branding succeeds only when the marketer remembers the tacit warranty associated with the brand. A print ad can include a URL and a short pitch that implies that something neat is to be had from logging on. But then, whoops —a page gets moved, an offer expires, whatever. Online branding continues to suffer because of these lapses. If you invite someone to your site to do something, see something, or get something, stay on track. If you invite someone to use your mobile application or visit your wireless site, deliver the value that your brand pledged. A mobile user, more than anyone, considers it a disservice if a brand doesn't live up to its reputation. Finally, remember that branding fails when the customer, visitor, or user has to think too hard to find out what the brand is about.

General Branding Concepts

Need a refresher on general branding concepts? As part of a primer on branding, Mike Bawden, president and CEO of consulting firm *Brand Central Station* (BCS), circulated the following list of definitions to agency members as a prelude to solving brand issues for agency clients. With Mike's permission, I've reprinted it here as your prelude to solving mobile brand issues:

BRAND: The identifying "mark" that a company or product makes in the mind of the customer that represents that company to the customer

BRANDING: The process by which a company or product positions its "mark" in the mind of the customer

COMMUNICATIONS: A two-way exchange of information between parties that involves listening, processing, responding, and evaluating

COMPANY: Any business, issue, employer, cause, and so on that needs to influence the behavior of a customer in order to advance their business and achieve their corporate vision

CUSTOMER: Any consumer, employee, business partner, investor, or peer who develops/maintains a relationship with the company's brand

MARKETING: The process of exchanging one item for another based on the agreed-upon value of the two items by the parties involved in the transaction

MISSION: The purpose of a company or product, in its own view

POSITION: The customer's perception (in other words, beliefs, feelings, and knowledge) of a brand

VISION: What a company or product is destined to become, assuming that it is capable of fulfilling its mission

VALUE: The worth of a brand in relation to other brands in the mind of the customer; it is assumed that a customer will always choose the brand with the higher value when forced to make a decision

©2001, Brand Central Station.

Many of these terms will be used throughout this chapter in the context of what works, what doesn't work, and what we still don't know about branding to mobile device users.

Talk to the Hand

Does room exist in the wireless realm for the concept of branding? That's a good question. When it comes to ad placements, do you ever define a brand's presence by the way it envelops a particular media?

On television, a brand can encompass the whole media experience. . . practically. While watching a TV commercial, you might only be aware of the brand message and nothing else for an entire 10 to 15 second spot. If the commercial is entertaining, your eyes and ears are involved in the branding experience. Two senses (eyes and ears) are involved in receiving the advertiser's message, unless of course you hit the mute button and get up to take a potty break.

On radio, the brand message might be peripheral to whatever else you are experiencing. If you're reading a book or driving the car, your ears take in the brand message while your eyes are engaged elsewhere. Or maybe your ears don't even get the message because you're probably gabbing with your passengers. And in print media, the brand message never has more than a slice of the media pie.

But if you're actually using a product, the message comes through like gangbusters. It's the interactive experience that reinforces branding the best. If the branded product is a vacuum cleaner, three senses—visual (your eyes), auditory (your ears, whether you like it or not), and tactile (your hands) are involved in the branding experience.

Now, where does that leave branding with regard to mobile handheld devices? Quite simply, the hand surrounds the brand. And because of that role reversal with the customer's senses, your brand might seem tinier or even timid. Wait— it gets more complicated.

Mobile Branding Concepts

Why is mobile branding so difficult? Industry politics and positioning, technological constraints, and user acceptance complicate the mobile world. Read on.

The Walled Garden: You Can't Get There from Here

The first time that I heard the phrase "The Walled Garden," I laughed. What a weird concept. Mobile telephone carriers each operate their own proprietary service networks. You see, there's this entire *garden* of great Internet content, but it's only available to the subscriber base that visits within the *walls* of each carrier's service. When the user scrolls through his or her carrier's content menus, your company's link might be absent. The user would have to manually enter your mobile URL into his or her phone's mini-browser, and that's no fun. Let's hope you did a good job of telling him or her how to find you.

Have you ever heard of anything so ridiculous? Well, yes. This type of brand exclusivity exists everywhere. Remember going into a pizza parlor and ordering a Coca-Cola? No dice. That's because that particular restaurant only carried Pepsi-Cola. How about television? Does *60 Minutes* air on the Fox Network? Is the same exact channel lineup on the local digital cable service available through a satellite TV provider? Heck no.

So, if such monopolies are fairly common, why are we so indignant when our user can't get to us easily through his or her wireless carrier? Maybe it's because Internet users don't have that problem, and wireless is just an extension of the Internet. A user of Netscape Navigator can access all the same Web sites as a user of Microsoft Internet Explorer, right? Oh, whoops—news reports make that statement inaccurate as of this book's writing. Okay, bad example. Here's a better one. AT&T WorldNet users can access the same content as *America Online* (AOL) users. No, that's not a good example, either. I can't get to AOL channels from the other side. Good grief.

Is the walled garden situation true for every aspect of wireless content? At least one carrier has bridged the gap for text messaging. AT&T announced that it was the first to "break the carrier barrier," in a company news release dated November 2001. Users of AT&T Wireless 2-Way Text Messaging can send messages across carrier networks, provided they know the recipient's mobile telephone number.

Impact on Branding

Walled gardens make your job harder when trying to reach mobile subscribers of different carriers. You can't create a branding experience for users who don't know that you exist.

Your Choices (Pick One or More)

1. Be more selective and choose placement on a few carriers that meet your precise demographic needs.

2. Negotiate with each wireless carrier separately to get as much mobile visibility as possible.

3. Save yourself time by working with a company that can do the negotiating for you.

4. Rely on a combination of traditional and online media to deliver the branding message so that users will seek you out no matter which carrier connects them to the wireless Web.

By the way, some industry watchers think that carriers could lose ground eventually. There's this thought from James W. (Jim) Caruso, founder and CEO of Atlanta, Georgia-based Media First PR, a high-tech public relations and marketing services firm: "The (telephone) carriers could have their whole markets taken over by people who are good branders." Jim told me that "someone with greater marketing power and the ability to sell could really take over from the carriers." Walled gardens aside, marketers can still make a dent in the wireless market if they grasp how to brand to mobile users.

Technology Perceptions

Rich media is a great tool for creating an interactive experience. Too bad we're not there yet. Rich and streaming media might be a common mobile occurrence in some parts of the world and for a few high-end users, but how many U.S.-based mobile users can see color or animated graphics on their devices right now? A year from now, what percentage of users will be able to receive rich media?

While I'm thinking about it, how often do users buy a new mobile device or perceive that they need a new device? Getting a new device is not like downloading the latest version of an Internet browser for free. Some industry folks claim that users, especially mobile telephone users, get a new gadget every three years. Others have told me that users hang on to devices much longer. Who is right? When bandwidth, devices, and marketers all catch up with the multimedia and wireless marketing hype, will users be ready?

Impact on Branding

Mobile technology limitations can inhibit widespread recognition of your mobile brand. Many mobile devices in use make companies look like they're marketing on the Web circa 1994.

Your Choices (Pick One or More)

1. Forego the rich media experience until the rest of the world catches up.
2. Deliver rich media and risk alienating users who can't see it.
3. Be more selective in the types of users you target and the level of rich media that you employ.
4. Revise your branding tactics repeatedly as technology and users catch up with your marketing needs.

Mobile technology changes at varying degrees. One thing's for sure—mobile branding activities are ongoing, requiring constant revision to keep pace with the market.

Name Recognition

Mobile handheld devices have limited screen sizes that vary from device to device. The name of your company, products, or services might not fit in every

Figure 5.1 "Marketing Wirelessly" can be an unwieldy brand name depending on the mobile device on which it appears.

case. As you can see in Figure 5.1, the name of my e-mail newsletter "Marketing Wirelessly" doesn't work for the Palm application launcher screen. The title is truncated and ends in dots. I'm not the only one with this problem, as demonstrated by an application called Pocket Cashier, seen in the same figure. In both cases, having a distinctive logo helps the situation but doesn't solve the naming problem entirely.

Impact on Branding

Long names look weird when truncated on mobile devices. Users might not recognize you right away if a device, mini-browser, or operating system truncates your brand name.

Your Choices (Pick One or More)

1. Rename your mobile brand to fit with mobile parameters.
2. Invent a complementary mobile brand name.

3. Tap into brand nicknames for m-branding applications.

4. Live with it. Lots of companies have this problem. Fixating on the length of your name will complicate branding issues further.

Logos

The logo for my newsletter "Marketing Wirelessly" looks great on a Web page, but I had to resize it considerably for use within the Palm operating system. That's when I noticed legibility problems. I tried to compensate by creating a negative image, but it didn't help much. In fact, I think the change made it look weird and somewhat unreadable. For the icon used in the Application Launcher, I chose a negative image of the graffiti letter "M." Yeah, I admit it. It's time for a major logo redesign if I'm going to continue to use "Marketing Wirelessly." But then again, on a mobile telephone, you can only see the logo half the time because not all devices support graphics.

Impact on Branding

Intricately designed logos might not translate well to mobile device screens. Your logo might look good on one device but not on another. In fact, your logo could disappear entirely.

Your Choices (Pick One or More)

1. If your logo works well in the mobile space, use your logo in its current form.

2. If your logo doesn't work well in the mobile space, use your logo in its current form and risk degradation or distortion.

3. Create another version of your logo for mobile branding purposes.

4. Use no logo at all in the mobile space and/or find other ways to brand your mobile image.

Mobile Branding in the Marketing Mix

So, now you know to forget about those pretty corporate identity elements. But if you can't always rely on the tried-and-true aspects of corporate ID—your company logo, official typeface, corporate colors, and all that jazz—what *can* you rely on for mobile branding, if anything?

Wireless branding requires the support of other media. The strength of a wireless brand might forever be linked to how well the customer recognizes you while he or she is doing and seeing other things. You might have to settle for how strong you can make your mobile brand through a well-designed print ad or an entertaining radio spot. You might have to settle for how well the user integrates your brand message into his or her lifestyle, rather than how often he or she recognizes you while tapping the screen of his or her handheld. So, admit it. Mobile brand building will have more success through a combination of all media than with a wireless device all by its lonesome.

Mobile branding *can* and does rely on intangibles to some degree. Wow, that's a scary thought. Can't put your finger on your company's personality? Can't recognize the feeling that customers have when they do business with you? You could be in trouble. Think about it. A user has certain expectations of his or her mobile device. In order to brand wirelessly, your products and services must meet those expectations. Therefore, your wireless presence should fill a need for the user, whether real or perceived. Notice how I said, "for the user" and not "for the marketer."

Your mobile branding efforts should convey sensitivity and awareness about your customer's needs. You want your customer to recognize the role that your company plays in making life better. You want your customer to become involved with your brand. Wireless marketing should instill a sense of satisfaction in the customer who uses your brand. Keep this goal in mind, and you're on your way to understanding the mobile branding experience. Believe me, many e-commerce sites today still look like the company doesn't care about or get this concept, which means that it'll be that much harder for the marketing team to transition to m-branding.

Well, you can't present a glittery image to most mobile device users, at least not for a few years, and your hands are tied as far as how much self-serving fluffy text users are willing to scroll through. You *can* design a mobile interactive experience that replicates the value that your brand has for the customer, however. Everything you do wirelessly should reinforce what you do to serve the customer in the physical world.

Analyze This

Before you think about conveying your brand to mobile users, take a moment to unearth aspects of your brand that appeal to your customers. Use this information to brainstorm about how to make it all work for mobile device users.

Personality Test

Take a look at the following personality characteristics. In each case, try to think of a brand or two, either online or not, that fit each keyword or phrase.

The asterisks on this list are noted by actual mobile brand positioning statements found in company promotional material.

affluent	expert*	reliable	speedy
affordable	gregarious	robust	tireless
authentic	practical	self-important	trust-worthy*
casual*	prestigious	showy	worldly
established*	punctual	simplicity*	youthful

Where does your mobile brand fit? Add your own words and repeat, looking for other mobile brands that have similar attributes. Take a look at how established brands extend characteristics to mobile devices. How did each of the following brands convey their personalities to the mobile user?

Casual simplicity. LandWare, Inc. says that Pocket Quicken is "the standard in mobile financial tracking software that makes managing your finances *as easy as* turning on your organizer," according to its Web site at www.pocketquicken.com.

Established expert. LapLink, Inc. is an *established* pioneer in the area of synchronization and file transfer. "With the introduction of PDAsync, we now extend our synchronization *expertise* to PDAs and mobile phones," said Mark Eppley, founder and CEO of LapLink in a September 5, 2001 mobile product announcement.

Trustworthy. In October 2001, Handspring announced the release of Blazer 2.0, a Web browser for Palm OS devices. The company highlighted its mobile product's enhanced *security* features.

Perceived Value and e-Commerce Economics

How much value can you provide to the mobile user? Take a look at your Web site. Perform a content and functionality analysis. Does the site have "stickiness"? Can you translate this "stickiness" to your current or future mobile presence?

Excite Mobile. "Get Excite on the go. Check your email, get the latest news, track your portfolio and more," reads the copy on its site at mobile.excite.com.

Hoover's Wireless. "All the business information you need, all in one place. Research 17,000 public and private companies worldwide," says the product description in the Web Clipping Application Library at www.palm.com.

Yahoo! Mobile Bookmarks. mobile.yahoo.com offers an extensive directory of mobile Internet sites. I can search through them while on my desktop computer, then add them to my own personal list of bookmarks just by clicking. Once I'm on my Web-enabled mobile telephone or PDA, I use the minibrowser or the Yahoo! WCA to access the bookmarks. This feature will save me a lot of keying and tapping.

Now, think about why you'd want to make your mobile site sticky. Industry statistics show that only a small percentage of first-time Web site visitors buy something upon first contact with a site. If the site provides value, the user will return. Return visitors are more likely to buy. If the user does buy, he or she is more likely to buy something again. These e-commerce generalizations could prove transferable to mobile commerce shopping patterns. Here are some examples that convey value to the mobile user.

Memorability and Impressionability

Will users remember you after they've logged off? How about before they even log on? How much does your media presence influence a user's decision to access your unwired site or buy your mobile products? Do you have a memorable brand experience that works universally? Look at how these brands create an impression for the mobile user.

Moviefone. It says that it's the largest movie showtime and ticketing service. AOL users recognize this brand by Keyword: Moviefone, as seen in Figure 5.2. With this much online visibility, they must be good.

Nokia 8260 Internet-ready telephone. "As featured in the hit movie *Charlie's Angels*," brags the promotional copy. Nice product placement. In fact, I remember seeing one of the Angels using it. I know that I don't look like Cameron Diaz, Drew Barrymore, or Lucy Liu, but I want one of these cool phones anyway.

Wine.com. In 2000, it became the first online wine merchant to launch a mobile commerce effort. Can you name any other online wine merchants?

Features and Benefits

What aspects of your mobile offerings can beat your competitor? Is there a good reason to visit you wirelessly or to use your mobile products? Here are some examples that answer these questions.

Figure 5.2 Moviefone maintains its presence in other media, including a keyword placement on AOL. (Moviefone screenshot © 2001 America Online, Inc. Used with permission.)

RIM's BlackBerry wireless e-mail solution and HP printers. Hewlett-Packard's Mobile Enterprise Printing application can help enterprises "increase the productivity of their mobile employees by making it easier for them to work with information while leveraging their existing wireless e-mail and document environments," says a September 2001 joint news release.

Yahoo! Local Sales. This section of the Yahoo! Mobile Web site, shown in Figure 5.3, promises the user that he or she can "access thousands of free advertised specials and promotions from your favorite local stores updated daily—all from your mobile phone."

USABancShares.com. Internet measurement firm Gomez rates it as the number one online checking account. See how USABancShares.com capitalizes on that advantage through its PDA application, as seen in Figure 5.4.

Sometimes a wireless brand has such a huge following in the physical world that its wireless presence is a foregone conclusion. Such is the case with The Sharper Image, a retailer that partnered with mobile solutions provider Bar-Point. See the case study found in this chapter for more details.

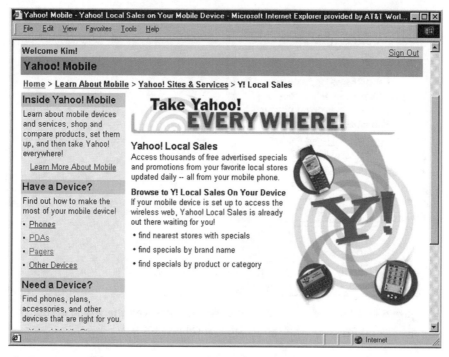

Figure 5.3 Mobile users can find nearby stores and specials by brand name and category just by accessing Yahoo! Mobile on any mobile device. (Reproduced with permission of Yahoo! Inc. © 2002 Yahoo! Inc. YAHOO! and the YAHOO! Logo are trademarks of Yahoo! Inc.)

The Usability Factor

What does a mobile branding experience need most? To answer this question, think about why users use mobile devices. Think about mobile customer satisfaction and how your brand plays into that. I think it has something to do with the following:

ACCESSIBILITY. People want to reach other people and access information more often.

CONTROL. People want more autonomy, freedom, independence, or whatever.

DOWN TIME. People want to be more productive and avoid wasting time.

FASTER, SMALLER, CHEAPER. People want to improve life on an ongoing basis.

INTERACTIVITY. People want to be involved with their lives and respect brands that understand that.

Figure 5.4 USABancShares.com's mobile customers can check their account balance in real time. (Copyright © 1999–2001 USABancShares.com)

SMARTER. People want to be prepared, do things better, and maybe answer all the answers on Jeopardy.

SOLUTIONS. People want simple solutions to everyday problems.

A good mobile brand meets one or more of these criteria. How does this information meet the mobile branding challenge? Let's take a look at how one consumer-oriented company handles it: Ralston Purina.

Differentiation: Your Mobile Uniqueness

There are certain traditional branding ideas that play well into the concept of mobile branding. One of them is finding ways to stand out in a user's mind.

Make Your Wireless Presence a Destination

Aside from competing with neighboring sites, bigger brands, and other distractions in the wireless world, marketers must devise a way to encourage mobile users to visit. This encouragement needs to come long before a user picks up his or her Internet-ready telephone or turns on his or her Pocket PC. How do you perform this task? Here are a few ideas:

The Sharper Image and BarPoint

When The Sharper Image decided to go wireless, it was not a big decision. The company's products attract the buyer who has enough discretionary income to buy high-end electronic toys and prestigious gadgets. And, because of the type of products available through a well-known print catalog, early technology adopters are The Sharper Image's main customer base.

Here's a little bit of background. One of the things about The Sharper Image that sets it apart from competitors is its position as a multi-channel retailer. Shoppers can find The Sharper Image just about anywhere these days. The company has a thriving wholesale image that extends to upscale retailers like Lord & Taylor and Bloomingdales. The company mails a monthly catalog. The company has stores in malls (lots of malls). The Sharper Image is even online, having launched its Web site way back in 1995. Obviously, these folks are on top of things brandwise. The company tries to make access to its multiple channels a seamless experience for the customer.

Adding to the strength of its brand, The Sharper Image is really a destination. I know this fact because every time I see a storefront, I want to go inside. I might even drive an hour or so just to spend some time in one of their stores playing around. But enough about my fascination with shopping there—you might ask why The Sharper Image decided to brand wirelessly.

"We thought it made sense that our customers would have the latest greatest devices. The nature of the wireless customer makes it a good match for our company. We feel it would be wrong if we weren't accessible through this fourth channel," noted Roger Bensinger, senior vice-president of corporate marketing and business development for The Sharper Image. Company executives feel that The Sharper Image customer expects convenient access to its products. So, pursue a wireless presence they did.

M-commerce was too new and immature, so company executives didn't want to take the risk by investing capital yet. Having seen what other retailers had done to set up applications for m-commerce, The Sharper Image knew that it needed the right mobile business partner.

Meanwhile, mobile industry player BarPoint had already contracted with most of the wireless telephone carriers for brand positioning on their top decks. BarPoint was ahead in the mobile marketing game because it had enabled 250 mobile devices to speak to its mobile service. It didn't hurt that BarPoint's CEO was also a fan of The Sharper Image products. The two companies became fast mobile friends.

To be honest, The Sharper Image doesn't really expect any serious sales volume in the short term from its mobile channel. This early in the m-commerce game, the experience is more like a branding exercise coupled with one more customer service outlet. How does it all work? Bensinger explains it as follows.

"If the user were to type in a CD player, our products would populate as options within BarPoint," he says, adding that if we were shopping in a Sharper Image store, "you would put an item in your BarPoint wish list." That means BarPoint becomes a mobile bookmarking service for future buying decisions. The user just enters the item code or UPC code for reference at a later time.

As far as corporate identity issues in the mobile world, Bensinger doesn't see a problem. The Sharper Image logo is based on Impact font, which means that it's only letters. Demonstrating products is another story. Before the sale, shoppers like to play around or examine items more closely.

"We'll start getting excited about mobile commerce when phones and PDAs can show graphics almost in real time," says Bensinger. Ultimately, rich media could enable consumers to get a closer branding experience, resulting in more product sales.

Invite the user to test drive your product. Invite the mobile user to log on to send a message or ringtone to a friend.

Tell the user what you know. If the user knows that your wireless site is a source of good information, he or she will be back.

Tell the user who you know. The old saying, "It isn't what you know, it's who you know!" is certainly relevant to wireless branding. Imagine that you want to become a portal of wireless event information. All of the links that you include that point to other sites, even competitive ones, add to your image as someone who is really connected.

Integrate Your Mobile Brand with Your Online Identity

How will you help the mobile device user remember you long after he or she has put down the device? Here are some ideas that play into the concept of mobile brand recollection.

Now, some folks separate their wired and wireless identities with different domain name extensions. The marketing staff might decide that BigJuicyDogTreats.com is for the wired Web site and then register BigJuicyDogTreats.net for the WAP site. (I made up those URLs. Feel free to take them if it fits your corporate identity.) For some reason, someone told these non-technical folks that they had to do it this way. I can name several dozen companies that didn't have to register a

Ralston Purina and the Mobile Cat Owner

When the Ralston Purina Company decided to launch its mobile version of CatChow.com, as seen in Figure 5.5, it knew that pet owners liked to take their pets along on vacation. In fact, Ralston Purina spokesperson Julie Kahn says that cat owners are becoming increasingly technologically savvy. Forrester Research provided some corroborating data that cemented the pet product company's decision to extend its brand to wireless users. According to Kahn, a Forrester Technographics survey indicated that 6.1 percent of North American cat owners currently own a PDA, a number that has doubled since 2000.

Purina had two goals in mind for launching its wireless presence. The company's primary goal was to gain experience in the wireless arena. At the same time, it could evaluate mobile usage among cat owners to determine future m-branding opportunities for other Purina brands.

The company's secondary goal was to stay connected with its consumers by "providing them with the cat care information they need, whenever and wherever they want it," says Kahn. The company had already experienced tremendous success with CatChow.com due to its rich content and community of experts. CatChow.com content addresses the physical, emotional, and nutritional needs of the cat. Feature articles and weekly cat tips top my list of interesting content. There are tips on traveling with cats and dealing with their special needs, as well.

Purina offers mobile access to CatChow.com through Web clipping service provider AvantGo. As for its decision to partner with AvantGo, Kahn cites audience penetration. AvantGo is "the largest wireless channel with over two million registered subscribers," says Kahn. Obviously, the popularity of an information provider that offers free services to the user becomes an important factor in reaching the most number of mobile device owners. Of huge branding importance was the fact that Purina became "the first AvantGo channel within the pet information space," emphasizes Kahn.

Visitors to the brand's long-established Web site are immediately informed of CatChow.com's mobile presence, as seen in Figure 5.6. An extensive cross-channel campaign at sister brand sites, like Purina.com and Tidycats.com, includes promotional links and mini-banners about CatChow.com's mobile presence.

So, what does CatChow.com offer the mobile cat owner? The brand's philosophical approach is about "enhancing the pet owning experience by providing them with the resources they need to care for their cats," says Kahn. The company wants to help cat enthusiasts provide the best care to their companions by furnishing the best information whenever and wherever it's needed. I'm a user and was glad to have the information at my fingertips during my last road trip. My tabby comrades George and Gracie tell me the Cat Chow AvantGo channel is the cat's meow.

Figure 5.5 Catchow.com to Go! is a new experience available to AvantGo mobile service users. (© Ralston Purina Company.)

Figure 5.6 A pop-up browser window on the Purina Cat Chow home page informs visitors about its mobile presence. (© Ralston Purina Company.)

new domain name for their wireless content. I can access their wireless site with the same address that I use in my desktop browser. That pretty much says it all.

You might also be tempted to choose a subdomain that conveys an extension of your brand, like mobile.ThisOldCompany.com or wap.ThisOldCompany.com. While similar subdomains work well for the wired Web, your user doesn't have that much time and patience to key in a lengthy URL or even guess at your mobile address. Here's my take on it. You sweated to establish a domain name that has brand equity. Use it, for goodness sake. You're better off tapping into plain old www.ThisOldCompany.com to avoid mobile user confusion. Have a heart-to-heart with your tech people if they suggest otherwise. Of course, the choice on how to handle your domains for wireless branding is up to you, but frankly, the simpler the better. Make it easy for your mobile customers to find you.

Leverage Mobile Design Features to Enhance Brand Imagery

Sometimes, the creators of a PDA application miss an opportunity to enhance the company's brand. They forget to change the way the application appears in the launch window, as seen in Figure 5.7. When the application developer overlooks using a source code reference to a logo or image file, the default image of a square diamond appears. This is a common oversight. A company logo, or a variation thereof, would make a stronger statement. Compare my example, by

Figure 5.7 Imaginary firm ABCDEFG uses the default Web builder icon in this version of its Palm OS® software.

fake firm ABCDEFG, to the ABC News logo and the "Ask" button service mark for Ask Jeeves.

Have you done any HTML or ever looked at Web page source code? Then you'll be glad to know that avoiding this little "boo-boo" is child's play. In Web clipping source code, the META tags PalmSmallIconFilename and PalmLargeIcon-Filename specify the graphic file to use when applications are displayed on a Palm OS device, as shown in Figure 5.8. How hard can that be?

Place Your Mobile Presence on the Top of the "Deck"

Here are several ways to position your brand so that it gains its share-of-mobile mind. Each has its advantages and disadvantages. Review them and see if they work for you or if a better approach is in order.

Product Packaging

Do you want a new user to think of you right after he or she buys a mobile device? Strike up a conversation with a handheld device manufacturer or two. See what it takes to have your software application featured in its bundled software package. Include your fliers in the product box if you can. With the cooperation of the manufacturer's PR folks, send out a news release to let the world know you're on this device's "hit parade."

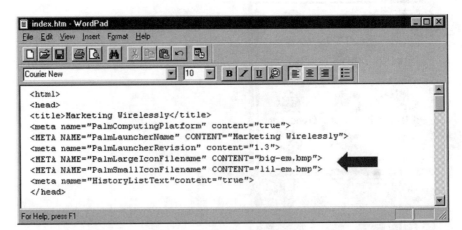

Figure 5.8 The source code for a Web clipping application shows how to specify a logo for the Palm OS® software launch window.

Advantages

1. You have an established base of mobile customers right out of the starting gate.

2. Your affiliation with another company appears as an endorsement to the user and builds your brand strength by association.

3. The user doesn't have to hunt you down to acquire your application.

Disadvantages

1. The latest and greatest version of your application might not be available to new users.

2. There's no guarantee that the user will open your application even after it's installed on his or her device.

3. This proposition could be pricey. Check with your intended hardware manufacturer for details.

Carrier Positioning

If you plan to deliver your content to mobile telephone users, you'll need to negotiate for position on the carrier's Internet content menus. For example, you might strike a deal with AT&T PocketNet or Verizon to place your link at the top of a list of entertainment providers or create your own unique menu. If your content has value not found elsewhere, this feature gives you extra leverage. Keep your eye on this space. Competition will heat up as more and more content providers jockey for position within the "walled gardens" of telephone carriers.

Advantages

1. Users will see you as they scroll through the content menus.

2. You don't have to work as hard to establish awareness among this carrier's subscribers.

3. Some carriers can convert and deliver your selected Web-based content to mobile subscribers, eliminating the hassle of creating a separate wireless site.

Disadvantages

1. You might not be the only content provider in your space on the carrier's menu.

2. There's no guarantee that the user will look at your content even after he or she finds you.

3. This proposition could be pricey. Check with your intended wireless carrier for details.

Portal Positioning

Take advantage of low-cost or no-cost ways to feature your mobile presence at major wired Web portals. This example, seen in Figure 5.9, shows how I gained visibility among Palm OS users by signing on as a software developer with Handango. I packaged back issues of my e-mail newsletter *Marketing Wirelessly* into a simple Web clipping application and uploaded it to my product directory at Handango.com. I wanted to create another distribution channel and make the content available to users who might want some reading at the airport. The result was my publication's increased visibility for a few wonderful days. By accident, I also discovered that Handango had a co-branding relationship with Lycos, as seen in Figure 5.10. Now, another of my mobile projects was visible on a second Web portal without my even trying.

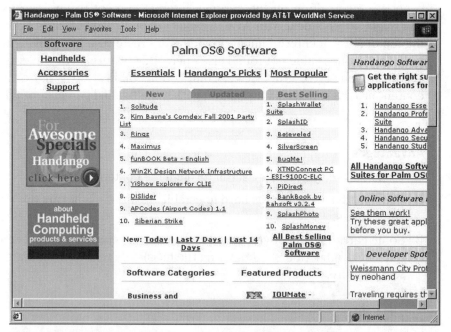

Figure 5.9 For about a week, the author was number two on the Handango new releases hit parade. (Copyright © 2002 Handango, Inc. All rights reserved. Handango is a trademark of Handango, Inc.)

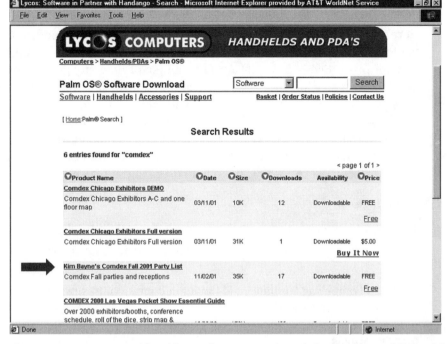

Figure 5.10 In partnership with Handango, Lycos brands itself as a portal for mobile users while providing some free PR to the author. (© Copyright 2002, Lycos, Inc. All Rights Reserved. Lycos® is a registered trademark of Carnegie Mellon University.)

Advantages

1. A portal can have more relationships than you know, and you'll be able to tap into that.
2. Many users come to the mobile Internet by way of their exposure on the wired Web.
3. The user doesn't have to hunt you down to acquire your application. Hey, I think I'm repeating myself.

Disadvantages

1. Search engines can be infamous for not displaying the latest description of whatever you have posted on the Web.
2. You have limited control over how your branding message comes across in some Web channels.
3. It can be difficult to trace the effectiveness of these types of co-branding relationships.

Application Launcher Positioning

Here's a cute trick. If you're putting together a WCA, you could use the META tag PalmLauncherName to designate a name that positions your application in a better place. See Figure 5.11 for an example of how city guide provider Vindigo got its name to appear first on my handheld. It appears that the WCA designer used a dash at the beginning and end of the name *Vindigo*. One can hardly blame them. After all, the company name starts with 'V' which positions its software lower alphabetically than most other companies. I thought it was such a neat idea that I followed their lead, renaming "Kim Bayne's Comdex Fall 2001 Party List" to "A Party List" to help users find it faster.

Advantages

1. When it comes to branding, who says that you have to play fair?

2. This process is very simple to implement, and it costs absolutely nothing to do.

3. When competing for handheld device recognition, this tactic can be pretty effective. . . for a while.

Disadvantages

1. Of course, the down side is that everyone else will catch on and mimic this tactic to some degree. Sorry, but the folks at Vindigo thought of this idea first. Everyone else is just a copycat.

Figure 5.11 Vindigo moved its Web clipping application to a more prominent position by tweaking its name.

2. It's kind of like hometown advertisers in the telephone Yellow Pages trying to outmaneuver each other by beginning their business name with "AAA." It looks kind of tacky.

3. And then there's the real branding issue: user perception. How will users feel when they can't find you in alphabetical order as expected? I had more than a few users mention that they didn't find my party list application right away after installation. One person installed it twice when he didn't see it. Whoops.

Focus On Brand Strength

Promote your most valuable brand attributes. In the upper-left corner of Figure 5.12, you'll see how the TITLE field on this screen accentuates one of the company's top services: tracking a shipment or package. The WCA designer used the TITLE tag in the application source code to name this page accordingly.

When promoting your wireless presence, use copy to solve a problem regardless of the media. Look at Figure 5.13 to see how America Online's Moviefone uses its catalog advertising to demonstrate how to access entertainment information. The Epocrates-branded Palm Vx uses its Web site to mention how it's

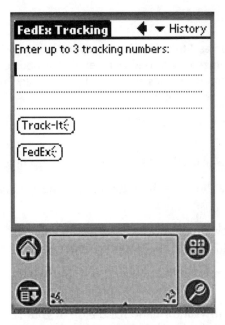

Figure 5.12 The title field for this page in the FedEx WCA emphasizes the purpose of this application. (© 2002 Federal Express Corporation. All rights reserved.)

Figure 5.13 Moviefone offers "easy access" to movie showtimes and tickets. (Moviefone ad © 2001 America Online, Inc. All rights reserved. Used with permission. Source: Affinity Publishing's Web Clipping Guide for Palm Handhelds, published by the Affinity Publishing Division of PennWell Publishing Company © 2000.)

the most popular handheld device used by healthcare professionals (Figure 5.14).

Here are a few more examples of how marketers are focusing on brand strength:

Amazon.com. "Would you believe there are 18 million items that you can buy on your Palm VIIx handheld?"

BarPoint.com. "Tired of drilling down for product info?"

Fidelity InstantBroker. "It's Time the Market Kept Up With You."

mySimon. "Instantly Compare Prices On Millions Of Products From Thousands Of Online Stores."

OAG Mobile. "Hold the power of travel information at the tip of your fingers. . ."

Prudential. "Only Prudential gives you so many ways to plan and manage your finances."

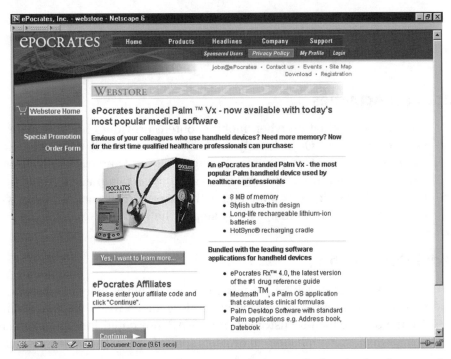

Figure 5.14 The ePocrates Web store appeals to a medical professional's sense of colleague acceptance and user need.

Travelocity.com. "Take Control Of Your Travel Destiny."

USAToday.com. "Your Connection to Your World, All Day, Every Day."

Tout a feature. Offer a benefit. Save the user money or time or both. Yes, mobile branding should promote the experience of the user in control.

Mobile Co-Branding

One aspect of wireless branding is how well it complements the branding of others. Although mobile devices are very personal in nature, your branding efforts could eventually focus on catering to a business partner plus its community of users, rather than individuals.

As prevalent as co-branding is in the online world, sometimes these marriages make about as much sense as these lyrics in the hit musical *Grease*: "We go together like ramma lamma lamma ka dinga da dinga dong." In other words, don't get together with just anybody just because it sounds neat. It could water-down your mobile brand.

When co-branding makes sense for your mobile presence, tap into these opportunities to distribute promotional materials, cooperate with advertising placement, or share in media relations duties. Here are a few examples.

Shared PR Activities

It's a win-win situation when mobile content providers hook up with mobile service providers. Occasionally, everyone wants to tell the world. See how location-based content provider Vindigo and food-and-travel reviewer Gayot got the word out in Figure 5.15. But Gayot doesn't stop its co-branding activities here. It has already hooked up with Sprint Wireless and AOL Anywhere to leverage mobile partnerships every step of the way.

Special Participation

Special wireless development programs, exclusive mobile merchandising promotions, and preferential listing in wireless media would be a good incentive for the sales channel customer. Your WAP site could include a directory of nearby dealers in alphabetical or geographical order. Those dealers that reach

---

BW2283   OCT 30,2001   6:34 PACIFIC   09:34 EASTERN

(BW)(NY-VINDIGO) Gayot Restaurant Reviews Now Available through Vindigo's Award Winning Location-Based Service; Gayot Launches on Vindigo's New Pocket PC Version

Business Editors & Hi-Tech Writers

NEW YORK--(BUSINESS WIRE)--Oct. 30, 2001--Vindigo, the leading developer of personal navigation applications for mobile devices, is pleased to announce the addition of Gayot to its roster of trusted, high quality content partners.
   Written by a team of savvy restaurant critics and food-and-travel experts, Gayot's high quality reviews will help Vindigo users hone in on the best places to dine in major U.S. cities.
   "We are thrilled to introduce Gayot to the Vindigo user base, starting with our newest product for Pocket PC devices," said Jason Devitt, CEO of Vindigo. "Gayot's professional reviews are exceptional, and we're pleased that they have chosen the Vindigo platform to distribute their content to mobile consumers."
   "We are delighted to bring our content to an entire new group of mobile users," said Alain Gayot, Editor-in-Chief at Gayot. "One of the key features will be the freshness of the reviews --

---

Figure 5.15 Vindigo's CEO and Gayot's editor-in-chief are quoted in a joint news release about the two companies' mobile offerings. (© Vindigo. Copyright © 1996–2002 GAYOT.)

certain sales volume levels could be eligible for enhanced listings in such directories.

Nested Branding

One complication of branding to mobile users is the co-branding that occurs quite by circumstance. Here's an example. I'm watching television, and I notice the big fat H logo in the lower right corner for the History Channel. In addition to being aware of this graphical treatment for the entirety of the program, I also notice the television brand (though less frequently), the brands mentioned during commercial breaks, and the identity of the individual program itself.

Compare this situation to the mobile branding experience. In the example shown in Figure 5.16, you'll see how nested branding messages have the potential to affect your individual mobile brand. I've labeled each brand by letter.

A. The Yospace SmartPhone emulator is a Web-based service used here to demonstrate mobile branding concepts.

B. The Nokia telephone skin is similar to a mobile telephone.

C. Finally, the user sees your brand, as demonstrated in the screen from Best Western's WAP site.

D. I forgot one. The fourth brand not seen here is the service provider, such as AT&T, Cingular, Sprint, Verizon, yada yada yada. In fact, the mobile user doesn't even get to your brand until he or she goes through this gatekeeper of mobile content. How's that for distracting the user while he or she is trying to meet you wirelessly?

It's possible that all these nested brands-within-brands can cause confusion about the identity of the brand owner. Keep that in mind when building your mobile brand and when choosing your co-branding partners. There's really no way to avoid this situation, because the telephone, the service, and the wireless Web site need each other. Just understand that nested branding is a very big part of the mobile marketing picture. You have to accept it and work with it.

Summary: Top Five Expert Tips

1. Keep your mobile branding efforts integrated with all your other branding efforts. Mobile branding can't make it alone—at least, not yet.

2. Be selective in agreeing to co-branding activities. They're a great way to extend your brand to as many users and communities as possible, but only if it pays off in real terms.

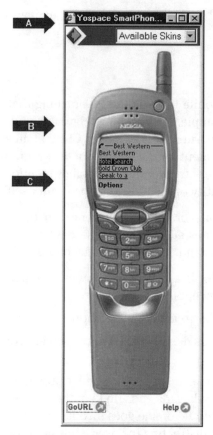

Figure 5.16 Stacked brands have the potential to either strengthen or weaken your mobile brand message. (SmartPhone Emulator © 1999–2001 Yospace Holdings Ltd. Used with permission. Telephone image © Nokia. WAP Site © 2001–2002 Best Western International, Inc.)

3. Find ways to position your brand for its uniqueness and value-added interest. Create an integrated approach to copywriting that fits into this mobile branding vision.

4. Focus on your traditional branding strengths, and translate these to the wireless world. Find what mobile users need and want, and give it to them.

5. Don't spend too much time on corporate identity concerns. A pretty logo is the least of your mobile branding challenges.

CHAPTER 6

Advertising without Wires

"One singular sensation. Every little step she takes. One thrilling combination. Every move that she makes. . . "

From the song "One" in the Pulitzer Prize and Tony winning Broadway musical
A Chorus Line

Wouldn't it be great if customers were so enamored with your message and so entranced with your imagery that they followed your company's every move? Given today's crowded advertising environment, such wishful thinking is hardly realistic. From bathroom stalls to elevator walls, advertising surrounds us. What options could possibly remain for the would-be wireless advertiser?

A few years ago, I logged into AT&T PocketNet with a loaner Ericsson R280LX mobile phone. Upon launching the Phone.com mini-browser, I was asked, "Are you a college basketball fan?" I answered "yes," and a wireless ad invited me to "Play the Tourney Pick-em game with AT&T Digital," revealing a sponsorship by Chevy Trucks. This novel approach to advertising was interactive, entertaining and—need I say it?—mobile. In order for my low-tech living room TV to deliver an interactive experience, I would have to be logged on to my laptop while sitting on the sofa. And that would hardly be comparable.

This early glimpse into wireless advertising is just a small indication of the future in store for this hot new media. Industry analysts anticipate that wireless advertising might well surpass $12 to $20 billion, depending on who you ask, in the next three years—a prediction destined to siphon dollars from more than just a few Internet and traditional media advertising budgets.

About This Chapter

This chapter will demonstrate how current wireless advertisers are targeting their intended audience. Does the title of this chapter mean that you won't be bothering with previous forms of advertising? Of course not—you'll see how marketers reach users anytime, anywhere, and when they *are* and *aren't* engaged with the wireless Web. This chapter will provide brief examples of how wireless advertising fits into the overall concept of establishing a wireless marketing presence. You'll also see how handheld devices are being used as a typical creative element in ad imagery.

Are you wondering what wireless advertising can possibly do for your company? Very simply, wireless ads can achieve any marketing goal that you can dream of, provided that you present tangible benefits to the user. There are plenty of examples of wireless advertising in action, all pictured on these pages. And in case you're wondering about guidelines for your ad creative team, the draft standards for wireless advertising, as summarized by the Wireless Advertising Association, are found here, too.

Before you begin reading, ask yourself this question: What is it about your products and services that can appeal to mobile device users? Review the advertising examples in this chapter and start making your list.

The Adoption of Wireless Advertising

The one thing that wireless advertising has over other forms of advertising is mobility. When you are on the Web, you rely on users to take action in your favor before they log off. Once they leave the office or home computer, the memory of your presence fades quickly. What better way to retain a customer's interest in your products and services than to use wireless advertising to tag along wherever he or she might go—reminding him or her gently as needed?

Besides the obvious business-to-consumer hook, what has driven the adoption of wireless advertising? Undoubtedly, the promise of additional revenue streams is one answer. Wireless advertising is a great way to leverage an already established customer base. And yes, telephone carriers have a captive audience in that regard—a built-in audience of loyal or obligated customers, depending on what kind of deal they agreed to at the beginning of the service contract. Verizon, Sprint, and AT&T are in unique positions to capitalize on that captive customer base. This opportunity is further enhanced by the continuing struggles of dot-com darlings around the world.

What Exactly Is Wireless Advertising?

When I first began to investigate the concept of wireless advertising, I encountered a pre-established definition of the term. Certainly, providers of wireless services, such as mobile telephone network providers, could easily stake claim, having been the first creators of wireless advertising. Their definition includes advertising the services of wireless communications networks to consumers. One can easily recall images of actress Jamie Lee Curtis, on television commercials in the United States, hawking a well-known mobile phone service—that's one form of wireless advertising.

Manufacturers of handheld devices, as in mobile phones and PDAs, could also call the invention of wireless advertising their own. Finally, if I wanted to further blur the lines of distinction, I could state that for anyone who has ever manufactured and/or marketed a wireless device of any kind. Perhaps even sellers of "walkie talkies," for example, could wear the wireless advertiser hat. All right—I stretched the definition a bit on that last one.

As with most things related to technology, definitions come and go—and in the case of online communications, definitions constantly, and often surprisingly, evolve. These days, when marketing mavens refer to wireless advertising, they might mean sending commercial messages to users of mobile devices. Still, wireless advertising might not be as obvious as you think. Sure, there are a few wireless directories for registering a wireless site's presence, but such registration doesn't really fall under the category of active wireless advertising, now, does it?

Defining the Wireless Ad

For the purposes of this chapter, I have defined a wireless advertisement as a commercial message delivered to and/or requested by the user of a mobile device. Examples of wireless ads, in no particular order, include the following:

- Short screens of commercial content that enable mobile device users to click through to a wireless site for more information

- Sponsored short text messages sent to the screen of a mobile device, such as headlined news alerts delivered to cell phones on a regular basis

- Logos and/or ad text coupled with selected wireless content, such as a local brew pub using m-coupons to make its presence known to users of a wireless dining guide

- Interactive ads, including a user survey displayed upon login, involving the user in learning more about a product in exchange for a nice discount or freebie

- A small static graphic or text-based banner ad surrounded by content in a wireless application or on a wireless site of sorts

- And yes, wireless advertising can even be defined as a brief voice advertisement delivered to users of mobile telephone services, such as those that provide driving directions through a voice-driven menu.

What is wireless advertising? It's the use of brand new media for reaching and targeting customers. It's the use of tried-and-true, or established media, to convince an audience to join you on the wireless Web. It's a way to provide product information to on-the-go people. It's an exciting way to build or enhance your traditional and online advertising presence. Wireless advertising is a new tool for your marketing mix.

A Few Wireless Advertising Concepts

SMS Text Messaging. The Short Messaging Service is used to deliver snippets of text-only content to the user's device screen. Using SMS, a wireless advertisement is sent directly to the opt-in user's pager or telephone. Most mobile telephones in use today can receive SMS with one exception—the user must subscribe to the text-messaging service with his or her mobile telephone carrier.

An SMS originator can be a marketing service that sends text messages in bulk to several users. M-coupons plus sponsored news and weather alerts are delivered in this manner. Another SMS originator can be an individual user who sends a message to a customer's telephone number by way of a service provider. For example, a user can address a message to another user's mobile telephone as though he or she is sending an e-mail. The TO: field might include the address 3035551212@mobile.att.net while the body of the message contains about a sentence of text.

How creative can you make SMS advertising? At this point, SMS is very limited. Graphics don't display, so forget about attaching that logo or product photo. And because the functionality of SMS ends at the point of destination, it is not practical to include a hyperlink to lead the user to a wireless site. SMS advertising can include the ability to dial a telephone number, but that's about it for now. Yeah, I know. That limited functionality could change like the wind . . . or as soon as you finish this sentence.

Push versus pull. Many forms of wireless advertising are based on, or should be based on, a concept of *opt-in*; that is, the user has the option of deciding whether he or she wants his or her name and number included on a particular list of customers. SMS text messages fit into this category. They're sent because the user specified that he or she is interested in receiving selected information, like alerts, at predetermined times (*push*).

Figure 6.1 A standard 468x60 banner appears on publishers' sites and instructs the consumer to enter the mobile phone number to receive a coupon. (Picture courtesy of Advertising.com. Copyright © Advertising.com, Inc. All rights reserved.)

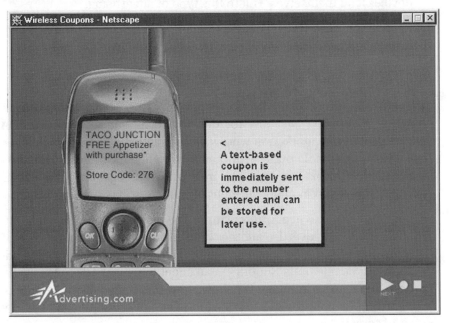

Figure 6.2 A text-based coupon is immediately sent to the telephone number entered and can be stored for later use. (Picture courtesy of Advertising.com. Copyright © Advertising.com, Inc. All rights reserved.)

Or perhaps he or she has responded to an offer to request additional information on the fly (*pull*). Often, a request for pushed mobile content is originated on the wired Web, as illustrated in Figure 6.1.

Mobile coupons. Mobile coupons can be text-based messages sent at the user's request, as shown in Figure 6.2. The user might request m-coupons by completing or updating a profile that specifies the user's preference for advertising type and frequency. A user can also obtain an m-coupon by clicking a link or replying to an offer. The m-coupon would then be sent by return broadcast or e-mail. M-coupons might be linked somehow to the user's current location and have an expiration time to encourage immediate action.

Location-based advertising. This concept of wireless advertising assumes that the user has either entered a current physical or geographic location (more user privacy and control), either by zip code or street address, or the mobile system has recognized the user's location through advanced location-aware technology (less user privacy and control).

Time-sensitive advertising. Location-based wireless ads with a short expiration time require users to take immediate action. Such ads might include an m-coupon for a lunch deal that's only good today from 10 a.m. to 2 p.m. Wireless marketers believe that the unique mobility of handheld devices lend themselves well to this type of advertising.

Now that you have those concepts under your belt, let's look at how they're being applied in the real world of wireless advertising.

Where Do Wireless Ads Appear?

Wireless advertising isn't just for delivery to mobile telephones, PDAs, and pagers. Enterprise marketers who wish to reach and serve mobile users must use a variety of media outlets for their advertising messages. From the following examples, you'll soon see that wireless advertising already appears in many different forms and in many different places.

Embedded in software applications. The developer of a popular software application can advertise another of its products by informing current users. See Figure 6.3 for an example of how QUALCOMM uses the ad-sponsored mode of its Eudora e-mail client to deliver ads to PC users. A drop-down menu in Figure 6.4 shows how this scaled-down version of Eudora software provides users with several of the same features of its full-sized version.

Figure 6.3 QUALCOMM informs its built-in market how to extend Eudora's functionality to a Palm™ handheld. (Eudora, Eudora Pro and Eudora Internet Suite are registered trademarks of QUALCOMM Incorporated. © 1999–2002 QUALCOMM Incorporated. All rights reserved.)

This discussion reminds me . . . when it comes to wireless advertising, take your time. You might be tempted to advertise a bare-bones version of your current product just to launch your wireless presence now rather than later. Such a hasty decision could disappoint or alienate current customers. QUALCOMM took great care in selecting the right features for its mobile Internet products. Oh, yeah, that's product development. Never mind. Let's get back to advertising. Here are some other places where wireless advertising appears.

Through Internet access services. The AT&T WorldNet Service i495 plan required wired Internet users to download special access software that delivered ad messages while connected. A service provider's software or portal could be used in a similar manner to promote your company's

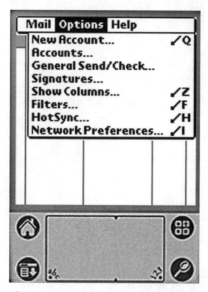

Figure 6.4 Eudora Internet Suite 2.1 supports POP, SMTP, HotSync®, multiple e-mail accounts, filtering, and filing. (Eudora, Eudora Pro and Eudora Internet Suite are registered trademarks of QUALCOMM Incorporated. © 1999–2002 QUALCOMM Incorporated. All rights reserved.)

wireless products and services to a user who just happens to be "wired" at the time. In the examples shown here (Figures 6.5, 6.6, and 6.7), Handspring pushes the adoption of its Visor handheld products with a series of different

Figure 6.5 The picture of a Visor handheld drops down from a toolbar on AT&T WorldNet i495 Service. (Visor image © Handspring, Inc. Used with permission. AT&T WorldNet i495 Service and ad toolbar © AT&T. Used with permission.)

Figure 6.6 Handspring informs AT&T users by advertising the features of the Visor Edge handheld. (Visor Edge advertisement © Handspring, Inc. Used with permission. AT&T WorldNet i495 Service and ad toolbar © AT&T. Used with permission.)

ads delivered to the Internet user. Clicking the ad message causes the browser to go to the associated Web site, which in this case is Visor.com.

On the pages of print media. Magazines, newspapers, and catalogs often contain advertisements for a company's wireless presence. The advertisements appear no different than any other print ad with the exception of its copy being targeted to current and future mobile users. Some print ads, like the one in Figure 6.8, promise to simplify the lives of Palm VIIx handheld owners by providing information wirelessly. Other print ads, like the one in Figure 6.9, offer wireless assistance to users in need.

Industry publications geared toward mobile users are also an excellent place to advertise your wireless presence. Quarter-page ads from manufacturers of software (Figure 6.10), hardware (Figure 6.11), and accessories (Figure 6.12) appear in the November 2001 issue of *Mobile Computing & Communications*.

Within the screens of Web clipping applications. A mobile user might tap through content screens while using a *Web clipping application* (WCA), sometimes known as a *Palm Query Application* (PQA). In the course of

Figure 6.7 Handspring makes AT&T users an interesting Visor offer. (Visor advertisement © Handspring, Inc. Used with permission. AT&T WorldNet i495 Service and ad toolbar © AT&T. Used with permission.)

Figure 6.8   An advertisement in Affinity Publishing's Web Clipping catalog introduced Palm™ handheld users to the wireless version of Ask Jeeves. (Ad © 2002 Ask Jeeves, Inc. Ask Jeeves is a registered trademark of Ask Jeeves, Inc. Source: Affinity Publishing's Web Clipping Guide for Palm Handhelds, published by the Affinity Publishing Division of PennWell Publishing Company. © 2000.)

reviewing the content, he or she might notice a mini-banner similar to one found in this Mobile Advertising Demo by AvantGo (Figure 6.13).

With product packaging. When I unpacked my Palm handheld device, I found a flyer promising me a free leather case for returning the enclosed reply card. Sorry, the postcard part is missing because I already sent it in before I remembered you might like to see it, too. Bottom line: I took the bait, got my free gift, and spent a few minutes on the telephone talking to a Fidelity representative who clued me in about how I could use Fidelity's wireless service to place stock orders, get quotes, and check account positions in real time. Yeah, it was a fair trade—my time in exchange for a useful gift. Sure, I'd do it again. Just ask me. Whatcha got? When I

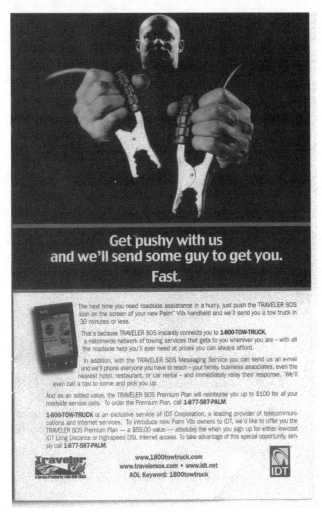

**Get pushy with us
and we'll send some guy to get you.
Fast.**

The next time you need roadside assistance in a hurry, just push the TRAVELER SOS icon on the screen of your new Palm™ VIIx handheld and we'll send you a tow truck in 30 minutes or less.

That's because TRAVELER SOS instantly connects you to **1-800-TOW-TRUCK**, a nationwide network of towing services that gets to you wherever you are - with all the roadside help you'll ever need at prices you can always afford.

In addition, with the TRAVELER SOS Messaging Service you can send us an e-mail and we'll phone *everyone* you have to reach - your family, business associates, even the nearest hotel, restaurant, or car rental - and immediately relay their response. We'll even call a taxi to come and pick you up.

And as an added value, the TRAVELER SOS Premium Plan will reimburse you up to $100 for *all* your roadside service calls. To order the Premium Plan, call **1-877-587-PALM**.

1-800-TOW-TRUCK is an exclusive service of IDT Corporation, a leading provider of telecommunications and Internet services. To introduce new Palm VIIx owners to IDT, we'd like to offer you the TRAVELER SOS Premium Plan — a $59.00 value — *absolutely free* when you sign up for either low-cost IDT Long Distance or high-speed DSL Internet access. To take advantage of this special opportunity, simply call **1-877-587-PALM**.

Traveler

www.1800towtruck.com
www.travelersos.com • www.idt.net
AOL Keyword: 1800towtruck

IDT

Figure 6.9 Another Affinity catalog advertiser offered to send help to unfortunate automobile drivers who were also wireless. (© 1-800-TOW-TRUCK, Inc. All rights reserved. Source: Affinity Publishing's Web Clipping Guide for Palm Handhelds, published by the Affinity Publishing Division of PennWell Publishing Company. © 2000.)

received my free leather case from Fidelity, they took the opportunity to include another marketing piece in the package.

On the pages of wired Web sites or portals. A search in the Yahoo! Web directory, using the keywords "palm software," produced several helpful links plus a banner ad for Handango's Security Suite, as seen in Figure 6.14. Once I refreshed my browser, I discovered Handango had even more to offer wireless users, as seen in Figure 6.15.

Throughout the wireless Web. While searching for information through the WCA version of answer site Ask Jeeves, the author discovered that a

Figure 6.10 Playing into the mindset of the mobile revolution, a LandWare print ad portrays a laid-back user of PocketQuicken. (© 1997-2001 LandWare, Inc. All rights reserved.)

publisher was a wireless sponsor of content, as seen in Figure 6.16. In Figure 6.17, a SkyGo user finds out about the flower business while browsing content. Notice how the FTD.com ad offers the user several choices, such as getting more information, saving FTD.com information to an address book, or adding FTD reminders to his or her To Do list.

The actions of early adopters of wireless advertising prove that at least some rules of marketing still apply. Wireless advertising—like any new media—is just one aspect of your marketing mix. There is no absolute equation for wireless advertising success, but one thing's for sure: the effectiveness of your wireless advertising program requires the use of several different tools that reach mobile users. You never know where your wireless audience might be. You might need to meet and greet users while they're online or invite them to join you in the wireless realm while they're doing something entirely different.

Figure 6.11 This print advertisement for a handheld keyboard offers mobile device users a free product. (© 1997–2001 LandWare, Inc. All rights reserved.)

What Do Wireless Ads Do?

For true marketing effectiveness, your wireless advertising must be structured to reach the right people with relevant content when it matters to them the most. Keeping this knowledge in mind, you can create wireless ads that accomplish one or more of the following objectives:

Create a Call to Action. For product or service offerings, a wireless ad can contain an invitation to purchase, either immediately or after more information has been delivered to the customer wirelessly. In this example from SkyGo, the Lexus automobile gets its share of wireless visibility through an interstitial advertisement (Figure 6.18). The Call to Action

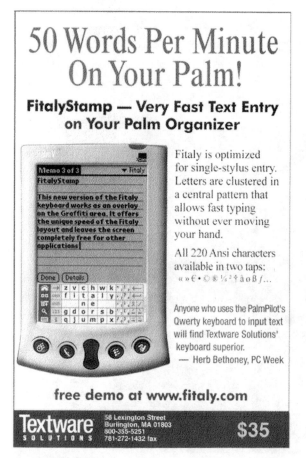

Figure 6.12 Textware Solutions reaches readers of an industry publication with its quarter-page ad for FitalyStamp. (Copyright © 1998–2001 Textware Solutions.)

invites the user to either ask for a follow-up e-mail with information or save Lexus to the user's address book.

Enhance brand awareness. A simple ad banner that merely informs can be part of a product launch campaign delivered to wireless users, as seen in Figure 6.19. The ad shown appeared on the results screen of a Web clipping application. Similarly, many enterprises leverage their mobile presence to deliver mini-banners from selected advertisers, including their own companies. You could use your wireless brand to generate additional revenue or barter for quid-pro-quo visibility by accepting advertisements, links or logos from paid sponsors or strategic business partners. Here is a short list of examples:

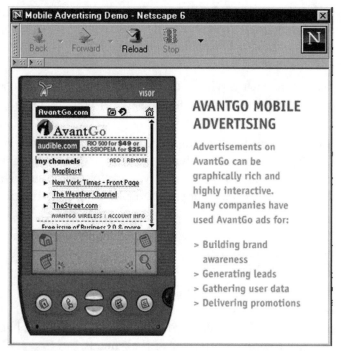

Figure 6.13 Using audible.com as an example, the AvantGo Web site demonstrates how a banner is placed within the AvantGo PQA. (AvantGo is a registered trademark of AvantGo, Inc.)

ABCNEWS.com includes a text-based link titled "Up to the Moment, Up to You" to advertise its own wired Web site.

Buy.com uses links titled "Top 10 Products For Palm Users" and "Palm User Specials" to promote selected products found within its database.

eBay tells handheld users the name of its application developer through a link titled "Powered by WorkSpot, Inc."

MapBlast! Includes logos of individual stores on location listings.

Generate leads for another marketing use. Your goals for reaching mobile device users might include gathering names and addresses for a future direct e-mail campaign or for telephone sales follow-up. Be careful about this one, though, because you can easily misinterpret a mobile user's intent. Make sure that you disclose any intended use of a mobile customer's information in advance. And don't forget: submission of mobile contact information by a user is not necessarily evidence of tacit consent for future marketing.

Include a hyperlink for more information. In response to a mobile user's clickthrough, you might wish to send mobile users a short product summary—or if your choice of mobile media permits it, lead them to your wireless site to make a purchase.

Provide entertainment with trivia. Your goal for reaching mobile users could include educating them about your industry or helping them remember your brand.

Meet a timely need for impulse buying. If your customers make buying decisions on the fly, wireless advertising might help. By being there when mobile users are in a buying frame of mind, you can close the sale. Need an example? Take a look at the case study for the NHL's Carolina Hurricanes in this chapter.

Deliver mobile coupons. Mobile device users might be more interested in trying out your company's offerings if you give them a discount. Established customers might want to have their loyalty rewarded, and a mobile coupon could be the "thank you" that they need.

Take a user survey or poll. Your interest in mobile users could include getting an opinion or two. Or, perhaps you'd like to look into user habits so that you can gear your wireless offerings to their needs.

Test knowledge with a user quiz. Depending on your company's focus, you might wish to dispel industry myths or reinforce your brand strength. A mobile user might view your quiz as a nice diversion that strokes his or her ego when answering correctly.

To put it in a nutshell, just about any advertising purpose can be revamped, refitted, and readjusted to meet the needs of both wireless marketers and their users.

Co-Branded Wireless Advertising

When it comes to advertising to mobile users, why go it alone? Cooperative placements are a great option. For example, users of Web-based e-mail might click and view a streaming video of a movie trailer for an upcoming movie, embedded in the image of a handheld device. For this wired Web-based ad, entertainment marketers could combine their promotional efforts with those of a device manufacturer, as parodied in Figure 6.20. Meanwhile, beauty site Reflect.com continues the industry-wide push for wireless adoption in a real ad seen in Figure 6.21.

Figure 6.14 Wireless software publisher Handango reaches mobile users through a keyword-related banner ad placement on a Web-based directory. (Copyright © 2002 Handango, Inc. All rights reserved. Handango is a trademark of Handango, Inc.)

What Is Your Wireless Advertising Message?

Here are a few basic messages delivered to potential and current mobile device users through advertising.

- Mobile devices are cool.

- They'll make your life easier.

- You can get on the Internet anytime and anywhere.

- Wireless gadgets make a strong fashion statement (see Figure 6.22).

- You'll be able to get work done even when you're not in the office because you'll be able to take a smaller version of something with you.

Here, let me elaborate on some of the messages that you might or might not wish to convey to wireless users. I might appear over the top on some of these suggestions, but then again, it's hard to contain my enthusiasm. . . or my lampoonery, for that matter, in evaluating some marketing campaigns.

Mobile devices are cool. Like most image marketing campaigns, wireless marketers want wireless users to know how cool they'll look when they sport the latest wireless gadget or application. If a user's social standing hinges on looking like a secret agent, they'll often perk up when they see or hear messages about how neat it will be to flash a new digital camera, tape recorder disguised as a pen, or even—gasp—the hottest Internet-ready doodad. If you're not marketing a handheld device, accessory, or piece of related software, you can still get in on this game anyway by associating your product or service with these nifty devices. Everybody say, "Oooh, ahhh."

Okay, I can hear a few of you booing me. Come on. I'm not suggesting subliminal advertising here. So, before I continue like an advertising wolf in sheep's

Figure 6.15 A Handango banner ad tells mobile users how to "travel lighter" by promoting popular travel software for the Palm OS® handheld. (Copyright © 2002 Handango, Inc. All rights reserved. Handango is a trademark of Handango, Inc.)

Figure 6.16 A publisher sponsors wireless content through the Ask Jeeves Web clipping application for Palm™ handheld users. (© 2002 Ask Jeeves, Inc. Ask Jeeves is a registered trademark of Ask Jeeves, Inc.)

clothing, I have to admit that most consumers today are more sophisticated than that. Knowing this fact, it's fairly obvious what your wireless advertising campaign needs. It certainly doesn't need to rely solely on an "image is everything" mantra.

Beyond the coolness factor, your advertising message needs substance. It needs timing. It needs a message that appeals to the user's desires, whether those desires include news and information, shopping, work productivity, or entertainment. In addition to the image advertising you might embrace to some degree, your wireless advertising message should convey tangible benefits to the mobile user. These tangible benefits need to address when he or she is away from home, away from the office, or otherwise out-of-pocket. In fact, I

Figure 6.17 SkyGo and FTD use an inline ad to provide several choices to mobile users. (Source: SkyGo. FTD.COM logo copyright © 2001–2002 FTD.COM All Rights Reserved.)

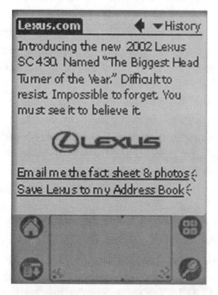

Figure 6.18 Lexus delivers its interstitial ad to mobile SkyGo users who are browsing through wireless content. (Source: SkyGo. Lexus logo © 2001-2002 Lexus, a Division of Toyota Motor Sales, U.S.A., Inc.)

even use my mobile devices at home when I'm too lazy or too tired to use anything else. So there.

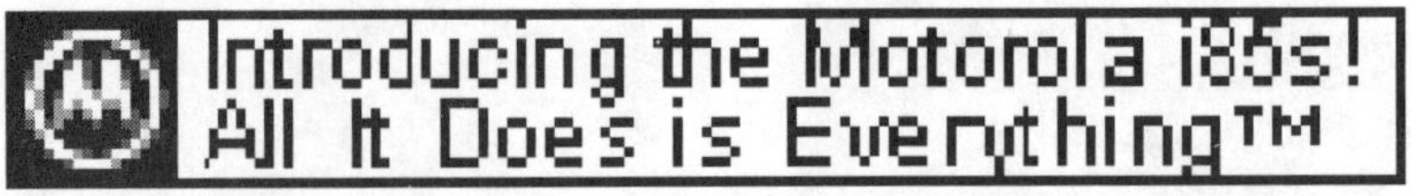

Figure 6.19 On another company's wireless application, Motorola introduces its product to mobile users in a very straightforward manner. (Advertisement © Motorola, Inc.)

Impulse Buying and the Carolina Hurricanes

Sports marketers know that many sports enthusiasts and event attendees decide at the last minute that they're going to a game. That's where Windwire, a wireless advertising and marketing network, came to the rescue of the North Carolina Hurricanes. The National Hockey League's franchise needed a new way to promote local ticket sales. Windwire offered the team an opportunity to reach a demographic with a taste for sports and a pocket of cash—that is, discretionary income for sports entertainment. Many mobile users fit that profile, plus they have a lifestyle that creates a need to buy tickets when and where it's convenient for them.

So, in the fall of 2000, the Hurricanes decided to go wireless. The wireless advertising campaign enabled the Hurricanes to reach local users of both PDAs and mobile telephones—plus it offered local users a great new way to get event tickets. This situation meant that eager, mobile-savvy sports fans in the surrounding region could now smash a beer can on their foreheads while simultaneously purchasing tickets wirelessly. (Just kidding, folks! I'm a hockey fan, too.)

When did the Hurricanes actually reach these wireless sports fans? When sports nuts were conveniently in a sports frame of mind. Duh! Oh, you want to know how this process worked? I'm getting to that. In any given sports franchise territory, there are a limited number of local wireless publishers that reach the right audience. Windwire chose wireless publishers in North Carolina, South Carolina, and Virginia to deliver the Hurricane's wireless advertisements. A local mobile device user who might be viewing relevant sports scores on a wireless device ran across the Hurricane ads in the normal course of reading content.

What did the wireless ad include? The wireless advertisement was a Hurricane logo complete with "call to action" text. The ad copy invited the user to click through to call Ticketmaster for tickets on the spot. Alternately, PDA users were pushed to Ticketmaster's wireless Web site for the same impulse buy.

Mind you, the Hurricanes weren't the only ones to rely entirely on the promise of wireless advertising. No slackers in the integrated marketing department, they bundled the ad campaign with television and radio placements.

By no means is this situation the end of the Hurricanes' wireless advertising story. Their program is more sophisticated than simply delivering a logo and a link or two. Ticket discounts and event codes contributed to measuring the return on their wireless advertising investment. So, if you had any doubts that the campaign was working, Windwire's system has the numbers to prove it.

What *were* the results? The Carolina Hurricanes' wireless advertising campaign boasted a response rate of between 10 and 15 percent, which is pretty good considering that the campaign was innovative, unprecedented, and pretty much an experiment. Compared to other forms of advertising, that's not too shabby.

Think about the demographics of wireless users. They're smart. They have money. They are predisposed to listen to you. Is your advertising message a fit? Here are a few more suggestions:

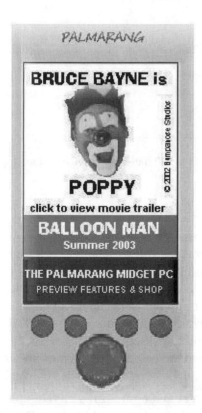

Figure 6.20 Fake companies Palmarang and Bumpanose Studios co-brand a mobile-themed Web advertisement featuring funnyman Bruce Bayne.

Figure 6.21   Reflect.com offers a free Palm™ m100 handheld to buyers spending $100 or more.

Mobile devices will make your life easier. Life was hard before we had mobile devices, right? (The author nudges you with her elbow.) Right? And if the user doesn't tap into the functionality of wireless devices, he or she might have no time left to spend with his or her spouse and kids. Hey, I wonder how many people know that mobile users can do all their bookkeeping on the train on the way to the office in the big city? That leaves Dad plenty of time to play football with little Jimmy when he gets home tonight. And, if a customer needs to catch up on the news, sports, and weather, wireless devices can help him or her do it when it's convenient.

Regular folks use mobile devices to reach companies anytime, anywhere. The day is packed with appointments and errands. There's no time to buy family tickets to that movie, and everyone needs a night out. So what will you do? Mobile devices enable users to buy admission tickets,

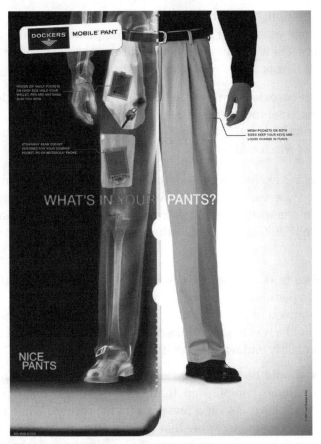

Figure 6.22 Dockers® Mobile Pant offers the user plenty of room for stowing wireless devices. (© 2001 by Levi Strauss & Co.)

purchase birthday gifts, and even send a sympathy card to Aunt Broomhilda while waiting in line at the grocery store, waiting for the loan officer, or relaxing in the office park at lunchtime.

Got insomnia? Get wireless. You can stay awake all night because the backlight on your PDA, mobile telephone, or pager lets you read news or play games in the dark while you are in bed. Your mother or even your spouse might never know the difference. Okay, my spouse will—but then again, anything that even remotely illuminates the bedroom can be a bother when he's trying to get to sleep. Let's move on.

Wireless devices make a strong fashion statement. If the latest fashions are any indication, tech-savvy folks love wearing clothes that say "I'm mobile." Established apparel manufacturers, and a few new garment kids on the block, are creating 21st century attire that fits into current lifestyles. Is a strategic alliance with one of these clothing companies on your agenda? Offering customers a new addition to their wardrobes could enhance a promotional event that is tied to a product launch.

Mobile users can get work done even when they're not in the office. If your marketing manager forgot to put those last-minute details into the conference presentation, now is the time for him or her to take advantage of the portability of wireless devices.

If you're not marketing exclusively to adults—that is, your market includes wireless-savvy kids, "tweens," and teens—your wireless marketing messages could appeal to their sense of boredom. Wireless devices can entertain users when the TV or Web isn't available. Do these benefits describe your customer's needs?

Users will be glad to take a smaller version of you with them. With a few exceptions, it's possible that every business on the planet will soon have a miniature version of its products, services, or Web site available for customers. I've found a few organizations on my own that one would never expect to find wirelessly and was glad that I did.

Savvy mobile users should be able to retrieve anything, write anything, buy anything, update anything, compute anything, and schedule anything they want. They should be able to tap on a few screens for results. While using a mobile device, the users wants to know that the resulting file or data will be compatible with everything at the home or office. They want to be able to accomplish more. And if a company's IT people are on the ball, enterprise users want the ability to upload forecasts and reports to the company's intranet. Your advertising can let them know how you can meet these needs.

Notice the customer-oriented theme here? Now it's your turn. When you think about it, you could probably tap into the creative side of your brain to put a sense of memorable entertainment into your wireless advertising campaigns, no matter what the product or service.

User Concerns

It's now time for a public service announcement. I'd like to shed some light on a very touchy subject: user privacy. Mobile device users have very real concerns about wireless advertising—all of which are legitimate.

According to a May 22, 2000 story in ZDNet's *Inter@ctive Week*, Canadian ad network Profilium has developed a way to "track wireless subscribers' habits and calling patterns, and the places they visit, in an effort to send targeted and personalized advertising messages to users." Reporter Meg McGinity reports that the habits of wireless subscribers are tracked throughout the Profilium network, a data mining move sending shivers up the average mobile user's spine. In its defense, Profilium maintains that its data is collected anonymously.

Sometime soon, *global positioning systems* (GPS) will be used to very precisely narrow down the location of individual mobile phone callers throughout the United States. No municipality will be without this lifesaving service. Emergency callers to 911 services who hang up too soon—whether out of fear or confusion—will be glad to know that help is still on its way. On the other hand, there are marketers who think the availability of this new technology will become another neat way to track unsuspecting users. Perhaps they'll want to send them a coupon for a free order of fries with purchase at the burger stand a mere block away.

Clearly, users can interpret the tracking of location and user habits as an intrusion. Whether the data is released to an outside company or not, the fact remains that someone can and will catalog this information. Such practices are always an issue for the user, no matter what is promised. No system is foolproof, not even the best-laid privacy plans of the most respected businesses.

Another user issue is how wireless advertising frequency might negatively impact workflow. Business users rely on the availability of Web-enabled devices to retrieve needed data in real time. Conceivably, the receipt of too many ads could reduce a mobile phone or PDA's efficient operation or value. At the very least, the user should always have the option to control the frequency of transmissions to his or her own device.

This time won't be the last that I bring up the subject of privacy. It's an important topic that's worth repeating several times.

Not So Fast

Unlike the Internet, implementing a wireless advertising campaign is not as simple as compiling a list of opt-in subscribers and e-mailing product notices and special offers each month, although it's a good place to start. If you have an established base of Web users, why not offer them the opportunity to receive your news or other useful content free and wirelessly?

But don't count your (wireless advertising) chickens yet. The acceptance of wireless advertising is still in its infancy. You must be very careful when advertising to mobile device users. A few legislators are even considering making unsolicited wireless advertising illegal. If passed, those will be interesting laws to enforce.

Watchdog efforts notwithstanding, if you care about your company's goodwill and reputation, take heed. Wireless phones, PDAs, and the like are very personal devices creating a bigger perception of intrusion among uninterested users. Imagine how frustrating the influx of unwanted advertising can be on a small yet portable device compared to the relative ease in deleting unsolicited e-mail. Although future studies might soon challenge this assumption, at this point too few subscribers are ready to reveal their precious mobile telephone number to individual marketers yet. In other words, proceed with caution. There's a long road ahead for both wireless device users and the businesses that plan to advertise to them.

As a personal example, I once signed up for weather-related text messages sent to the screen of my cell phone. Unfortunately, I lost the Web address of the weather news provider and had no way of discontinuing the alerts when my needs changed. My telephone carrier was of little help in stopping the SMS spam, other than suggesting that I eliminate text-messaging service entirely. To be honest, the weather alerts weren't the worst part. It was the unwanted accompanying ad headers. They took up so much memory on my antiquated cell phone that I couldn't delete them fast enough. Eventually, the weather alert provider realized that it had forgotten to brand its free wireless content properly. Finally, it inserted a Web URL in the header of the messages—enabling me to log on and cancel the annoying twice-daily blurbs.

So, Are Users Ready or Not?

While you're formulating your strategies and tactics for overcoming market resistance to wireless advertising, consider the following statement. Acceptance for wireless advertising might already be a foregone conclusion in some markets.

In December 2000, wireless marketing firm SkyGo, Inc. released the results of a study done in Boulder, Colorado on the acceptance of wireless advertising. Study responses were compiled in five separate online surveys. The findings from SkyGo's Wireless Marketing Study suggested that not only were users ready for wireless advertising, but they welcomed it. To help put this study in perspective, SkyGo mentioned that 65 percent of the study group were actively browsing the Internet wirelessly anyway—a number much higher than the then current WAP user population.

Based on a four-month trial with more than 1,000 opt-in consumers, 60 percent of the participants believed that wireless ads had informational value. By the way, study participants received their cell phones without cost as part of the study, but at least 27 percent were quoted as saying they would consider changing to a wireless service provider to continue receiving wireless advertisements.

Now, if this situation sounds like a bunch of wishful thinking or marketing hype to you, you're not alone. I had the same skeptical reaction at first. It's hard to believe that consumers would willingly pay for the very thing they fight to avoid on the Web. Of course, as with any marketing program, the two key factors in determining whether or not a user is interested in receiving ads lies in the following:

1. Users expressed an interest in receiving specific ads; that is, ads met predefined needs for information.

2. Successful ads are "targeted, compelling, convenient, and interactive," says Daren Tsui, co-founder and CEO of SkyGo.

To further shed some light on its study, SkyGo followed up with this data:

- Sixty-four percent of WAP ad alerts were read by recipients.

- Alerts generated an overall ad recall rate of 58 percent.

- Fifteen percent of all wireless ads resulted in action or planned action.

- Interactive ads had click-through rates of 52 percent.

- 2.9 percent of ads results in a purchase, either online or offline.

- 37 percent of participants opted to provide credit card data for use in an m-wallet.

What's in It for Me?

Sometimes a little incentive can go a long way in encouraging user acceptance. For example, Australian-based Wireless Dynamics offers a service called DynamicSMS that actually pays users to receive SMS advertisements. In essence, the user receives messages in exchange for a percentage of the company's advertising profits.

First, the mobile user activates his or her account on the Web. After activation, the user completes a lifestyle profile to help the ad delivery system target advertisements accordingly. Finally, registered users must use viral marketing techniques to refer their friends and family to the service.

As the Web site says, "The key to DynamicSMS is to get as many people to join as you can before anyone else does. The more people you get to join (at the higher commission percentage)—the better." DynamicSMS denies that its service is a pyramid scheme, preferring instead to call itself a "network marketing business."

In its favor, DynamicSMS promises that advertisers do not share in the personal information provided by the user. Another good incentive is their promise that the user can deactivate his or her account at any time, deleting all references to personal information. Just in case you're wondering, only decent folks may advertise on the network. Sorry, no porn peddlers allowed.

Interested advertisers can contact the company through their Web site at www.dynamicsms.com. You'll be interested in knowing that Pricewaterhouse-Coopers is listed as the auditing firm for the calculation of commissions and advertising distribution.

WAA Advertising Standards

You might have noticed how device manufacturers are using images of handheld devices as so-called windows into the world of the wireless Web. By placing the image of the device in the advertisement, users might already feel that they're plugged into the unplugged phenomenon.

The *Wireless Advertising Association* (WAA) is one of those entities spearheading the establishment of standards for wireless advertising. Given the seemingly endless variety of devices, networks, and protocols available, I don't envy them. To put their agenda in perspective, you should know that the WAA's board of directors includes movers and shakers from just about every corner of the wireless world, including luminaries such as AT&T Wireless Services, AOL Mobile, MSN Mobile at Microsoft, OmniSky, Vindigo, SkyGo, and so on. You can read more about this organization at www.waaglobal.org.

On June 26, 2001, preliminary draft standards were released. Oh, and just so you know—GSM stands for the Global System for Mobile communications. For your quick reference, here are the standards.

GSM SMS Standards

These were previously determined by the European ad standards working group and apply only to messages carried over GSM mobile networks, predominant in Europe and much of the world outside the United States and Asia:

Zagme's Location-Based Ads

If you're shopping in the United Kingdom, you might be an opt-in recipient of wireless ads at a nearby shopping mall. In November 2000, wireless content provider ZagMe launched an opt-in wireless service for shopping center customers. Pairing with technology developer Adeptra, ZagMe delivered personalized versions of ads in the form of text messages to individual shoppers via their mobile phones. These wireless promotions, complete with expiration times, are designed to attract users into select stores.

Members registered with the free service by providing only a mobile telephone number. A shopper interested in more personalized offers is invited to provide additional details, including preferences and favorite stores. The user activates the service both upon entering a participating shopping mall and through location-aware sensitivity linked to selected retailer's storefronts. Brand-name mall advertisers include The Gap, Pizza Hut, Reebok, Warner Bros. Cinema, and The Body Shop, which were able to send offers, gifts, and prizes to users during their shopping excursions.

Zagme reports the following results:

- One in five people completed a transaction after receiving an alert.

- User conversion rates reached as high as 20 percent.

- The average value of sales transactions for participating retailers increased.

- User demographics varied, increasing wireless advertising's appeal to a wide range of retailers.

- Sponsorship: A message that is up to 34 characters in length (two lines of text on most phones), designed for sponsoring content which precedes or follows the ad unit

- Full message: A message of up to 160 characters in length, typically delivered as standalone

Non-GSM SMS Standards

These standards will apply to all SMS messages carried over other mobile networks, such as *Code Division Multiple Access* (CDMA) and *Time Division Multiple Access* (TDMA), the predominant systems in the United States.

- Sponsorship: A message that is up to 34 characters in length (two lines of text on most phones), designed for sponsoring content that precedes or follows the ad unit
- Full message: A message of up to 100 characters in length, typically delivered as standalone

WAP Standards

Interstitials

- All standard sizes listed here can be run as interstitials.
- An 80x31 pixel interstitial will run full screen on a four-line high display.
- Should time out at five seconds
- User must have the option to skip the ad.

Comments

"Content friendly" standards are designed for publishers or carriers who require some non-ad content to appear on the opening screen of the device.

TEXT ADS	NOTES
15 Characters (Fixed)	Content Friendly
30 Characters (2 lines fixed)	Content Friendly
34 Characters (1 line of Marquee/ Times Square* text)	Content Friendly /SMS Standard Compatible

GRAPHIC-ONLY ADS	NOTES
80 x 8 pixels	Content Friendly
80 x 15 pixels	Content Friendly
80 x 20 pixels	Content Friendly
80 x 31 pixels	Designed to run full screen on a four line high display

- Marquee or Times Square formats utilize groups of words that appear on multiple screens (left to right) to enable the display of an entire phrase on a single line.

GRAPHIC PLUS TEXT ADS	NOTES
80 x 8 pixels plus one line of text (see text specs above)	Content Friendly
80 x 15 pixels plus one line of text (see text specs above)	Content Friendly
80 x 15 pixels plus two lines of text (see text specs above)	Designed to run full screen on a four line high display
80 x 20 pixels plus one (or two) lines of text	Designed for larger screen devices

Note: I-Mode standards will be derived separately as a future project.

PDA Standards

Comments

"Supported" formats are in use by the industry but not as widely as "recommended" formats. These will be re-evaluated as usage grows.

Wireless Ad Serving

Internet marketers can easily place a banner advertisement on a given Web site, sponsor a text message in the header of an e-mail discussion group or list, or even purchase a keyword or two at any number of search engines. There

PALM OS	POCKETPC OS	COMMENTS
Recommended		
150x24 pixels	215x34 pixels	
150x32 pixels	215x46 pixels	2 lines of text
Supported		
150x18 pixels	215x26 pixels	1 line of text
150x40 pixels	215x58 pixels	3 lines of text

Source: Wireless Advertising Association, www.waaglobal.org

are an endless variety of choices for businesses interested in tapping into the marketing power of the Internet. All that's needed is knowledge of your online market, such as where your customers are most likely to congregate, and you're well on your way to reaching interested buyers. On the wired Internet, you can decide between multiple, ongoing placements at the most expensive of general-purpose sites or a few short ads appearing for a limited time within a few low-cost e-communities. And now, we give you some disclaimers about wireless advertising.

The Good, the Bad, and the Ugly

On the wireless Internet, you have far fewer advertising creative and delivery choices. Not every mobile device can recognize and display the same wireless ad, which means that you might have to develop ads for multiple platforms. Comparatively, when it comes to recognizing and displaying a graphical ad banner on the Web, the difference between Microsoft Internet Explorer and Netscape Navigator is minimal.

Unfortunately, many mobile devices on the market today use black-and-white screens with limited sizes and graphic capabilities. In other words, they have little or no accompanying graphics. When advertising to mobile devices, you rely more on the power of your ad copy than on the power of your ad layout. Yes, I know—plain text can be ugly. There's nothing like having online history repeat itself. Don't worry—it'll get better eventually, just like the wired Web.

While you're planning your new wireless promotions, ask your Web-based users to opt-in to receive your text-based missives. I hope that you're willing to put at least some money into attracting new customers. Marketing your wireless presence to an established base limits the number and type of people you reach to those you already know.

Another approach to wireless advertising would be to buy media at sites that already have a wireless presence, such as ABC News, Amazon.com, Ask Jeeves, and eBay. These placements, on the wireless version of the sites, could extend your targeted advertising efforts. You must decide whether such placements will capture enough attention for your needs.

To reach the broadest possible number of wireless users, investigate wireless ad networks. Just like their wired cousins, wireless ad networks deliver ads to hundreds—no, thousands—of opt-in wireless users. These could be the interested people who you don't know yet but would like to meet. They have already expressed an interest in meeting companies just like yours. Wireless ad networks have technology infrastructures in place to deliver your wireless message across a broad range of sites. Some networks can deliver the same wireless ad in several different formats, saving you development time in creating ads for multiple mobile platforms. That's the good news.

Summary: Top Five Expert Tips

1. Keep wireless ad copy compelling, interactive, and immediately useful to the recipient. An offer by itself doesn't necessarily meet the useful criteria.

2. Leverage your existing marketing presence to invite established customers to use your wireless products and services.

3. Look into wireless ad networks to save development time and to garner the broadest reach to new customers.

4. Investigate an advertising network's privacy and data mining practices beforehand.

5. Always base your wireless push advertising on opt-in user preferences for content type and frequency.

CHAPTER 7

Delivering Content to Wireless Devices

"You see, we never ever do nothin' nice and easy. We always do it nice and rough."

Singer Tina Turner, talking at the beginning of the song "Proud Mary"

When I launched my first personal wireless site, I had much to learn about mobile users' wants and needs. To be honest, I wanted my first m-content publishing experience to be *nice and easy*. I looked around and found one of those do-it-yourself free sites for hosting WAP content, namely mpresence.com. Consequently, launching my first project was very simple and pain-free. I just clicked through the menus of a browser-based editor as noted in Figure 7.1, cutting and pasting selected material from my wired Web site. I was convinced that I had somehow bypassed most entry-level issues related to joining the wireless publishing revolution.

"But where's the value proposition?" you might ask, referring to the importance of my WAP site to the typical mobile user. Well, there was none. My site was, to borrow a phrase, *nice and rough*. I created a quick-and-dirty WAP site for the sheer fun of it. I was just playing with the concept of wireless publishing. But I also wanted to brainstorm about whether or not a wireless site would be fit for my particular business model as a writer. More importantly, I wasn't sure that I was ready to commit any real time or money to the venture. I didn't even have a plan. Obviously, my first attempt at wireless content served no one but me. After accessing and wading through my site—as you'll see referenced in Figure 7.2 on a Web-enabled Ericsson mobile phone using the AT&T PocketNet service—I knew that I had a long way to go in attracting interested visitors (back to the drawing board).

Looking back at other early mobile sites, I know that I wasn't alone. For many companies, early wireless content paralleled wired content found when the commercial Web first launched. Most marketers published on corporate Web

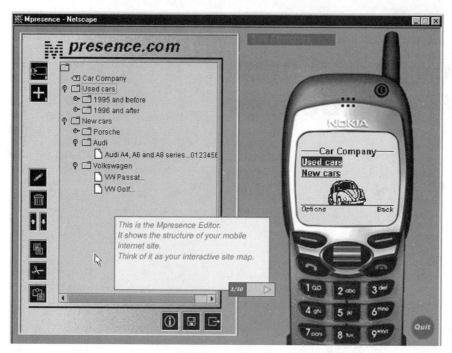

Figure 7.1 The Mpresence.com editor simplifies the task of creating a small business or personal WAP site. (Site hosting courtesy of Mbasics. All rights reserved.)

sites by grabbing old documents and converting them to HTML, all the while changing barely a comma or period. Navigation was minimal. Graphics were rough. Page layouts were rudimentary at best. Eventually, technology advanced—then Web marketers became savvy about copywriting, design, and functionality. The wired Web matured.

You might know from your past Web publishing experience that repurposing brochures word-for-word doesn't work well for electronic media. That's because Internet-capable computers, HTML, Java, and other well-known tech-

Figure 7.2 Kim Bayne's first mobile site at mgo.to/kimbayne as seen through an emulator application found at Yospace.com. (Site hosting courtesy of Mbasics. All rights reserved.)

nologies exist to create a memorable interactive adventure for Web surfing customers. To complicate content and site architecture matters, users have higher expectations of Web sites than they did a few years ago. Web browsing in the 21st century has tainted and predisposed them to faster access, animated graphics, scripts, and so on. Wireless user demands about mobile site content and functionality will follow the same evolution as the e-marketing bar continues to rise. What satisfies mobile device users today will become ho-hum and perhaps less useful tomorrow. As a mobile content provider, plan to field and respond to impatient inquiries by enthusiastic yet early adopters. But most of all, you should plan to adapt.

About This Chapter

If you're hoping that this chapter will help you code pages for a wireless site, you've come to the wrong place. That would bore the marketing side of your brain. Besides, a primer on WML, *Handheld Markup Language* (HDML), or some other handheld language would be outdated long before this book's publication date. Not to worry. There are several resources, both online and offline, designed to train ambitious and qualified folks in optimizing content and code for mobile devices as referenced in Figure 7.3, including FAQs on font sizes and page widths. This book isn't one of them.

But take heart. This chapter will provide an overview of what to expect when you start tackling your first wireless publishing project. You will learn which wireless content is important to mobile users, what current content delivery choices exist, and the different ways that other content providers are meeting the challenge. Finally, you will think through the process of delivering the type of wireless content that your mobile users really want.

Content Formats and User Access

Content delivery on the wired Internet can be done several ways, depending on your users' needs and preferences. These can include the following:

SMS text messages. These opt-in e-mail alerts include updates on news, weather, sports scores, and so on sent directly to the screen of your wireless device. Normally, the user signs up at your Web site to receive selected information, as in Figure 7.4. To avoid the wrath of small screen users, each mes-sage should contain no more than a very small snippet of information boiled down to its essence. The number and frequency of these items should be lim-ited, and you should provide the user with choices in this area.

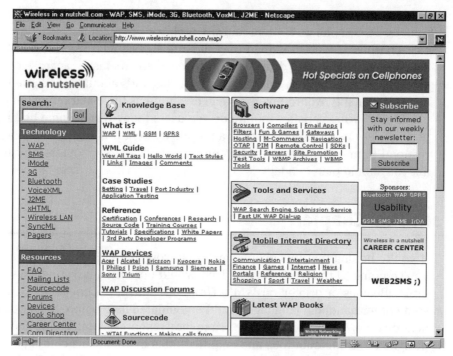

Figure 7.3 Wirelessinanutshell.com is but one of many developer resources found online.

Mobile devices are personal devices and should be treated with respect. Wireless spam is a growing problem. You do *not* want your corporate image associated with this awful phenomenon. Never ever sell, trade, or give away your users' cell phone number to anyone for any reason. Do *not* betray your users' trust. The Wireless Developer Network at www.wirelessdevnet.com has published a Top Ten List of SMS Etiquette, provided by TheFeature.com. While the article focuses purely on the consumer end of using SMS, it does contain one excellent piece of advice for marketers: "Remember that SMS can be traced."

Wireless Web site. Unfortunately, wireless subscribers cannot access all the sites on the wired Web. Only pages, directories, and sites coded in wireless lan-guages can be found. That's the main reason why you have to undertake a new site development project. How do visitors ever get to your wireless site? Mobile device users might scroll through content menus provided by their carrier or enter your URL directly into their mobile devices. Just make sure that you let everyone know that you exist somehow.

Personalization and location-based delivery. Content delivery options are often driven by two main activities: a user's express interest to receive selected information and/or a content provider's knowledge of the user's

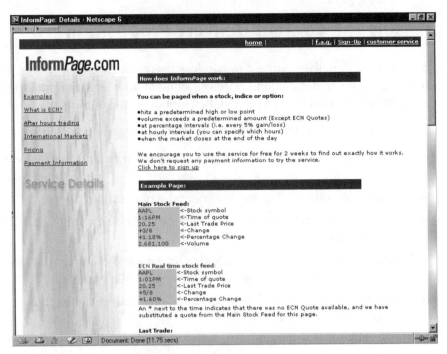

Figure 7.4 Mobilestockalerts.com, powered by InformPage.com, sends current stock prices to opt-in subscribers for a two-week free trial. (Copyright © 1998–2001 Inform-Page.com, LLP. All rights reserved.)

current geographical position. Personalization can be done on the Web upon user registration. Subsequent changes to wireless content preferences can be done with or without wires.

Voice retrieval. There is a certain percentage of mobile users who will never surf the wireless Web. How are you going to deliver your content to them? Voice interaction solution provider Conversay provides software development tools for speech-enabled applications. Lycos provides a voice version of the Web through a toll-free number. The world of wireless Web access by voice is just beginning.

Web clipping and synchronization. If you own a Palm, you know about this feature. Here's a very simple explanation. There's no way that you can down-load all the sites and content that you'd like to see onto one tiny device. There's just not enough memory or time. If you're traveling, certain modes of transportation prohibit you from using wireless capabilities, so you're stuck with what's already there. Just before you head to the airport, stick your handheld in the cradle and let your PC or Macintosh, plus a neat application or two, do all the work. Data will be transferred to your device, and you're good to go.

Addressing the Content Delivery Proposition

So you want to deliver content to wireless users, eh? Let's take a look at some of the keys to understanding wireless content delivery. I've put together a straightforward checklist to put you in a mobile frame of mind.

Before you tackle any wireless content project, you must (in no particular order):

- Assess your position relative to the value of your competitor's wireless content, if any.

- Research the market demand for your type of content.

- Appraise your current content library for its relevancy, value, and usability for mobile users.

- Evaluate your current staff, marketing agency, and other vendors for expertise relative to creating and delivering mobile content.

- Estimate the amount of money, time, and physical space that it could take to make content mobile-friendly.

- Determine which device-specific users will be able to read your content.

- Resolve whether selected wireless content will be complementary to, an integral part of, or separate from your wired content.

- Create new content that uniquely serves mobile users' wants and needs.

- Understand content delivery limitations and how they relate to formatting, readability, and user input.

- Choose how the user will subscribe to, receive, download, or otherwise gain access to your mobile content.

- Decide whether your content will be served statically as a Web clipping, dynamically in real time, or both.

- Create an administrative system for maintaining and updating wireless content.

- Build, buy, or borrow a technical system for delivering mobile content to either single or multiple platforms.

- Locate one or more partners or channels for extending content delivery, content branding, and other related activities.

- Leverage one or more strategic relationships for content promotional activities.

And even after everything mentioned here is said and done, you still have to perform the following tasks:

- Convey the value of your content offering to the mobile device user.

- Find a way to close the content acquisition "sale."

- Encourage mobile users to visit your company elsewhere—perhaps on the wired Web, at the mall, during a conference, or in person.

- Create a mechanism for receiving feedback from mobile users for improving content offerings.

- Keep your mobile content accessible, relevant, and timely on an ongoing basis.

- Continue revising your content delivery strategy to meet your user's changing wants and needs.

- Remain informed about how technology, market conditions, and your competitors' movements affect your content delivery choices.

Now, take a moment or two (or three or four) to jot down some brief bulleted answers or thoughts related to these items. You don't have to be precise right now. The idea is to help you understand that there's more to content delivery than simply throwing together a Web clipping application or pointing a user to a wireless service provider. By the way, these two (WCAs and service providers) aren't bad strategies by themselves. Just know that there are more details to this project than first meets the eye.

Real Cities and AT&T

In March 2001, Knight-Ridder's Real Cities Network announced that it had teamed with AT&T Wireless to deliver local news, sports, and entertainment content to AT&T Digital PocketNet users in 15 markets. You see, Real Cities had this established—and successful, I might add—content strategy of using multiple delivery channels to reach its audience. They thought, "Hey, why don't we work with a prominent player in the wireless arena?" It is a nice deal if you can get it.

Anyway, adding AT&T to the mix further cemented Real Cities' marketing position as a provider of local content. Plus, it enabled them to meet mobile users' needs for "on-demand, up-to-the-minute, localized information," said Dan Finnigan, president of KnightRidder.com, as quoted in a company news release.

Apparently, AT&T thought the content delivery proposition was a good deal for its users as well. It just so happens that they wanted to work with high-quality local content providers in order to increase the overall value of its PocketNet service to current users. Hey, it's a tough world out there—and somebody's got to do it.

Tackling the Wireless Content Project

Are you putting together a plan for this aspect of your e-marketing program? Start by defining the why, who, what, where, and how of your wireless content project:

- *Why* do you want to deliver wireless content?
- *Who* will be your wireless content users?
- *What* are the content interests in your wireless market niche?
- *Where* will mobile users access your information?
- *How* are you going to fund this project?

Why: Choosing to Deliver Mobile Content

First, consider the following reasons to either include or not include mobile content publishing in your marketing mix. Second, review each reason, consider the source, and then determine how it applies to you. Third, keep in mind that the United States, Western Europe, Japan, and other areas are worlds apart regarding the present and future of wireless content. Market studies and content preferences might not apply to all mobile users in all geographical areas.

Reasons to Embrace M-Content Publishing Now

If you don't get on the wireless content bandwagon now, you could have a tough time catching up. New handheld devices are emerging hourly. Yes, I admit that's a bit of hyperbole, so here are some real predictions to ponder:

- Does your content type or hierarchy work well with the short menus, mini-browsers, and small screens found on most Web-enabled cell phones? In the future, mobile phones will become the most pervasive handheld device according to a report titled "Wireless Market to Take Off in 2003," an April 16, 2001, Vision Report by Jupiter Media Metrix, Inc.
- Wireless portals are but one of the many mobile presence strategies in place today. If you're planning on developing a wireless portal, worldwide revenue for your mobile model could grow from $747 million in 2000 to $42 billion in 2005 (so says independent research and consulting company Ovum).
- Partnerships for mobile content delivery are growing. A brief titled "AOL Mobile Will Bring AT&T Wireless To Consumers" (Forrester Research, June

28, 2001) reports that AOL Mobile and AT&T Wireless expanded their association "from a mobile portal deal to cobranded data service."

Reasons to Be Wary or to Wait

Wireless content publishing might seem like a cool idea, but just think how frightening it will be to waste your marketing budget on a pipe dream. There I go again—fear mongering. Don't take my word for it. Take a look at these insights:

- Metered wireless content access as referenced in Figure 7.5 or subscription-based models could limit the number of customers you can attract via mobile devices. According to "Wireless Marketing: Rhetoric, Revenues and Reality" (Ovum Research, June 11, 2001), it's unclear whether users are willing to pay for wireless content.

- But even if your customers are willing to pay, income from mobile content might not be worth the effort. Data revenues will only be 4 percent of overall mobile revenue, according to "Mobile Internet Realities," a May 2000 report published by Forrester Research.

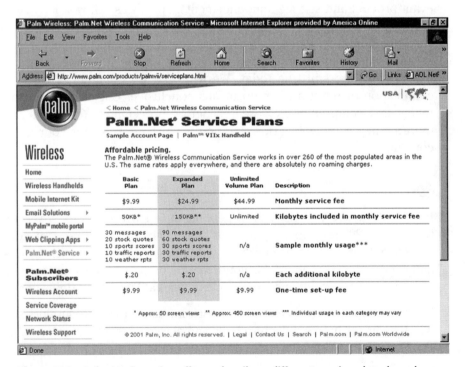

Figure 7.5 Palm.Net® service offers subscribers different service plans based on individual usage.

- Serving content to mobile device users promises to be a money-losing proposition for a couple of years due to a lack of revenue, according to Jupiter Media Metrix in a February 14, 2001, Vision Report titled "Mobile Content and Applications."

- In the study "Wireless Internet Content: Any Content, Any Device, Anywhere" published in May 2000, The Shosheck Group concludes that the structure of WAP and SMS make "differentiation and branding of wireless content" nearly impossible.

Who: Mobile User Numbers

Who are you trying to reach? As you might know, not all of your wired visitors will become wireless ones immediately. You should be able to encourage a good percentage of them to request your wireless data at some point, however, perhaps through offers of SMS content alerts. In addition, many mobile users will first discover your unplugged presence while browsing the menus of a carrier's wireless portal. To serve them content that they want and will use, you must understand one thing: Who are these people?

A sampling of user numbers, including age breakdowns, usage studies, and relevant product and service announcements, appear as follows. For a snapshot of initial mobile Internet use and companies that were banking on the future of wireless, skim this brief list. But before you run off and build a wireless marketing plan based on this information, ask yourself whether these market observations are still true today. We will offer a disclaimer: This now-dated compilation of reports is by no means conclusive. Check the Web for more recent and comprehensive research before proceeding. You might find that there's a new wireless market that you wish to consider for your untethered content.

Age

Harris Interactive reports that 42 percent of GenWireless survey respondents (ages 15 to 29) are mobile phone or pager users, plus 27 percent additional respondents had plans to purchase within the year. The August 2000 survey indicated that 36 percent of this youth market uses its devices six times or more per week. Forty-six percent use mobile devices at least three times per week.

College campuses are installing network infrastructures to support students' wireless device habits in lecture halls and classrooms, reports Cornell University News Service in a March 8, 2001, issue of the *Cornell Chronicle*.

Lest you feel that certain age brackets are being underserved, I have more news for you. Wireless NewsFactor reports that disposable cell phones are being marketed to seniors, according to a March 14, 2001, story titled Startup Pitches Disposable Phones by Jay Wrolstad. Norway-based Screen Media is marketing FreePad, a mobile Internet appliance as "Grandma-tested" (LinuxDevices.com, August 29, 2000). The design, which has been patented around the world, is being lauded for its simplicity, as seen in Figure 7.6.

Ethnic Group

In the April 2001 issue of *Marketing to the Emerging Majorities*, Verizon Wireless revealed a wireless content partnership with African American e-community Afronet.com. Afronet content includes daily news updates, daily tips from AfricanAmericanHealth.com, personals, entertainment, hip hop news, a monthly calendar of related events around the world, and a dining and entertainment directory.

Gender

RCR Wireless News reports that men talk more than women on mobile telephones. In a 2001 Cingular Wireless survey, male mobile phone users talked 35 percent more, averaging 372 minutes per month. Women used their mobile phones for voice communications 275 minutes per month. In the June 18, 2001, article, Cingular reported that men and women matched in their wireless Internet use.

Figure 7.6 The patented FreePad is a wireless Internet terminal designed for e-mail, video, Web browsing, and phone calls. (Design has been patented in most countries of the world.)

Geographic Location

More than 50 million Latin American Internet users will access the Internet wirelessly by 2005, says Jupiter Media Metrix. If you're delivering content to the United Kingdom, you have some competition. In June 2000, iTouch announced its wireless entertainment portal targeting children in the United Kingdom, according to Kids Marketing Report. By 2010, mobile Internet use will bypass voice mobile telephone use in the United States, reports The Seamless Media Survival Guide in March 2001. The report by Myers Reports, Inc. claims that mobile phone users in North America "will nearly double" by 2004, as noted in Figure 7.7.

Job Title

Medical professionals are now using PocketScript, a speech-driven interface for wireless PDAs, according to a story in *Wireless NewsFactor*, (J.B. Houck, February 6, 2001). Doctors are now able to retrieve patient records and access prescription information. In an article titled "Wireless Industry Writes Prescription for MDs," Houck reports that the ability to monitor patients' vital signs, such as pulse, temperature, respiration, and blood pressure, remotely through the use of mobile devices could soon become a reality.

Sexual Orientation

GayWired.com claims the title of being the first gay and lesbian site to offer wireless access to its users in 2000. AvantGo mobile Internet service is the go-between for users to add the GayWired channel to their mobile content preferences. A guide to dining and nightlife in New York called GayGuide can be found at www.tagtag.com/gay.

North American Wireless Subscriber Forecasts (in millions)	
2000	107.0
2001	129.5
2002	154.0
2003	178.0
2004	203.0

Figure 7.7 The number of North American mobile phone users will double by 2004. Source: The Jack Myers Report: "The Seamless Media Survival Guide," March 2001.

What other groups exist that could benefit by having access to your wireless content? Make a list of them now and then, for competitive research and future content development planning, and research the availability of relevant digital content on both the wired and wireless Internet.

What and Where: Content Choices and User Habits

"Given the limitations of the medium, wireless users want tiny packets of hyperpersonalized information, not boiled-down versions of generic information," wrote David Haskin, managing editor of *allNetDevices*, in an early 2001 article posted to wirelessadwatch.com.

Ultimately, your success in deploying wireless information could rest on your ability to offer quick accessibility, compelling applications, and useful on-the-go content rather than a scaled-down version of your wired Web site. If by chance your wired Web site resembles data that you should deliver to the mobile world, more power to you. You'll still have to create unique functionality or additional information to drive users to your mobile site repeatedly. By the way, it helps to know where mobile users are most likely to access your wireless content . . . while leaving the office, at home on the sofa, on the road, or elsewhere.

Content Ideas and Players

In one of those great movie moments, actor Woody Allen produces Professor Marshall McLuhan from behind a lobby sign in order to squelch the misinformed ramblings of a nearby moviegoer, as seen in the classic flick "Annie Hall" (1977). He then challenges the blowhard's alleged knowledge of McLuhan's works.

"You know nothing of my work," McLuhan intones, taking the know-it-all down a few pegs. When I first saw this scene, the audience howled with delight. We would all like to have instant access to the source of our discussions when someone is misinformed, challenges our credibility, or is just plain arrogant. Woody's character wishes that life could be like this scenario. Guess what? *It is now.* But even if you don't have the same neurotic tendencies as a Woody Allen character, you must agree that mobile content is empowering, and it's a user-centric world.

Entertainment

Imagine that pop boy band O-Town is about to open in the summer at various venues throughout the United States. Local fans need to know when tickets go on sale so that they can be the first in line to camp out at the box office. As an entertainment marketer, you could offer wireless users the option to sign up for ticket alerts based on zip code. Remember to publish retrievable snippets of tour news and celebrity gossip for wireless surfers, too. At the concert, wireless teens will be the envy of all their friends.

Sample content providers include the following: Citysearch.com (city-specific movie and event guides), Hollywood.com (stage, screen, and celebrities), Ticketmaster (music, art, and sports event tickets), ClubFONE, Froghop (games), MysteryNet.com (interactive mysteries), AstrologyIS.com (horoscopes), and Jokes.com (what else?).

Financial Services

Your company's biggest investor is stuck in an airport when he hears a young couple mention that your stock price took a dive this morning. Imagine how much calmer he'll feel after checking your current price in real time. If you have his permission, make it a habit to send him financial updates via SMS to keep him informed. By the way, that young couple just got married and was wondering if they'll be able to buy a house after the honeymoon. Any chance that your content can answer that question right now?

Sample content providers include the following: Ameritrade (investing), Hoover's Online (public and private company data), CBS.MarketWatch.com (real-time stock quotes), Homes.com (national real estate listings), Countrywide Home Loans (loan applications and approval), and Progressive.com (auto insurance quotes and comparisons).

Food and Drink

Annette is in the car. There's nothing to eat in the house, no time to plan a menu, and she wants to shop for dinner before her husband Alan starts heading home. Help Annette figure out what to make for dinner while she's at the store. Or, perhaps it's Friday night and company employees are going downstairs to that new karaoke bar. The HR guy wants to order an unusual drink, but the bartender has never heard of it. Help the bartender impress his new customers. Serve cocktail recipes to the PDA in his back pocket.

Sample content providers include the following: Kraft (recipes on the go), Allrecipes.com (recipes, menus, and meal planning), and M-Cocktails (a searchable database of cocktail recipes).

Health

During the summer months, hoards of vacationers head to the mountains or lakes for a few days of outdoor fun. While at the seashore, young Bruce cuts his foot on a piece of glass left in the sand. What can Mom do to prevent infection before heading to the nearest emergency room? Oh, no. Bernice just had an asthma attack from all the excitement. Wouldn't you like to be there to help them? Make your great medical advice available via the mobile Internet.

Sample content providers include the following: HealthAnswers (news, tips, and tools), HealthGrades (emergency services), and MD WAPNet (traveler's health tips and vaccination information).

News

We all joked about the hold-up in the 2000 U.S. Presidential election. What's the real reason why we can't confirm the next leader of the United States? I overheard a reference to Grandma Rita who lives in Broward County. Busy people don't have time to wait around for a world event that drags on like an O.J. Simpson trial. The news on the car radio only provides the briefest details as we drive to the grocery store. Help users retrieve the latest story on a Web-enabled cell phone while waiting in line to check out.

Sample content providers include the following: Ft. Lauderdale Sun-Sentinel (breaking local and national news from the southern Florida daily newspaper), ABCNews.com (general news from the broadcast TV outlet), WSJ Interactive Edition (business news), *The Chicago Tribune* (Chicago daily newspaper), CNN Mobile (general news from the Cable News Network), and LA Times Mobile (Los Angeles daily newspaper).

Reference and Education

Michael's term paper is due next Monday. The Greyhound bus heads back to campus at 7 a.m., and there's no time to check facts at the library. You can help this college student avoid an F by serving academic content to the wireless Web. Remember those long car trips as a kid? A bit of trivia would be nice to have on hand—especially when it incites hour-long debates. Start publishing to the wireless Web if your content is useful for research or even for just passing the time.

Sample content providers include the following: Britannica.com (encyclopedia), Dictionary.com (foreign language dictionaries, thesaurus, and writing resources), Merriam-Webster (dictionary and thesaurus), Colleges.com (vocabulary), The Gallup Organization (public opinion analysis), Qwest (Yellow Pages), and Yahoo! People Search (White Pages).

Shopping

Have you ever met a condescending computer salesperson that insisted that the hardware or software you seek isn't as good as you believe? If so, you'll understand why your Web users would like to take your comparative product reviews along with them on their next shopping trip. For bargaining purposes, it wouldn't hurt to provide up-to-date pricing, too.

Sample content providers include the following: mySimon.com (consumer comparison pricing), CNET's News.com (computers and electronics product reviews), BarPoint.com (product information by UPC code), ConsumerRE-VIEWS.com (consumer product reviews), and Switchboard Nearbuy Merchandising (products at local brick-and-mortar stores).

Sports and Games

Is The Rock quitting WWF, or is that just a nasty rumor? Wrestling fans will appreciate knowing, especially if they can pull in the latest while lounging on the sofa during TV commercials. Those of us cheering in the stands at a baseball game would like to check out player stats to add to our enjoyment, too.

Sample content providers include the following: ESPN.com (football, basketball, hockey, baseball, and so on), CBS SportsLine.com (scores and news), and VegasInsider.com (sports gambling).

Travel

Some people can find their way around high-tech devices but can't find their way home, even while driving behind a neighbor's car. How will they keep their sanity in a strange city when trying to find the hotel in a rental car? Allow directionally challenged users to retrieve door-to-door directions from a Palm device or cell phone. Help users check tomorrow's flight during down time in a hotel room. While you're at it, some of us are having trouble getting the desk clerk to understand our needs. Your content could help.

Sample content providers include the following: MapQuest.com (door-to-door directions and maps), Alaska Airlines (flight schedules), Sabre.com (planning), Fodor.com (local travel and reference guides), Hazar.com (translation services), 10Best (a virtual concierge), and Besttoilets.com (bathroom finder).

Weather

It's the Fourth of July, and U.S. families are heading over to the symphony in the park event for the annual fireworks display. Was that a drop of rain? Now locals are concerned about that weekend camping trip. At an outdoor festival, weather updates aren't readily available unless one has a wireless device. Sure, users can look at the clouds and give it their best guess, but most would rather check a reliable source. Perhaps your meteorological data can serve their needs.

Sample content providers include the following: The Weather Channel (current weather conditions and five-day forecasts—) and The Weather Underground (ditto—see Figure 7.8).

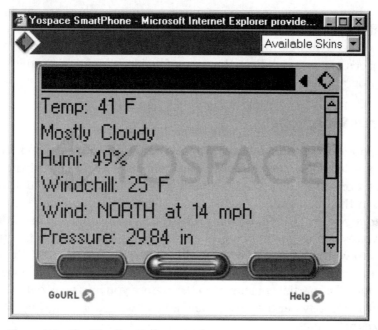

Figure 7.8 The Weather Underground as seen on a manufacturer-neutral Yospace emulator. (Copyright © 2002 The Weather Underground, Inc. SmartPhone Emulator © 1999–2001 Yospace Holdings Ltd. Used with permission.)

How: Funding Development and Deployment

Who is going to pay for your wireless content and its delivery? You can debate whether it's a good idea to charge wireless users. That choice is up to you. Certainly, by offering free content you'll attract more users. But if users don't pay, will they respect you in the morning? And who will foot the cost for writing, editing, delivery, site development, hosting, technical support, and so on?

Strategically, you must study how your market and its users perceive wireless content fees. Medical professionals might interpret user fees differently than college students. Attorneys might have more discretionary income than secretaries and therefore are less willing to balk at fees for business-related information. Many wired Web users think that paying for content stinks and might take this view into the wireless world. You need to find out. Beyond user studies, the value of your professional content is of prime importance.

If your content is highly coveted, for example, it's available nowhere else, and you might get away with charging users. You could also delay charging users until wireless access fees are restructured (if at all). Changes in how the telecommunications companies charge for wireless service plans could open the doors for more content payment models.

Like most budget-minded marketers, you're wondering how to pay for it all. After that, you want to know how to maintain profitability for your wireless content (or even, in light of no or lagging content revenues, how to maintain your project's ongoing viability). Here are a few ideas for keeping your wireless content program in the black.

Offer Paid Subscriptions

Here's an option. Offer a fee-based wireless version of a free, wired Web site. Charge for selected delivery options: basic content is free while enhanced content is not. Concerned that you don't know how to manage content delivery and payment in this manner? In August 2000, RightsMarket launched its *digital rights management* (DRM) software for Windows-powered handheld devices. The software ensures content control and usage rights by using authentication protocols to verify the user of a handheld device. Its first product, RightsPublish, offers content publishers the ability to charge users based on a variety of payment models: "partial consumption (try before you buy, view only, view and print, and so on) pay per use, expiration, and subscription," reports the *Canadian Corporate News*.

Charge Nothing

Publish free content and forget it. Obtain grants to fund development and maintenance. Better yet, consider your wireless presence a Web promotional expense. If you can point wireless users to your wired site to register for personalized wireless services, you've got their attention and their personal information. Now you can use it for e-mail marketing purposes (with their express opt-in permission, of course). When users get to the Web, serve them paid ads. Meanwhile, you'll grab share-of-mind when visitors access your wireless content while on the go. That could give you an edge over a competitor who hasn't grasped the concept of reaching mobile users. Being a wireless information philanthropist can net your company more than is readily obvious.

Sell Advertising and Sponsorships

Offer a free version of wireless content supported by paid advertising. If you send SMS messages, add a tag line to tell everyone who paid for content delivery. Some mobile devices can support graphics, so if a client's logo can be converted for wireless use, that's another revenue bonus for you. If you develop a wireless site, add converted images to selected areas of that site. If you keep it to a minimum, you won't offend mobile users—and this funding option will enable you to offer free wireless access to your wired customers as a bonus. Contact existing clients and partners to see whether they would like to piggyback off your wireless publishing plans. These companies could sponsor certain portions of your wireless content.

Find a Partner

Keep development costs down by partnering with someone in the know. Sign up with a wireless network to deliver your content for relatively low or no cost. Media sources Bloomberg, Dow Jones & Co., and *The New York Times* have teamed with AvantGo, according to a March 2000 Advertising Age Special Report titled "Media Eye Mobile Marketing" by Adrienne W. Fawcett. AvantGo and OmniSky offer mobile users customizable choices for adding content channels to their wireless devices.

Leverage Your Uniqueness

Convince wireless carriers like AT&T, Sprint, and Verizon that your content is so unique and so useful that subscribers actually need it. Allrecipes.com managed to secure this relationship with a few carriers. Similarly, carriers might be willing to grab selected content from your wired site, convert it, and deliver it to the wired Internet at no cost to you. Remember to appeal to each individual carrier's content positioning strategies when you pitch your content proposition. This risk-free arrangement could also land you a prime position on portal menus, saving you a bundle in promoting your site to thousands of new users.

License Your Content

Do you have great content that you would be willing to share, on a paid basis, with other wireless enterprises? In February 2001, AirMedia announced its Wireless Hub, a service designed to introduce content providers and distributors to each other. The business-to-business marketplace concept can help you sell information that can generate revenue for your wireless venture. Content providers include AccuWeather.com and Nando Media, for starters, according to a company news release. An added bonus is AirMedia's ability to transcode content and deliver it to more than one type of device.

In the April 2000 report titled "Executive Summary of Internet Content: Not Just for the PC," Yankee Group analysts predict that content developers will continue striking deals with "alternate device manufacturers, wireless carriers, and content delivery enablers to push content out to new devices." According to the report, users could still want access to your PC-based content on their mobile devices—an observation that might affect the content selection process for your company.

Charging for wireless content is not an all-or-nothing proposition. You could embrace a variety of options to fund your wireless content publishing, only to change your revenue strategy in a mere month or two. If watching Web-based content providers has taught us anything over the past several years, content, access, and subscription models do change. . . constantly.

Development Options

Content conversion and delivery issues might have been a challenge the first time that you launched a Web presence or added additional e-marketing activities. Well, you're in for another shock. The wireless world supports but a few HTML tags. What about graphics? Your logo might not look so hot on a Web-enabled cell phone. Remember the format and layout compromises that you made the first time your company published on the wired Web? Just wait. Even after you convert company prose to something useable on the unplugged Web, developing forms for simple wireless customer inquiries or surveys could make you grit your teeth.

Talk about dealing with multiple standards. Thank goodness that the wired Web wasn't this bad. Wireless formatting languages include *Wireless Markup Language* (WML), *Handheld Device Markup Language* (HDML), *Compact Hypertext Markup Language* (Compact HTML), iMode, *Extensible Markup Lanugage* (XML), and *Extensible HyperText Markup Language* (XHTML). Fortunately, several companies offer development tools to help you avoid learning these languages, thereby shortening the time to launch your mobile information service.

I'd like to dissuade you if you're not truly qualified to tackle the project of wireless site design and its associated hassles. After reviewing dozens of wired Web sites over the years, I'm convinced, by and large, that in-house development by amateurs leaves much to be desired, even with the coolest of tools. To put it bluntly, the best option for marketers who wish to remain marketers is experts who can handle such projects for you. Your technical support staff might already know about configuring servers to handle wireless languages. Many new media agencies are versed in tackling wireless Web site development. Ask to see examples, then tap into their expertise. Chat with content networks about their capabilities. A few are mentioned in this book. You don't need to know any WML. If you choose a network or carrier to convert your data and your site is compelling enough, you might even be able to negotiate for better rates in HTML transcoding and mobile delivery.

Before you ask someone to pull together a quote on wireless Web development and hosting, have a little fun. Log on to one of those free wireless sites. Play around with your content just so you have an idea of what questions to ask and how to tell vendors what you want. Pull up the site on your mobile device and see where the issues lie. Playing around with these free services won't hand you all of the answers, but at least you'll understand a bit more about dividing and conquering content for the wireless Web.

Do-it-Yourself

You can create a wireless site by using your desktop computer and a browser. One problem with this approach is the amount of energy that you'll expend cutting and pasting content. For personal home pages, these sites are a pretty cool first step, but for business purposes they might not be the best choice. How much time will you spend informing unknown users that your wireless content exists? Wireless sites without a partner, such as a carrier or network on their side, are like islands—hard to find by most mobile customers. Fortunately, central directories of wireless content, á la Yahoo! and Lycos, are popping up daily, but that might not help much. Ever hear of walled gardens? Selected telephone carriers charge a premium to users for accessing individual wireless sites not part of their planned wireless content menus. The following resources offer a combination of free tools for creating pages, hosting sites, and redirecting URLs:

- Beaker.net
- Buzzed.com
- Mpresence.com
- TagTag.com
- Wappy.com

Service Providers

The following companies can provide a turnkey network solution for delivering wireless content to your users:

- AvantGo
- Geoworks
- GoAmerica
- OmniSky
- Vindigo

Questions to Ask about Content

Using www.mgo.to/kimbayne as an example, I can safely say that few people want to scroll down repeatedly on a telephone keypad to read long paragraphs found in someone's biography. That's because most devices aggravate users with weird ergonomics, limited memory, and screen size problems. In addition, time is money. Access time is money, too. Mobile users are turned off by content that is too long and ponderous. Users can and prefer to read certain data back at the office. So, forget that long-winded about.html page for your mobile site. There's no reason to read it in a taxicab or while traveling by train. Sure, a few people do visit these pages during the daily commute, but such content is too bulky and static to maintain on-the-go user interest for long. Now, contemplate these questions.

User Preferences

What do your wired Web site visitors like most about your existing site?

Which section gets the most documented hits and has the longest page views?

Would wireless users be willing and able to pay for your current content?

Would users be willing to pay for different content?

Content Use

What is a typical clickstream progression for your wired Web site?

Can your content be arranged to create a similar wireless user experience?

How and when do users access your wireless content?

Is your content type and frequency suited to the following:

- Real-time access (surfing) to wireless sites
- Web clipping (pull content) applications
- SMS text messaging (push content)
- A combination of these

Can you format content for the least amount of independent interaction by the user so that he or she is not forced to buy a keyboard attachment for the handheld?

Content Suitability

Does your content read well or make sense without the graphics (at least for now)?

Is your content suited to the instant information needs of mobile users?

Is the content dynamic enough to both attract mobile users and keep them coming back for more?

If it is not, can you create new or revamped content to meet mobile users' needs?

Are there reasons to offer wireless content different from your wired content?

Does the depth and breadth of your content lend itself to user personalization?

Market Research

What general and market-specific data (surveys, polls, studies, and research) can you use to support your interest in publishing content to wireless devices?

Have you surveyed your Web site visitors (Figure 7.9) to determine the following:

- Their wireless preferences
- Their content interests
- Their usage needs
- Their device ownership

Also, you should ask the following questions:

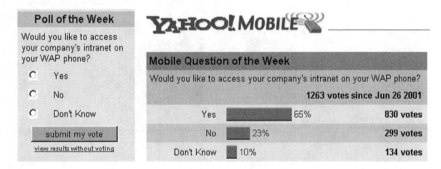

Figure 7.9 Yahoo! Mobile tracks users' interests through its Poll of the Week. (Reproduced with permission of Yahoo! Inc. © 2002 Yahoo! Inc. YAHOO! and the YAHOO! Logo are trademarks of Yahoo! Inc.)

- What type of wireless content is available from your Web-based competitors?
- What type of wireless content is *not* available from your Web-based competitors?

Device Support

Are your current Web-based visitors mostly users of:

- PDAs
- Two-way pagers
- Web-enabled mobile telephones
- Other devices

What is your content strategy for different devices? (Figure 7.10)

Do you prefer to roll out device support one device at a time?

Do you plan to deliver content to multiple devices, and if so, over what time frame?

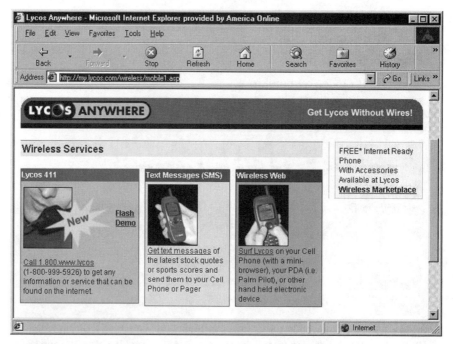

Figure 7.10 Lycos Anywhere users can access wireless content in different ways, including by voice. (© Copyright 2002, Lycos, Inc. All Rights Reserved. Lycos® is a registered trademark of Carnegie Mellon University.)

Device Suitability

For which mobile devices is your content best suited?

Are there any devices where your content would not be a fit?

Would your wireless content look better on a tiny cell phone screen or on a palm-top device?

Repurposing

How much editing is required to make your content easy-to-navigate wirelessly?

What are some ways that your content can be restructured for easier use by mobile users?

How much time will content reworking take?

How will the reformatting of pre-existing data affect your scheduled wireless launch plans?

Would it be more cost effective to develop new content?

Outsourcing

Are you or your in-house staff capable of handling the technical demands of delivering content to your chosen wireless devices?

Can you find a solutions provider to help you easily and cost-effectively deploy your content to multiple wireless devices?

Adaptation Is the Key

As you continue to evaluate your wireless content selection, consider the following information. Your content should be flexible enough to allow for additions and changes as delivery options improve. After you decide that certain content is not suitable for mobile devices, you could change your mind a year from now. If you wish to charge users for mobile content, for strategic purposes you might find it better to foot the bill until you have stronger content to offer.

That's because the wireless industry is heading toward greater innovations on a daily basis. By the time you finish this chapter, the ability to stream audio and video to mobile devices could be a reality. Banking on the future of wireless multimedia, telephone carriers were already testing rich user interfaces via 3G technologies in 2000. Companies like PacketVideo are positioning to push the wireless streaming media envelope by serving content to video-enabled wireless devices. Regardless, mobile users will ultimately decide whether they want to spend time downloading your nicely formatted product literature. Meanwhile, carriers will continue to acquire additional spectra, build better network infrastructures, and release new supporting products geared toward making the wireless Web as exciting as the wired one. Voice-activated search capabilities will improve substantially—another area in which you should look for formatting your wireless content. Mini-browsers should become more intuitive (one can only hope). All of these elements will affect how you approach your initial and follow-up deployment of wireless content. One recommendation, however: Avoid painting yourself into a corner regarding future wireless content. Build flexibility into the user experience. Make your content scaleable. Plan for the future.

Now, stop what you're doing. Make no more mental notes about how to approach your forthcoming wireless content project. Instead, become intimately familiar with how different content sites are perceived, accessed, navigated, read, and digested on a variety of handheld devices. Beg, borrow, or purchase a handful of both run-of-the-mill and unique mobile gizmos and gadgets like the one in Figure 7.11, and get some hands-on knowledge. Go to your nearest mall and ask to see working models of Web-enabled phones by Ericsson, Motorola, Nokia, or whatever. Check out the content menus of at least three wireless Web carriers: AT&T Wireless, Sprint PCS, Verizon, you name it. Don't take anyone's word for how the

Figure 7.11 Mobile Internet devices continue to get smaller, as demonstrated by the Timex Internet Messenger Watch. (Copyright © 2001–2002 Timex Corporation. All rights reserved.)

A Few Thoughts about Paper

Now that you have your wireless content plans under control, do you have to worry about paper anymore? Well, that's not an easy answer. You do and you don't. Come on. Can anybody control how and when users print content? Remember when we realized that Web users were printing our Web pages to show others and to scribble a few notes? We cringed at the thought of how awful our pages must have looked, because most of us had designed them for the Web. Yeah, the same thing is going to happen to wireless content. Trust me.

Electronics for Imaging, Inc. already has this network of printers located in offices, hotels, business centers, and whatever. In October 2001, the company announced its intent to make printing stations "as accessible as ATMs," according to a company news release. EFI's PrintMe Networks enable Palm PDA and Blackberry users to print documents from their mobile devices without any drivers or special software. Users can e-mail, upload, or beam documents right to a network printer or fax machine. The company hangs around trade shows and conferences like Comdex to entice mobile users to print stuff on the spot (heavy sigh). You get the picture. Oh, well. It could be worse. It could be raining.

mobile content experience looks and feels from device-to-device or carrier-to-carrier. I guarantee that you'll gain a better understanding of what users want.

Summary: Top Five Expert Tips

1. Be realistic when selecting the right content to serve a mobile user's needs.

2. Make wireless content timely and relevant. Dynamic rather than static information is the key.

3. Investigate both low-cost and no-cost options for jump-starting wireless content delivery when time is short. Use growing interest in your initial content offering to justify a better program for future marketing budgets.

4. Admit it when you can't manage content delivery yourself. Experts can save you time and trouble and help you avoid looking like an amateur.

5. Leverage existing partnerships and develop new ones to deliver your content to the widest possible audience.

CHAPTER 8

Untethering Public Relations and Publicity

"Let's give them something to talk about . . . a little mystery to figure out."

Singer Bonnie Raitt, voicing the lyrics of the song "Something to Talk About"

Bonnie Raitt was on the right track when she suggested feeding a few folks noteworthy news, even though she was referring to gossip. From a public relations perspective, news can make or break a business. Public relations people really want to give journalists something to talk about, at least in a positive and businesslike sense. Wireless communications has the potential to make news—in other words, professional news research, media coverage, and analysis—work better for all concerned. You'll find that you can leverage wireless as the definitive tool for creating a buzz. It's no mystery that wireless is fun to embrace when it comes to figuring out PR.

But first, I have to ask the following question. What is it about new technology that inspires marketers to cheer while journalists sneer? After all, new media tools exist to help everyone work more productively. Perhaps it's the way that businesspeople often jump on the bandwagon of technology before it is ready for implementation. Lack of etiquette and understanding can frustrate and annoy the gatekeepers of public opinion with beginner mistakes, so please proceed cautiously when using wireless in your public relations plan.

Back in 1994, I read interviews with select journalists about the then-embryonic Internet PR trend. At the time, a few veteran news professionals shunned e-mail news releases as insignificant fare, promising to delete them upon receipt without a second thought. Fortunately, the tide turned. It's a good thing that most reporters decided to accept online PR activities a few years ago—otherwise, many publicists would still be unsuccessful at getting ink. These days, however, there are too many news releases and not enough real news. From my perspective, e-mail releases are run-of-the-mill, and it's time to evolve. Now there's a new media mistress in town—

wireless technology. You can either enter the 21st century in news dissemination or get left behind.

About This Chapter

This chapter won't teach you how to convince journalists that your company is worth writing about, nor will it guarantee that your news has value. That part is up to you. If you're looking for a primer on writing e-mail news releases, you've come to the wrong place. This book isn't your answer, either.

Let's assume that you've done Internet PR. You get it, and now you want to take your PR program to the next level. This chapter is your checklist of ideas. In this chapter, you'll find case studies of innovators on both the agency and client sides of wireless PR. This chapter will help you recognize the smart side of wireless PR while cautioning you against the dumb side. You will read comments from journalists who expect you to tread lightly when it comes to reaching them via personal wireless devices. You will get an opportunity to brainstorm with me about ways to incorporate wireless devices into your company's PR plan.

Wireless PR is moving fast. Most of these suggestions could be common practice by the time you read this book. For example, wireless news dissemination is a done deal already. Most major news outlets have found a way to inform users wirelessly. Your next step is to learn how to join them. Ready? Let's begin.

The Mobile Reporter

The concept of using wireless devices for news reporting purposes is apparently old hat for some. In 1998, *Online Journalism Review* wrote about mobile computers in a story titled "Wearables: The New Computer-as-Clothing Line" by Neda Raouf. The author speculated that in the future, journalists would be "armed with equipment to rival the likes of James Bond." The article goes on to quote a professor at the *Massachusetts Institute of Technology* (MIT) as imagining that "every book you've ever read, or any argument you've ever had or any legal thing you ever read (could be) available immediately." Riter Raouf says that for journalists, such access would be priceless.

In July 2001, Jeff Houck, a writer with Wireless.NewsFactor.com, interviewed Liz Pulliam Weston, a personal finance writer for *The Los Angeles Times*, about her use of mobile devices. In an article titled "Finance Writer Counts on Her PDA," Liz is mentioned as using her Palm IIIx for just about everything—from reading daily newspapers to finding movie schedules to doing mundane chores like grocery shopping. Weston is sold on the power of her mobile organizer because it "makes it easier to work from home or on the road." Apparently, once a reporter starts using mobile devices, there's no stopping him or her.

The September 11, 2001 terrorist crisis in the United States inspired television networks to latch onto wireless devices as a way to deliver the news more quickly to television audiences. CNN has been able to broadcast footage of U.S. military actions through the combined use of a ruggedized mobile videophone and a mobile satellite link. The videophone's small form factor is quite a change from the bulky cameras used by video crews for years.

And, if the mobile momentum among various press corps members wasn't enough, PR practitioners are also involved in encouraging the adoption of wireless devices among journalists in the field. In a January 2001 e-mail sent to my attention, Wireless WebConnect! at www.wwc.com offered to loan me a high-speed wireless modem during a show-related promotion. The offer was made to reporters traveling to cities where the high-speed network was available at the time, which included Atlanta, Baltimore, Dallas/Fort Worth, Denver, Detroit, Houston, Manhattan, Minneapolis, Philadelphia, Phoenix, San Diego, San Francisco, and San Jose.

Five Good Reasons to Unplug Media Relations

1. **Creativity.** Wireless communications can help you be more creative in your media relations. Sometimes revamping your marketing materials for new media forces you to look at it in a whole new light. You see errors that you didn't notice before. You see ways to make content flow better. You recognize material that's out of date and ready for the circular file or the recycle bin. If you're still stuck on the wired Web, take a moment to open your desktop browser. What do you see? You see a browser jam-packed with unorganized and long-forgotten bookmarks. Make your wireless pressroom interesting, exciting, and useful—and it could well surpass your wired Web activities.

2. **Accuracy.** Wireless communications can give you a last chance to correct reporting errors before they happen. How many times have you found yourself unable to reach a reporter just before he or she went to press? Tell him or her to check by wireless access for the latest information before filing the story. Send him or her a quick message pointing the journalist to

clarifying information. What about the point you made in the last interview? Boy, it'd be great to simplify it and avoid having a product feature misinterpreted. Use wireless and you could decrease the number of times that stories appear in print that make you cringe.

3. **Accessibility.** Wireless tools give people the ability to deliver or retrieve news "as you like it." Do these situations sound familiar? Your media contact is in a cab on his or her way to a COMDEX Fall press party, and he or she is planning to file a story on the ride there. The managing editor of that newly launched technology magazine is sitting in a coffeehouse near PC Expo sipping lattès with a colleague. Where did the time go? He just missed your press conference. Somewhere in a meeting room at an AMA conference, a boring speaker drones on behind a lectern. And that journalist in the audience could have been sitting in your presentation instead. Your company might have something useful and interesting to say to all of these mobile people if you could only reach them. Reporters in each of these situations might have a Web-enabled phone or a wireless PDA. They might even have one of those other handheld devices without wireless capabilities that can be synchronized each night through Web clipping applications. Guess what? In almost every case, you can provide more current information to these people than what they received from you the last time you made contact.

4. **Opportunity.** Wireless tools can reach the media first before your competitor beats you to the punch. Don't drag your heels on this one. What are you waiting for? Wireless tools are a cool way to communicate with everybody. By the time you finish this book, everybody will know it—even your younger brother's girlfriend who babysits for the local business editor. For that matter, my hair stylist already uses a PDA to schedule hair-cutting appointments, so he knows it, too.

5. **Synchronicity.** What's good for a reporter is also good for other people, too. Business and trade analysts, investors and financial institutions, and just about anybody who has a vested interest in keeping track of your company's news will appreciate access to your press material via wireless devices.

Conducting Wireless PR

Conducting public relations via wireless devices can be done in several ways, depending on your media contacts' needs and preferences. Here are a few examples to ponder:

SMS text messages. If your targeted media contact is a financial analyst or reporter, you might consider offering alerts that include IPO announcements or stock prices. Depending on your disposition, you can either send an alert to the individual yourself or direct him or her to one of several sites, such as PrimAlert provided by www.primalert.com (a real-time financial alert service based in the United Kingdom). According to a July 6, 2001 news release, the service offers access to information on "all European and major U.S. stock exchanges." Although PrimAlert's target user includes financial institutions, Web and wireless portals, and individuals residing in the United Kingdom, this service could be a useful tool to leverage for IR activities. Don't assume that you have to be the originator of everything in your wireless PR arsenal. It's nice to be able to refer media contacts to a reliable outside source once in a while. Look around. There might be a financial news alert service that could be a potential wireless partner to some degree.

Southern African news portal IT Web enables its 50,000 readers to send news headlines to pals via SMS. This Web-based feature is enabled through a technology supplied by Cape Town-based global marketing company Clickatell. While reading a news item, the Web site visitor can click "SMS this headline" and the news brief is transmitted immediately. Imagine using this idea to encourage visitors to create a word-of-"mouse" news distribution service to enhance your PR efforts.

Wireless Web site. Take a look at the chapter on content for more ideas in this area. Meanwhile, whether you need a temporary measure for one press event or a long-term solution for an ongoing wireless PR program, you might be able to get by with what's already in place. You might have already discovered that the majority of reporters in your industry rely more on PDAs than on Web-enabled phones for their mobile news and information (or vice-versa). If you know that PDAs are the bee's knees for sure, you might not have to create a WAP site just yet. I happen to know from personal experience that I didn't need to do anything extra to make my husband's schedule available to my Palm VIIx before I got on an airplane a while back. On the road, it was nice to know when I could reach him. As a subscriber to AvantGo, I just added the exact page from his Web site to my channels.

You might think that this scenario doesn't translate to the PR world, but it does. The other day, a reporter inquired about getting a few pictures of my better half, Bruce, as "Poppy the Clown" in action for a human-interest story. The reporter didn't know when he would be able to schedule a photographer to come out. And Bruce's schedule can change daily, depending upon how many people are desperately in need of balloon animals. I asked the writer if he had wireless access, and he confirmed that he had a Palm handheld. I pointed him to Bruce's appearance schedule by talking him through the wireless options. The photojournalist caught up with Bruce when he needed him, and the rest is history. In other words, if I can perform this task with something as niche as my husband's hobby, you can perform this function with something even more critical to your business survival.

Another access solution—one that doesn't require me to sync a device to an unavailable computer—is to use a mini-browser to enter a specific Web-based URL. The basic version of the DPWeb browser is downloadable for free from www.digitalpaths.com. By the way, take a look at Figure 8.1. Notice in the lower right-hand corner how MSNBC Mobile is a sponsor of DPWeb? Keep that in mind the next time you wonder how to make your wireless presence pay off.

Now back to the browser. Using the DPWeb browser helped me recognize some mobile-specific glitches in site coding, ones that were easily fixed and didn't affect the Web-based layout much. At the very least, I knew that calling my significant other around lunch on August 15 would be a wasted call, as shown in Figure 8.2. Your media contacts might run into a similar situation while trying to reach a company executive, and it would be a good idea to

Figure 8.1 Users of either Digital Paths' basic or deluxe wireless browser can access the pages of wired Web sites in real-time. (Browser Copyright 2000 Digital Paths. All rights reserved.)

Figure 8.2 I might be one of the few individuals who accesses a clown's schedule wirelessly. You might want to access your executive's speaking schedule.

proactively direct them to either a mobile-friendly schedule or the Web, as shown in Figure 8.3.

Piggybacking off someone else's turnkey wireless solution could be the short-term answer you seek while you're planning for a more elaborate and satisfying wireless presence. Create a FAQ document at your wired site containing simple instructions so that mobile-novice journalists can access selected areas of your site while on the road. A word to the wise: At the time of this book's writing, graphics and frames did not display well in some wireless browsers. Knowing that, consider pointing mobile reporters to Web pages with minimal graphics and straightforward text. It might even be worth revamping selected pages for this purpose or even creating a special directory on your regular Web site for storing mobile-friendly pressroom pages. Sure, you can always hire a programmer to create a downloadable wireless application or contract with a service to access and convert the HTML content of your Web-based pressroom, but if you're out of time, AvantGo and DPWeb are two possible answers.

Personalization and location-based delivery. Each time I access certain sites on my PDA, I notice my device sending location-specific details to the server in question. I set it up that way, but you might or might not have the same experience. Once my location information is out there, it could mean

Figure 8.3 Now that I mention it, SkyGo's Web-based speaking schedule is easily viewable with the DPWeb browser. (SkyGo Web site Copyright © 1999–2002 SkyGo, Inc. All rights reserved. Browser Copyright 2000 Digital Paths. All rights reserved.)

that I'd be greeted by an unsolicited message someday. Here's how it can happen.

When designing a Web clipping form for a PDA application, the programmer can add a code or two to determine the mobile user's location when connected. The code can be used to discern the user's current zip code. The application sends its best guess on the user's location to the application provider's server. It's not rocket science, but it works.

Who knows just how accurate and usable location-based wireless services will become eventually? From a public relations perspective, however, I would imagine that most journalists don't want their personal locations tracked and fed to marketers or their buddies, especially if the identity of the mobile user is obvious.

Imagine an investigative reporter gathering material for a crime exposè or a war correspondent in a foreign country trying to report on the resistance movement. In either case, it would really stink to have a secret location revealed when the reporter needs to keep a low profile. Who knows how loose-lipped an employee can become when he or she doesn't understand the gravity of the situation? Tracking the current locations of individual journalists who access your wireless pressroom could create other problems that I can't even foresee.

Are you a fan of government conspiracy theories and their alleged influence on freedom of the press? Then there's nothing I could suggest that would trump your imagination.

Now, if wireless location information is aggregated and not connected to a certain user, then location tracking might be acceptable to some degree in your wireless PR program. Let's say that your office is in Phoenix but your exhibit booth is in Dallas. How many journalists are accessing your wireless pressroom from Dallas, for example? If you're tracking access, you might notice more groups of users accessing your wireless pressroom from Dallas the week of the show. This information could be used to change things a bit when you formulate your next news distribution strategy.

Meanwhile, I'd avoid anything that smacks of tracking the exact locations of individual reporters, even if some really cool technology for doing so becomes available tomorrow. It's a stupid idea, and I can't think of a single valid reason to use location-based tracking on individual media contacts. Feel free to make fun of me in the future if and when someone proves me wrong. At this writing, that's my view and I'm sticking to it.

So, how do you make sure that your media contacts get the right content? Personalization is the obvious choice here. If you're offering an opt-in news service specifically to wireless journalists, make sure that each person has access to and control over his or her individual profile. And don't make the mistake of collecting data that you don't have a right to know, even if you think your company policies are designed to prevent abuse. Guidelines and intentions change, as do executives at the helm—so don't tread dangerously.

Voice retrieval. Sometimes a reporter's eyes are just too tired to read one more news release. After pouring through piles of press kits, opening and deleting dozens of untargeted e-mails, and sitting through hours of press conferences, it might be nice to just pick up the phone and get the news that way. Did you forget that wireless PR includes talking and listening on mobile phones? No, I didn't think you did. So consider creating a voice-activated version of your pressroom for those editors and writers who have no more time than a few glassy-eyed moments to find out what's what and who's where. Another idea would be to advertise your wireless presence on a voice retrieval system frequented by journalists. Do you know of any? Make the call.

Web clipping and synchronization. If you already own a Palm-type device, you know about synchronizing Web-based data and other information to your handheld. And if you got to this paragraph but didn't read about my cheap attempts at mobilizing Web-based event schedules, then shame on you. Go back and read that stuff. It contains good ideas to use as inspiration for your own wireless PR program, even if you're not doing PR for a clown.

The Wireless PR Survey That Wasn't

In July 2001, I attempted to conduct an informal e-mail survey. Let's just say that it was a loosely based opinion poll. OK, I don't really know what to call it. Anyhow, it was supposed to clarify for you, for the world, and for me what journalists want and don't want from a wireless PR program. I figured that it wasn't too early to get started on establishing some type of benchmark for wireless PR manners among folks who care. That's what I had planned to do with the wealth of useful information that I was sure was forthcoming. I wanted to share it all with you.

Here's my research-gathering method, flawed as it was. I posted requests for participation to moderated journalism-related e-mail lists and e-mailed a few dozen contacts. I pointed them to a Web page to complete the questionnaire form. The e-mail-to-Web poll was, in my humble opinion, a bust. Barely anyone participated, and I was too cheap to follow up by telephone. Sound familiar? If you've ever done this badly at research, don't worry—this book is for publicly admitting my foibles, not yours. Do what I say, not what I do.

I kept thinking that surveys were passè, my survey was lame, or a little bit of both. It could have been that journalists didn't trust me because I used to do PR. It could have been that the answers to the questions were rather self-evident. I could have deployed the survey wirelessly, but the questions were too long. Yeah, that's it. Wireless deployment would have made sense. Duh. Or it could have been that most journalists suspected me of compiling some agency spam list, which by the way I wasn't. In fact, I vaguely remember a response to that effect. Whoops! Well, back to the drawing board. Good thing I didn't mortgage the house to launch that ill-conceived project.

During this short-lived opinion sampling, for lack of a better title, I asked reporters about their preferences for wireless PR activities. Their answers were not earthshaking. As predicted (by just about everyone with any common sense), no one likes the idea of unscheduled calls by an unfamiliar PR person to his or her mobile telephone, regardless of how the phone number was obtained. Similarly, not one soul thought that unsolicited SMS messages were cool, no matter how convenient for the sender. But you knew that already.

By now, you realize how unscientific this whole exercise was for me, but I did manage to get a few comments to share with you. Although the sample was small, I would stand by the following answers anyway just because, from my own experience as a writer on the go, I know them to be true.

Joao Manuel Oliveira, a journalist in Portugal, advises PR professionals to never to perform mass wireless SMS mailings of "all kinds of information" but instead limit wireless PR communications to the distribution of interest-targeted and/or personalized content.

"Remember that (the) mobile phone is the last medium," Oliveira continued. "It is personal and journalists aren't supposed to work 24 hours. (They) need time to rest." He cautions PR agencies and clients to "always ask first if you want to use the journalist's wireless connection" for your marketing communications.

Freelance writer Willie Schatz wrote that the rules for contacting him via a mobile device are "the same as for contacting me via any other medium:

Rule #1: If it's not NEWS, I'm not interested.

Rules #2 and #3: When in doubt, see Rule #1."

As far as what types of wireless PR content would be accessed more often by reporters, the small group that responded indicated that they would consider accessing and using press kits, company backgrounds, and event press registrations on mobile devices when they became available. Well, for some industries, mobile press kits are here now, as you'll soon discover. Hey, how about that third item—event registration? Now there's a good idea. Allow reporters to RSVP for your press party via PDAs and Internet-ready phones while at a show. You never know which last-minute press confirmation will net your company its best coverage.

Beam it Over, Scotty!

I kept telling everyone that I wasn't "doing paper" in this trade show. My feet and back were killing me, and I wasn't in the mood to lug any more junk back to my hotel room. So when solution provider Bluefish Wireless offered to beam its Comdex Fall 2001 press kit to my Palm VIIx via its IR port, I took the bait. The access point was a small white box that sat right on the Bluefish exhibit counter in the Palm Solutions Pavilion. Just take a look at Figure 8.4. An overview of their technology, an explanation of market opportunities, contact information, and a helpful little section called "Viva Las Vegas" were beamed over for my reading pleasure. The activity took fewer than 20 seconds, and my arms didn't feel any heavier for the experience. Simultaneously, Bluefish managed to position itself as the only application in a new category that it had created on my handheld.

Figure 8.4 A visitor to the Bluefish Wireless booth downloads information to a wireless Palm™ handheld. (Bluefish Access Point Copyright © Bluefish Wireless Inc. Photograph © 2001 Kim M. Bayne. All rights reserved.

Tackling the Wireless PR Project

Are you putting together a plan for this aspect of your e-marketing program? Start by defining the *why, who, what, where,* and *how* of your wireless PR project:

Why do you want to use wireless in your PR program?

Who will be your wireless media contacts?

What are the wireless contact preferences of individuals on your media list?

Where will mobile reporters and authors access your information?

How can you make a writer's job easier?

Conducting PR Wirelessly

There are several reasons to transport your public relations functions to the wireless world. Your industry and your unique approach to public relations can dictate what's appropriate or feasible to untether. Or, maybe you just need some assistance in recognizing when wireless PR is a good choice.

Four Situations that Need Wireless PR

Using wireless communications could give you an edge over your less-savvy competitors. If you plan to make your PR program wireless, here are some thoughts.

Situation #1. You work in the pharmaceutical industry, and you're constantly on the road. Your executives are constantly out-of-pocket, too. Time stands still for no one. Pretend that you just checked your e-mail and discovered a need to arrange a telephone interview between your vice president of marketing and a freelance writer. The writer is under deadline for a feature story on new medications for children with Attention Deficit Hyperactivity Disorder. The freelancer lives in Arizona, you're at a health care convention in Colorado, and your VP is at a drug company meeting in New York. What time is it in each location? How can you schedule the interview, conference in on the interview at the right time, and avoid time zone confusion? At several places on the wireless Web, you will find time zone converters and meeting planners. For example, you can use your Web-enabled cell phone to access Intouch World Time at wap.intouch.co.za/nk/time/ and have the information at your fingertips.

Situation #2. Your publishing house is launching a new book. It's all about mobile communications, so it makes sense to publish a book excerpt or two wirelessly to stimulate book sales. As part of your book promotional efforts, you strike a deal with a wireless platform provider to make your content available to targeted wireless users. Besides promoting books, you also provide publishing news and interviews with authors. As an example, the Books@Random Mobile Edition is available now for Palm Computing and Windows CE users. Users of mobile book excerpt services love them. According to one Books@Random subscriber quoted at AvantGo.com, the downloaded or clipped excerpts make great reading while on an airplane.

Situation #3. You might have noticed how some reporters attend major events and leave with boxes, luggage carts, or even shopping carts filled to the brim with press kits. Some reporters will hand you their business card and ask you to mail the kit to them so that they don't have to lug it back. Other reporters cram multiple FedEx boxes full to capacity, shipping them back to the office at their publications' expense. Still other reporters sit in the working pressroom foraging through the contents of paper press kits, gleaning business cards and relevant news releases. The pressroom floors at many major shows are often a mass of discarded paper. Oy vey.

"It's so last century to do this," quipped Mark Hass, CEO and founder of PR firm Hass Associates, observing that many press members "are abandoning the traditional ways" of obtaining and dealing with press material. Everything a reporter needs to write a story can now be found on notebooks or Palms. If for no other reason than saving the thousands of trees needlessly chopped down each year to make wasted press kits, please go wireless.

Situation #4. Now, close your eyes while I paint a scene for you. Wait, wait, wait. Don't close your eyes. You won't be able to continue reading this chapter. Just use your imagination. OK. You're at the hospitality suite. Someone wants a copy of your product release, but the press conference was yesterday, you gave out all the press kits, your marketing coordinator is at Kinko's, and your own personal stash of releases is sitting on the floor of some unknown taxicab somewhere. Avoid this situation altogether by preparing for wireless dissemination before you go to the show. Rewind.

You're at your desk and thinking ahead to all the possibilities at an upcoming press conference. Open a news release and copy and paste the text-only body copy into a notes file in your desktop organizer software. When you synchronize your desktop with your handheld, the file will be transferred to your mobile device. How can this feature help? Users of Palm OS handhelds can beam data by pointing the *infrared* (IR) ports of their devices at each other. Now imagine discussing your latest product announcement with a reporter on the floor of a trade show. The industry journalist hasn't seen your release but wants it. Save him or her some time and effort by providing the text right here, right now, effortlessly. He or she will thank you for not loading him or her down with paper, and you'll thank the journalist for using your content to avoid typographical errors that occur when rekeying data.

Wireless News Providers

Someone had to be the first to deliver news wirelessly, whether through an agency with direct-to-the-journalist connections or through a media outlet. Who has already embraced wireless news delivery? If you're looking for reporters who might be more sympathetic than normal, here's a hint. It's a safe bet that early-adopters are educating staff to accept the forthcoming wave of wireless public relations activities.

A sampling of media outlets appears as follows. Some have established a presence for Web-enabled mobile phone users; some have concentrated on Web-clipping applications; and others have focused on real-time access. Some news media outlets are delivering content in as many wireless ways as currently possible.

For a snapshot of initial broadcast, print, and Web-based news disseminators that were anticipating a rosy wireless future, skim this brief list. By the way, the following list is by no means complete. But before you run off and start converting your online pressroom to a mobile site, ask yourself if your target media list is ready and willing.

Case Study: PR21 and Openwave

Interactive PR firm PR21 has been providing wireless reporting on media coverage to its agency clients for a few years now. Delivered to a client's PDA or mobile phone, reports include highlights of the latest news of the day and article synopses. Company executives can read the full text of selected pieces by clicking or tapping on a headline, as noted in Figure 8.5.

Figure 8.5 PR21's Media Tracking Report for Openwave provides its client with on-the-fly access to relevant media clippings. (Source: PR21)

Articles and news are captured and updated daily for PR21 clients. The image management firm also generates a synopsis highlighting what's important in the context of relevance to the client's marketing communications program. PR21 includes counsel and analysis around the wireless content, such as how to address industry news and trends as questions come up.

With Palm VIIs and below, clients can synchronize report information from their desktop PC. With the Palm VIIx and other wired PDAs, users are able to read updates throughout the day. Clients can either view a report the day that it's published or retrieve past reports by selecting the Article Archive, as noted in Figure 8.6.

continued

Figure 8.6 Users of PR21's media tracking report archives can reference past data by month. (Source: PR21)

On November 20, 2000, following its recent merger with Software.com, mobile Internet software provider Phone.com announced its relisting on the NASDAQ market as Openwave Systems, Inc. Its agency PR21 was at the helm for its media tour.

"We had scheduled on their behalf a number of interviews with the broadcast media in New York for the morning of the listing to help kick things off," recalls William Jefferson Black, vice president of *Competitive Intelligence Services* (CIS) with PR21, Chicago. It was a tight schedule—PR21 had planned a different media briefing nearly every half hour. Fortunately, PR team members, with access to mobile phones and PDAs, were armed with the latest industry news, enabling them to respond to or benefit from media coverage while on the go.

As Openwave executives made their way through the broadcast circuit of CNNfn, Bloomberg, and Reuters, PR21 fed updates on the latest news to its busy client in half-hour intervals. Reports included references to competitors as well as how the media was reporting on OpenWave's relisting efforts. In addition, PR21 included broader industry news to provide perspective.

"We had a team moving from broadcast studio to broadcast studio," recalled PR21's Black. Using a Sprint PCS cell phone, PR21 was able to send updated text-based reports with a synopsis of key news and information to team members. The reports included the ability to drill down into the full text of a story.

Don Listwin, Openwave's president and CEO, was on hand during the intensive media tour. PR21 used its wireless reporting service to update Listwin on an ongoing basis about how things were being received by different media outlets, providing counsel as the morning progressed. Later in the morning, while they still were conducting interviews, the market began to change.

That day, the NASDAQ was down about 11 percent—so OpenWave's message evolved to include how the opportunity fit into the broader market context. Executives had the information needed to allow them to expertly address how Openwave's relisting was unique compared to other Internet companies at the time.

Figure 8.7   PR21 partners with Burrelle's to combine traditional news monitoring with wireless PR services. (Source: PR21)

To obtain news clippings, PR21 works with Burrelle's Information Services (as referenced in Figure 8.7). Burrelle's media monitoring system sends relevant articles into a database, then PR21 pulls from the database and combines materials into one delivery package to run a report. With Burrelle's and PR21 teaming behind the scenes, PR21 generates a front-end delivery system—a personalized media report on the PR21 Web site.

continued

PR21's wireless PR service resides within a secure extranet environment. Each client gets a unique login and password, restricting them to their company-specific account. Clients can either access the report on the Web or by wireless device. At the time of this book's writing, PR21 directed its clients to AvantGo.com with instructions to add a unique Web-based URL as a new channel to individual wireless accounts, as noted in Figure 8.8. The agency plans to discuss "a more robust agreement" with AvantGo as wireless client interest grows.

Figure 8.8 PR21 directs a handful of agency clients to create a link to Web-based media reports using the Custom Channel Wizard on the AvantGo service. (AvantGo is a registered trademark of AvantGo, Inc.)

PR21 has many wireless industry clients that appreciate the agency's leverage of technology-based tools. Clients like home appliance manufacturer Whirlpool Corp., Skil Power Tools, and alcohol beverage company Jose Cuervo aren't necessarily impressed with wireless functionality for marketing yet, according to PR21's Black. But when the agency mentions its capabilities to mobile communications carrier Sprint, wireless location services provider SignalSoft Corp., and Openwave, "it really resonates with them," he says. "They appreciate that their agency partner gets wireless and can use it."

PR21 executives are enthusiastic about its agency's mobile services and future potential. Some clients are using the information to "arm the sales guys," according to Black. "They're taking it right to the field," he says.

Case Study: Hass Associates and General Motors

Technology marketing firm Hass Associates, Inc. conceived a plan for its client, General Motors, to use Palm technology at automotive events, such as the 2001 *North American International Auto Show* (NAIAS) in Detroit. The GM NewsCenter, a custom software application for the Palm platform, uses a menu-based system to present what would otherwise be the bulging contents of a very large press kit.

Hass empowered both journalists and GM executives alike by providing wireless PDA access to a full map of the auto show, an event schedule, GM press contacts, press releases, and other show-related material, as noted in Figures 8.9 and 8.10. Rather than limit PDA offerings to plain text, Hass designed its system to give users the ability to navigate the show floor by dragging around exhibit booth outlines in their PDA window, as noted in Figure 8.11.

Figure 8.9   The GM News Center offers automotive journalists a list of content choices to support their news gathering efforts. (Source: Hass Associates. © General Motors Corporation. Used with permission.)

Every year, the Detroit Auto show attracts journalists from around the world—and the mood among reporters on the show floor is highly competitive. There is also a tradition of "turning car unveils into theatrical events," noted Mark Hass, CEO and founder of Hass Associates, adding that there's a "one-ups-man-ship among exhibiting automakers." Every year, exhibitors try to improve upon last year's efforts in courting the automotive press.

continued

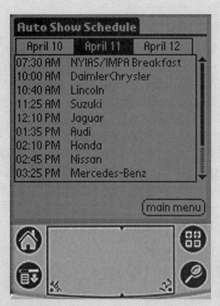

Figure 8.10 An outline of the auto show schedule, complete with event details, keeps reporters on track during the busy show day. (Source: Hass Associates)

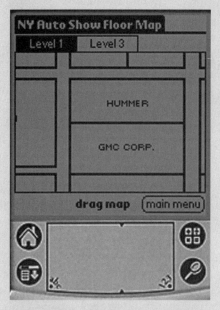

Figure 8.11 An interactive map of the New York Auto Show enables Palm™ handheld users to move exhibit booth outlines to find their way around multiple show floors. (Source: Hass Associates)

Hass Associates proposed the notion of establishing show site "beaming stations," which would enable interested users to bring a Palm OS device to a kiosk to receive beamed media information. At the kiosk, journalists were able to receive the GM News Center.

"It was a really cool project but it turned out to be bigger than we imagined," admitted Hass. With a "very strong technology and Internet component," one of the agency's teams includes software engineers who "come up with cool ideas for companies who want to use online communications in their marketing communications," he said.

"In a lot of ways, [the wireless media kit] attracted more attention than a lot of other activities in the [Detroit auto] show," reported Hass. The wireless PR strategy and tools helped GM deliver a technology message outside the context of its products.

To be fair, Hass and GM aren't the only ones embracing wireless news dissemination at automotive industry events. Automotive marketplace MSN Carpoint, the official Web site of NAIAS 2001 in Detroit, linked up with AvantGo to provide behind-the-scenes wireless coverage of new concept and production vehicles, complete with photos. Carpoint's AvantGo channel included Digital Showcases on Toyota/Lexus, The GM Experience Live, and Ford plus a full schedule of unveilings and press conferences for Volvo, DaimlerChrysler, and Volkswagon, to name a few companies.

As you can see, I get sidetracked easily when it comes to wireless. Anyhow, let's go back to the real focus of this case study: Hass and GM. Other PR challenges for automotive PR professionals include finding ways to minimize the cost of distributing automotive press kits, which are very expensive to produce. For large automotive shows, marketers might have to prepare thousands of press kits. And while the GM wireless media kits didn't include any multimedia files, it still contained quite a bit of information, such as new vehicle specifications. To maintain media interest, the GM News Center is continually updated for each show. In addition to Detroit, the Palm application was used for media days at the Los Angeles Auto Show, Chicago Auto Show, New York Auto Show, Salon International de l'Auto Geneve, IAA: Frankfurt International Motor Show, and the Tokyo Motor Show.

"Anything in Word or black and white form is included in the news center," Hass said. For journalists not attending the show, content is also available from the GM media site, as seen in Figure 8.12.

Apparently, journalists who use wireless press kits "love (them), especially the contact lists," according to Hass. Reporters have all the basic information needed to write a story right in the palm of their hand (pun intended).

continued

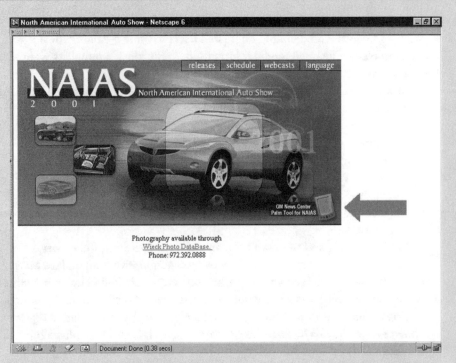

Figure 8.12 Visitors to GM's NAIAS Media Center can download an application to install the press kit on their Palm™ handheld, Visor, or other handheld device. (© General Motors Corporation. Used with permission.)

Hass, a former Deputy Managing Editor of the Detroit News, has seen a remarkable number of journalists using mobile technology over the years. Still, he claims that European journalists are "a lot less open to this. They tend to do things more traditionally." For example, at the Geneva auto show, Hass observed European reporters taking paper press kits in addition to accepting the mobile material. In Geneva, Hass helped GM in providing wireless press content in three languages: French, German, and English.

But the agency's use of wireless technology didn't stop there. For the Full Line Preview, an event where automotive journalists travel to see vehicles before the rest of the world even knows that a model exists, Hass came up with another idea.

"We gave all the journalists a color Cliè (Sony handheld device) to use during the show," he said. "The notion was every year reporters get a package of material to take with them." This time, reporters received a Cliè with the press material preloaded. The agency delivered high-resolution content on a memory stick. Hass plans to continue this activity for each new auto show, sending journalists a new memory stick with new data. Plans to use Bluetooth technology at future auto shows are currently in the works.

Case Study: Vocus Public Relations

In March 2001, online news service PR Newswire revealed its award of a $30 million software development contract to PR software developer Vocus, Inc. The new project would help the public relations industry "better target and track journalists," according to Sara Kehaulani Goo, writing in *The Washington Post*. In Goo's March 23 article, Rick Rudman, president and chief executive of Vocus, is quoted as saying that the new product, soon dubbed Vocus Public Relations Management Software, would help PR practitioners avoid "blasting out information." The article referenced how e-mail news releases had reached the status of spam and were considered ineffective.

Vocus' wireless PR services include a communication tool that helps PR practitioners deliver news directly to journalists who are interested in specific content. Journalists who use wireless for e-mail can receive the information on their mobile device. Vocus also manages a WAP-enabled Web site so that journalists can visit an organizational newsroom to view content from a wireless PDA.

In the article, Rudman said the product enables PR professionals to maintain histories of conversations with the media while tracking individual beats. This function assists PR agencies and clients in targeting reporters more effectively, increasing the possibility of press coverage.

From the PR practitioner's viewpoint, the Vocus PR service is a far cry from telephoning the office to ask a PR intern to look up a journalist's e-mail address or phone number. Vocus promotional material touts the service's abilities to "look up a journalist, issue a news release, respond to press inquiries, whether you're traveling, at a meeting or at home." The PR user can use a real-time Web-browsing application on a wireless PDA, such as Internet Explorer, enter vocuspr.com, and log onto the site by using a password, as shown in Figure 8.13. The user can now choose from several areas as seen in Figure 8.14, depending on his or her on-the-road PR needs.

Imagine that a reporter has telephoned on deadline while you were out of the office. The voice mail message was truncated for some reason, and you don't have a telephone number handy for follow-up. Using the Vocus PR system, you can locate contact information on any reporter, such as *Washington Post* Staff Writer Sara Goo, as shown in Figure 8.15. After searching, a list of possible last name matches is presented, as shown in Figure 8.16. Individual records contain detailed contact information, such as pitching profiles, activity logs, and past news coverage on the exact reporter, as shown in Figure 8.17. Users can also send individual e-mails to reporters through the system.

continued

Figure 8.13 Clients of Vocus Public Relations log on to the application by using a PDA, as seen in a Palm™ VIIx handheld emulator session. (Source: Vocus PR)

Figure 8.14 Several content choices are available to mobile PR professionals using the Vocus PR service, as seen in a Palm™ VIIx handheld emulator session. (Source: Vocus PR)

Figure 8.15 Finding a reporter's e-mail address is done by ticking a checkbox on the Vocus PR Find Screen, as seen in a Palm™ VIIx handheld emulator session. (Source: Vocus PR)

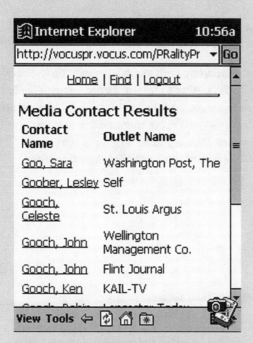

Figure 8.16 Several choices of journalists are presented as a result of searching with the Vocus PR wireless application, as seen in Internet Explorer. (Source: Vocus PR)

continued

Figure 8.17 Sara Goo's contact information is found through the Vocus PR wireless application, as seen in Internet Explorer. (Source: Vocus PR)

Kay Bransford, vice president of marketing with Vocus, doesn't see the service becoming a news portal for journalists, similar to Internet Wire, which distributes news content via AvantGo, as seen in Figure 8.18. Vocus PR's model is designed to help PR professionals deliver the news in a more targeted manner. In summary, the Vocus PR Web site writes, "Vocus Public Relations Wireless software allows professionals to have a virtual PR office at their fingertips."

Newspapers

Germany's *Die Rheinische Post*

Norway's *Aftenposten*

Swiss newspaper *Der Bund*

The New York Times

Salon

The Wall Street Journal

The Washington Post

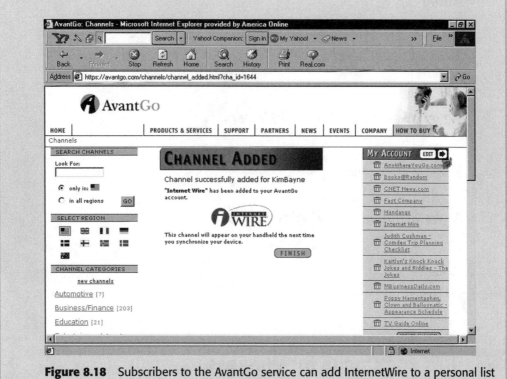

Figure 8.18 Subscribers to the AvantGo service can add InternetWire to a personal list of channels by clicking a logo on the InternetWire home page. (AvantGo is a registered trademark of AvantGo, Inc.)

Magazines

Fast Company

Latinamerican Wap Magazine

Wireless News Magazine

Television

ABC News

BBC News

CNN

MSNBC

Radio

Syndicated talk show host Art Bell's program.

"Talk is Cheap," a New Jersey-based, hard-core, punk radio show on WRSU 88.7 FM

Webzines and E-Mail Newsletters

CNET News.com

MbusinessDaily.com

News Syndicates and Wire Services

7am.com

Bloomberg

PR Newswire Europe

The Do's and Don'ts for Wireless Media Relations

Do raise awareness among reporters about your wireless presence. Publicize it in your press kits, and mention it on the telephone. Reference it in the editor's note at the bottom of every news release. Imprint your wireless access information on a PDA stylus or leather organizer case to give to your media pals. They'll use your gift and always have your wireless information at hand.

Do create supporting content and tools to serve mobile reporters' real needs. Look for ways to make life easier for writers who use your information in their reporting efforts. Ask them what they fantasize about to make their journalism job easier, and use these ideas to create better press information to deliver wirelessly.

Do ask reporters about their individual preferences for mobile communication. Don't assume anything. When considering how to use the mobile contact data you've been entrusted with, choose to err on the side of caution rather than exuberance.

Don't share a journalist's mobile phone number or service address with anyone —period.

Don't send unsolicited SMS text to a reporter for any reason. Make sure that you have permission before you send that first text message. If you ever come across a list of wireless device numbers for sending pages or messages to members of the press, run—don't walk—to the nearest trash can, or hit Ctrl-D immediately.

Do target your SMS messages appropriately. Avoid the mistakes of Internet marketers who continue to send e-mail news releases to the wrong people. I can't tell you how many communications I continue to receive from PR agencies in the wrong industry after I have repeatedly asked to be removed from their lists.

Do limit the number of SMS messages sent each month, regardless of the topic. If you do get a reporter's consent to send news-related wireless alerts, keep it to a bare minimum. Don't abuse the trust.

Do allow reporters the utmost control over their opt-in SMS subscription. No one wants to feel like there's no way to stop an intrusion. And sometimes, news that was interesting last month is no longer the case. Someone might change beats, making your press communications no longer relevant to their news gathering interests (and possibly a nuisance).

Don't telephone journalists to ask whether they received your SMS text. In doing so, you're defeating the whole purpose of using certain media to reduce costs. If you can't help yourself and feel the need to call anyway, then stop sending SMS. You're not ready for the uncertainty of wireless communications.

Don't send full-text news releases by SMS. Some Web-enabled mobile phones can only handle a limited amount of characters. Even with the bigger screens, long news releases are not a fit for such devices. Summarize, cut, edit, and boil the news down to its essence. Save the longer version for access by PDA users or Web visitors at their discretion.

Do use a variety of tools to deploy and publicize your wireless PR presence to reporters. The more you have, the better. You can never tell, until you do the research, which writer is missing out on accessing your wireless content.

Register Your Wireless Site

You want search engines? We've got search engines! Several wireless hosting services offer Web-based help for marketers who need to get the word out about their sites. These automated submission services behave just like the consolidated submission services that you use to register a landline site. But if you'd rather do it yourself, here is a list of resources that point users to wireless sites, either through the Web or wirelessly.

- www.2thumbswap.com
- www.4metawap.com
- www.alloutwap.com
- www.andanza.com
- www.anywhereyougo.com
- www.ccwap.com
- www.coodies.net
- www.djuice.com
- www.ewap.it
- www.gelon.net
- www.gixom.com
- www.jmwap.com
- www.journalduwap.com
- www.jumbuck.com
- www.lewap.com
- www.m-browse.com
- www.m-find.com
- mfinder.cellmania.com
- mobile.yahoo.com
- www.mopilot.com
- www.mywaplink.com
- www.orktopas.com
- www.palowireless.com
- www.pawgo.com
- www.phortal.com
- www.site-wap.com
- www.snap.com
- www.sowap.com
- www.streetm8.com
- www.submitwap.com
- www.superwap.nl

- www.wannawap.com
- www.wap.co.uk
- www.wap.com
- wap.phonevalley.com
- wap.raging.com
- www.wapall.com
- www.wapaw.com
- www.wapjag.com
- www.wapjump.com
- www.wapjump.org
- www.waply.com
- www.waponthenet.com
- www.wap-reviews
- www.wapring.net
- www.wapspy.com
- www.waptiger.de
- www.wapwarp.com
- www.yospace.com

Summary: Top Five Expert Tips

1. Create a wireless version of your press materials to save steps . . . and a few dozen trees.

2. Tie wireless content into all other PR materials to encourage an ongoing dialogue between you and members of the press.

3. Encourage company executives to publish their calendars in a mobile-friendly format so that you can schedule interviews around their availability no matter where you are.

4. Tap into wireless information to feed updated news and analysis to your executives for that next broadcast press tour.

5. Location tracking sounds like a great idea for opt-in customer marketing, but it could alienate journalists who access your wireless pressroom.

CHAPTER 9

Enabling Mobile Commerce and Sales Functions

"Please turn on your magic beam. Mr. Sandman, bring me a dream."

From the 1954 top 40 hit song "Mr. Sandman," as sung by The Chordettes

While watching yet another TV commercial touting the future of mobile commerce, my mind began to wander. I imagined how monetary transactions could someday be affected by wireless communications. By the time my young daughter reaches high school, I might beam the digital equivalent of a few dollars to her PDA rather than open my wallet to fork over the cash. At least I won't be wondering what she did with the money. With any hope, she'll show me an itemized mobile trail of where she blew her allowance—rather than answering my motherly inquiries with, "Gee, I don't know." Well, so much for wishful thinking.

Today, similar dreams of a cashless society echo in the writings of futurists and science fiction authors, much like the lyrics of a cute romantic ballad mirror lonely-heart wishes for that perfect date. Lately, I've been reading about the promise of beaming credit card numbers from my handheld to a cash register terminal, which could save me the trouble of fumbling through my wallet. Still, I must remind myself that even the 20th-century dream of a *paperless* society has yet to be realized. Yes, you're right—I complained about that in my first book. Apparently, some still-cryptic aspects of human nature continue to prevent true progress from happening. C'est la vie.

But what can mobile tools do to makes sales and finance better in the near future? Hmm. Let's see. The limitations of off-site sales crews can be minimized with the addition of applications geared toward customer relationship management. Field service personnel in certain industries can access important company records, such as product inventory that can be checked in real time. Company agents can conduct inquires into rates and provide service quotes in an instant. Consumers can use down time—in a taxi, in a dentist's waiting room, or on a mall bench while waiting for his or her spouse to finish shopping—to manage personal banking transactions. And I've barely scratched the surface.

Well, I've done enough espousing the virtues of mobile sales and finance functions. It's time to talk about what's real now. To reuse a well-known hamburger joint ad slogan, "Where's the beef?"

About This Chapter

This chapter will provide insights into how wireless devices can help mobile commerce and sales-related activities. Such activities can include online commerce via handheld devices as initiated by either the user or sales person.

We'll ponder some of the resistance of users to conduct mobile commerce and provide a thought or two on how to make the concept of mobile shopping more palatable. How does the customer perceive the mobile point-of-sale? That's a good question—one that we will touch upon here.

If you have your own products and services, you'll want to investigate mobile wallet applications, which we cover briefly. If you're a content provider or games developer, look into micropayment or pay-per-use solutions. Finally, if you have no concrete product or service offerings of your own, you might wish to sign on with a sales affiliate program and sell someone else's wares. We'll tell you about the front-runner in that area.

Why Mobile Commerce Scares Us So

Every week I read another announcement about wireless payment solutions, servers, applications, or related technology. In the wireless realm, companies have caught on quickly about the need for mobile commerce solutions.

Software advancements aside, customers aren't fully sold on the concept of conducting mobile financial transactions. Psychologically, customers might not be ready to do business that way. There's the mobile brand perception factor. On the small, grayscale screen of a Palm VIIx handheld, a company's logo just doesn't have the same impact that it does on the Web. Personally, I believe that if you have an established relationship with a customer in the real world and/or on the Web, you've got no problem with this one.

Perhaps it's the unknown. Where does the credit card number go, and can someone intercept it? Who hasn't had a few paranoid fantasies about some loitering criminal sniffing wireless networks with a laptop? After all, to the average person, wireless communications do not seem nearly as secure as wired ones. Come on, now. Surely, it's a lot scarier to let your 16-year-old son borrow the car than to send credit card information over a wireless network.

But look how long it took for e-commerce to catch on. Sure, there will always be Luddites and hesitant customers. No matter what you believe about the future of wireless transactions, you must be realistic about who's really shopping wirelessly. For now, early adopters are *the market* for mobile shopping, and that might even include your 16-year-old. So, let's concentrate on making these mobile-savvy folks happy. Let mobile users know that you respect them by finding a secure and simple way to accept their orders. The rest of the market will eventually follow.

Improving Transaction Security

To truly take advantage of mobile commerce, servers and systems must incorporate tight security measures and technologies at the online point-of-sale and during all transmission activities. From a marketing standpoint, promotion of a secure environment for mobile shopping not only appeals to shoppers but it can also deter the unscrupulous (at least, those who can't hack into systems, anyway).

Mobile Digital Certificates

Ericsson inked a deal in February 2001 to embed VeriSign digital certificate technology into Ericsson's WAP-enabled mobile telephones. This deal means that a user of these mobile phones is assured that selected sites can be authenticated through VeriSign's wireless server digital certificates. The user feels more confident about the wireless transaction, knowing that the wireless server in question is kosher—making it nice for the end user who doesn't want to do mobile financial gymnastics just to complete a purchase. This situation is quite a wireless marketing coup for the banking, retailing, and brokerage industries.

Are you installing your own wireless server? VeriSign is one of those companies that can help you in your quest for a wireless server digital certificate. But don't let me bore you with the technical details of secure wireless servers and associated software. Just know that this area is one that you'll need to consider, especially because these costs will increase your marketing budget.

PIN Numbers

According to an August 2001 press release by Visa International, nearly 90 percent of 16- to 18-year-old shoppers in the United Kingdom dislike signing charge card slips at the point of sale. Visa's research indicated that these young shoppers prefer a *personal identification number* (PIN) to a handwritten signature, believing PINs to be a more secure and an evidently quicker method for payments.

Visa undertook the study as part of its efforts to reduce credit card fraud. Survey respondents indicated that retailers that use PIN numbers for *point-of-sale* (POS) systems are more modern and perhaps more in tune with younger shoppers' shopping preferences and needs. Whether you're empowering your customer base or arming your mobile sales force, chat with your IT people about whether adding another layer of user-entered identification, like a PIN number, is useful, feasible, and necessary for your mobile commerce needs.

Who You Are

Another way to enhance security for financial transactions is to make sure that there are multiple keys in place to guarantee a user's identity. A combination of approaches could include scanning a credit card, asking the user to enter a PIN, and asking the user to put his or her thumbprint on a device. From the user's viewpoint, these three steps are as follows:

Credit card = what you have

PIN data entry = what you know

Thumbprint identification = who you are

Currently, portable credit card scanners for Palm handheld and other mobile devices are available through companies such as Cardservice International and LinkPoint International. I saw them in use at a trade show recently. The neat little devices slip over the bottom of the PDA. But they are more practical for sales representatives than individuals.

Biometrics technology, which relies on fingerprint or iris scans, is not an integral part of the average mobile handheld device. Still, a few companies are working on making mobile transactions more secure by incorporating these three transaction elements, if not more. It could be a while before the average person gets the word and even longer before he or she combines them for mobile commerce. Consider it something to keep in the back of your mind.

Understanding the M-Commerce Point-of-Sale

You might ask, what exactly is the POS? According to investorwords.com, the financial term point-of-sale refers to the "physical location at which goods are sold to customers." For a Girl Scout selling cookies door to door, POS simply means the next-door neighbor's doorstep. In a retail store, a broader definition of POS might include the beloved cash register and related hardware, software, and other technologies such as bar code and receipt printers, show floor kiosks with access to product information, and of course, the store itself. Hey, why not? These items exist at the point of selling and certainly contribute to and/or encourage a sale.

What is the main difference in the POS concept between yesterday and today? Historically, the retailer had decisive control over the POS environment. Travel back to yesteryear in the American West. Because time machines aren't a reality yet, just use your mind's eye. Got the image? Good. See that sign in the store window over there? Blue fabric is on sale today. Posting signage to increase visibility along the main street of a small town, the owner of a general store entices interested townsfolk to stop by and look around. If he planned well, the shopkeeper could move tables with goods—in other words, leverage the positioning of displays—around his store aisles to reinforce his message of quality. Once Mrs. Brown and her brood came through the door, Shopkeeper Truesdale had ample opportunity to engage them both visually and verbally. Such rudimentary knowledge of POS has been handed down and refined by generations of shopkeepers, long before the likes of Buffalo Bill rode into town.

As a 21st century e-retailer or e-tailer, your window dressing might well be enhanced by a broader concept of POS. National magazine and prime-time TV ads stoke the fires of recognition with the brief mention of a URL. Once the spending public stops by your online store, your POS presence is dependent on Web-based fonts, colors, layouts, graphics, and innovative, interactive functionality.

Nowadays, with mobile shopping moving quickly into the minds of ravenous consumers, there's a new marketing mindset to embrace. One interesting concept of mobile POS is as follows: instead of having the POS envelop the customer, as in a store setting, the customer's hands envelop the POS. With POS real estate reduced to the smallest territory imaginable, the e-marketer must now learn to overcome the elusive and migratory nature of POS within the wireless sales environment. And, if the concept of POS as a moving, Lilliputian target weren't enough, the typical rules for closing a sale itself have been rewritten. Leveraging the POS for an m-commerce venture is much more than translating sales functions from the store to the Web to the mobile device.

Arming Your Mobile Sales Force

How do you overcome the restrictive and migratory nature of the mobile POS? One way to capitalize on the inherent characteristics of the mobile POS is to arm your field sales force with wireless devices, applications, and peripherals instead of relying on the mobile customer to call all of the shots. In essence, you take some of the purchase control away from your customers and put it back where it belongs—in the hands of your trained sales people. This approach minimizes many of the downfalls of electronic commerce: poor customer service, abandoned shopping carts, and credit card fraud (to name a few).

How do you do that? The first two examples that come to mind are fairly straightforward:

Sales orders. Using an Internet-ready telephone, a palmtop device, or wireless laptop, your sales crew can record sales transactions, verify credit cards, process all kinds of payments, and issue receipts.

Field sales support. Given the right tools, your mobile sales force can access enterprise applications, calendars, and other data such as purchase records, order processing systems, task lists, customer contact lists, meeting schedules, and raw sales leads. This information can be found on your company's Web site or on a secure intranet. In some cases, it's fairly easy to make information mobile-friendly or accessible to the mobile sales person. In other cases, you might need the help of a custom or off-the-shelf application.

Mobile-Friendly Access for the Simple Stuff

If you have a knack for HTML, then you'll love this feature. Web pages can be made mobile-friendly for your marketing and sales people just by "dummying down" the source code. That's not an insult to someone's intelligence, honestly. It's more of a commentary on the current state of readying simple content for even simpler wireless retrieval. Take my word for it, I did it very quickly in preparation for a business trip, as shown in Figure 9.1. Think how quickly you can pull together similar mobile-friendly code for your sales force.

Notice how boring the page appears visually. That's because I wanted to be able to view the site on the browser I installed on my PDA, but I also wanted to repurpose those same pages for a *Web clipping application* (WCA). Once the basic HTML was in place, it was relatively easily to build a simple WCA for those same pages (see a screen shot of the scrollable Palm device home page as pieced together for Figure 9.2).

I've found that creating a simple WCA is a neat way to make all kinds of information portable, from my *Marketing Wirelessly* newsletter to my conference presentation to my daughter's knock-knock joke collection.

Yes, you can perform this task, too. I promise you. If you're interested, WCA building tools can be found in various places on the Web. Like their HTML edit-

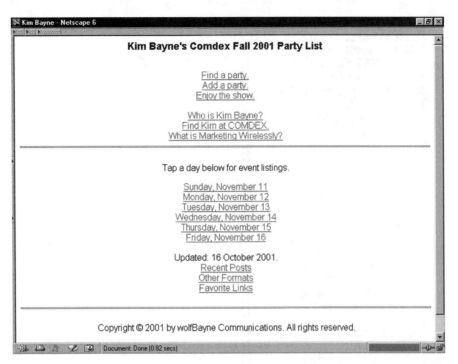

Figure 9.1 Due to its plain HTML, Kim Bayne's Party List on the wired Web can be viewed through the mobile browser on her PDA.

ing ancestors, these applications come in various flavors depending on how sophisticated your needs are. One example, Palm's WCA Builder for Windows—available to registered members of Palm's Developer community—takes no time at all to master. Once you get a tool like this one, you just tell it to grab the main index.htm page from a directory on your hard drive. The application uses document links to find the other files and images in that directory, then puts it all together for you.

Anyhow, once I built the WCA or *Palm Query Application* (PQA) and uploaded it to my Web site, I told other show attendees by an opt-in e-mail list. Attendees could each download the file for installation on their devices. My Web site even provided users with instructions for viewing the document in other formats, depending on their preferences. I'll show you that FAQ in the chapter on customer service if you're interested. Now imagine doing the same cool thing for your mobile sales force by using internal phone lists, price lists, product specifications, FAQ sheets, and so on. Start brainstorming about the different ways you can repackage sales-related content. It doesn't get any easier than this!

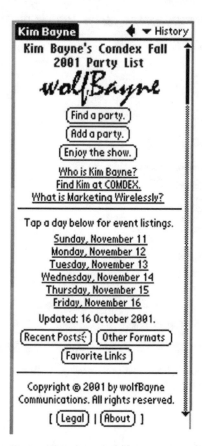

Figure 9.2 Kim Bayne's Party List enables Palm™ VIIx handheld users to view prepackaged data yet access updates on the wired Web.

Contact Managers

Years ago, I became an avid user of ACT!, a contact manager application from Interact Commerce Corp. Interact has since extended its product line with ACT! Link for Palm OS handhelds. ACT! Link is free for downloading, so you can use it right away if you already have ACT! on your desktop. Your sales staff might have its favorite brand of contact manager. I'll bet that there's a wireless version waiting in the wings.

Handspring, Palm, and Sony handheld users can use the wireless version of their PC or Macintosh-based contact manager to keep track of updated customer histories and notes and to grab data from designated groups. Bundled with a wireless service, wireless contact management applications enable sales people to obtain information from a centralized location. A few applications have the added bonus of enabling news, stock quotes, and weather based on individual preferences.

Synchronization Software

Several sales people I know have the habit of synchronizing everything—their mobile devices, their desktop applications, and a Web-based personal information manager account. Starfish's TrueSync Plus enables users to synch it all very neatly from the desktop, as seen in Figure 9.3.

Case in point: I once left my PDA in my hotel room but was too far away at the conference center to go back to get it in time for a meeting. Trouble was, I did not have the details with me—and for the life of me, I was having a "senior moment" and couldn't remember the names of the people I was to meet. Fortunately, this conference center had a bank of Internet-connected PCs in the pressroom. I logged into my account at Yahoo! and accessed my calendar, complete with minor details like the executive's name. Duh. Thank goodness I synchronized all that data before I got on the airplane.

By reminding your marketing and sales department to synchronize their wireless devices regularly, you'll improve efficiency and create a backup for emergencies. So, use me as an example and tell your mobile sales force to back it up.

What about your company's sales force? Someone might need to meet with Heather, your sales director, but can't reach her on the road right now because she's on a flight. Rather than wait for Heather to call in for messages, an assistant

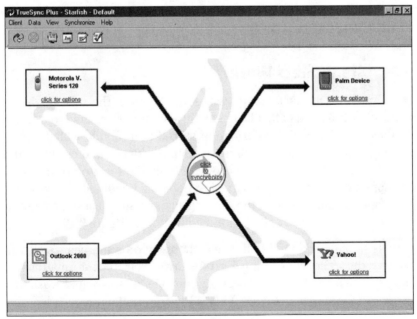

Figure 9.3 TrueSync Plus helps a user keep multiple copies of his or her schedule in several places. (© 2001 Starfish Software, Inc.)

or secretary can update her online calendar and send a heads-up e-mail to her wireless device as an alert. If she brought the right cable with her, she'll find the appointment in place after she synchronizes her data. That little trick could keep her from double-booking sales appointments.

Mobile Wallets

So what drives mobile commerce? Obviously, a key component of any mobile commerce transaction is its payment channel. Think mobile wallet, digital wallet, or virtual purse applications—whatever you choose to call this user-centric application. In use in many parts of Europe and Asia, mobile wallets are available for mobile phones, PDAs, and pagers. If your online presence generates or plans to generate income from mobile users, look into how this feature will affect the sales transaction.

For both the merchant and the customer, one advantage to using an m-wallet is the shortened sales transaction time, similar to the convenience of using a Web-based e-wallet. Think about the number of key taps needed to complete a mobile transaction. Now think about how annoying, and sometimes impossible, it can be to enter a credit card number on a handheld device. Now think about completing the data entry process again with your shipping address and telephone number. Disgusted yet? By reducing the frustration factor inherent in wireless data entry, mobile wallets increase the likelihood that a customer will make a mobile purchase.

How Do Mobile Wallets Work?

Depending on the exact mobile wallet application, the user might enter personal and/or financial data, like checking account or credit card information, as referenced in Figure 9.8. Information stored in a mobile wallet could include the user's full name, billing address, shipping address, and credit card numbers for each account listed (see Figure 9.9). Such data is stored in a mobile software application, perhaps on his or her personal handheld device, or on a desktop computer that transfers the data during synchronization, as demonstrated by the bogus data that I entered for a colleague in Figure 9.10.

After the mobile customer is finished shopping on a merchant's site, he or she taps open the wallet application for transferring selected information to the wireless purchase form. For added security, m-wallet software might ask the user for a password (as shown in Figure 9.11), a PIN, or another unique identifier.

The existence of mobile wallets helps bring the wireless user that much closer to the one-click shopping concept. Some solutions providers are betting that such

Case Study: Boston Duck Tours and E.E.S. Companies

Boston Duck Tours, a land and water tour operator, worked with E.E.S. Companies, Inc. of Natick, Massachusetts to create a Palm-based mobile application that enables sales agents, located anywhere in Boston, to book tours. Duck-Links is a customized version of POS/OE 4 PDA software created by E.E.S.

Boston Duck Tour sales agents use their individual Palm VII devices to:

- Select tours by date and time, as shown in Figure 9.4
- Check seating availability
- Enter ticket quantities, as shown in Figure 9.5
- Process ticket payments (see Figure 9.6)
- Authorize credit card transactions
- Print invoices, as shown in Figure 9.7
- Issue ticket receipts

The ability to process the completed transaction by wireless device also means that sales inventory is always current. The entire mobile POS solution includes a Palm VII handheld, a portable receipt and ticket printer, and a credit card reader.

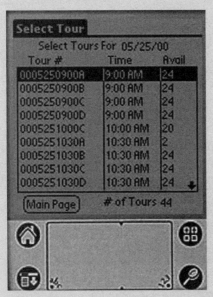

Figure 9.4 Duck-Links enables the sales agent to select a tour by date and time. (© 2000–2001 E.E.S. Companies, Inc.)

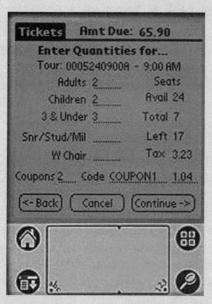

Figure 9.5 Ticket availability is easily checked through the Boston Duck Tours mobile sales application. (© 2000–2001 E.E.S. Companies, Inc.)

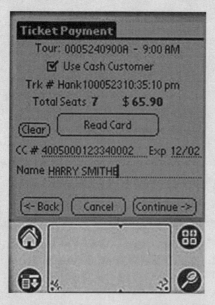

Figure 9.6 The Duck-Links application enables the sales agent to process ticket payments by sending data to a secure server. (© 2000–2001 E.E.S. Companies, Inc.)

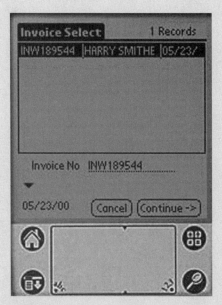

Figure 9.7 Boston Duck Tours invoices are easily printed by selecting the right record. (© 2000-2001 E.E.S. Companies, Inc.)

Previously, Boston Duck Tours tickets were sold in one location only. In season, guests waited in long lines—an annoying factor of popular tourist attractions. That all changed now that Boston Duck Tours can use Duck-Links to set up an impromptu ticket booth on the fly.

Another side benefit of a mobile POS sales tool is its ability to increase efficiency. Without immediate access to inventory, sales agents in the hospitality and travel industry often overbook or underbook tours, hotel rooms, shuttle services, and so on. Because Boston Duck Tours went wireless, it has been able to minimize such problems while decreasing tourist frustration. By placing the point-of-sale into the hands of its city-wide agents, Boston Duck Tours overcame both the limitations of its sales operation and a few pet peeves of mobile commerce.

There is one interesting side note. Depending on the sales environment, not every employee is suited to using wireless sales tools while on the go. At the Boston Duck Tours site, I noticed a job listing for *Guest Service Representatives* (GSRs). The position requires an "energetic team player to work indoors and outdoors," one special qualification that you might consider when forming your wireless marketing team (as addressed in Chapter 4).

Figure 9.8 SplashMoney organizes the PDA user's personal financial data, such as credit cards and bank accounts.

helper applications will encourage mobile impulse buying. Meanwhile, most mobile users are slow to develop the habit of using a mobile wallet application. And those who have used mobile wallets before aren't quite confident enough to

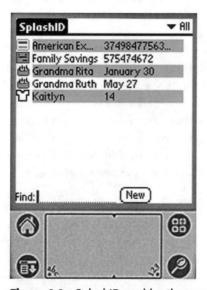

Figure 9.9 SplashID enables the user to add intimate details such as credit card numbers, bank accounts, family birthdays, and clothing sizes.

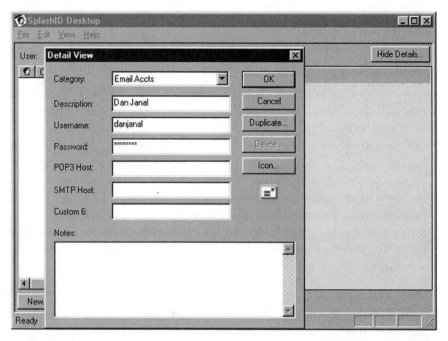

Figure 9.10 The SplashID Desktop application makes data entry much easier and enables data transfer to the handheld device during synchronization. (© 1997-2001 LandWare, Inc. All rights reserved.)

Figure 9.11 SplashMoney records a user password for added security. (© 1997-2001 LandWare, Inc. All rights reserved.)

purchase big-ticket items, which could impede m-commerce's bottom line. Finally, certain products and services might not lend themselves to the notion of the mobile wallet concept. A few industry pundits claim that user resistance is futile. So, hang in there. M-wallet acceptance should gain momentum eventually.

The best mobile wallet application supports a variety of payment channels—credit or debit cards, micropayment, or pre- and post-paid accounts. A few vendors have even added features that store user preferences and other files, like body measurements or clothing sizes, frequent flier numbers, and airline booking interests. The SplashWallet mobile wallet application for Palm OS is bundled with a photo album for viewing personal images. Another example of a mobile payment application with jazzy user-oriented features is the SNAZ Mobile Wallet. This device enables shoppers to save multiple details from different merchants to lists. Lists can then be sent to friends and family. An added bonus is the software's ability to comparison shop through the SNAZ merchant network.

But forget about all the bells and whistles for now. Your best bet is to find a mobile wallet solution that is seamless and pain-free to integrate into your mobile site, not to mention instills confidence in your user base. That could be SNAZ or it could be something else, depending on your user's wants and needs.

The Centralized versus Decentralized Debate

Now, about those security issues. Sometimes mobile wallet data is stored in a centralized server location, managed by a telephone carrier or digital cash company. But sending information between multiple parties—the user, the m-wallet server, and the merchant site—can increase security risks. In spite of vendor assurances that such solutions are secure, there are no guarantees with technology. This situation can contribute somewhat to the user's perception that mobile commerce isn't what it should be.

One choice might be to keep all data on the user's device and only transmit selected information as needed directly to the merchant. On the flip side, storing such data will increase the size of the mobile database residing on the user's device, which could affect device performance and deny space to more noteworthy applications. And if the device is lost or stolen, it's too easy for a crook to hack in and walk away with a new identity.

Before choosing a mobile wallet partner for your m-commerce venture, evaluate your user's experience with online shopping. Skittish and novice mobile users might not like a solution with a mobile-middleman interface. You might wish to build user education into your customer service process to help heal the wounds perceived by stories of stolen identities and network sniffing.

In order to promote mobile commerce, you must respond to your customer's need for a simple yet secure payment solution. If you're a small mobile player, think about leveraging someone else's payment solution instead of building your own. Make friends with a mobile wallet solution provider who will serve as the conduit between you and the customer's payment channel. It's well worth the formal introduction.

Mobile wallets can increase sales by making the buying process easier. Mobile wallets take merchants out of the verification loop while still providing several options for customers. Mobile wallets can prevent fraud and increase user privacy. Lead your customer to a partner with mobile financial processing capabilities, and that's one less part of your wireless presence to worry about.

Wireless Micropayments

Picture a teenager standing in front of a vending machine. With no change in her pocket, she manages to procure a can of soda simply by pressing a few buttons on her mobile phone. Yes, we've all seen the TV commercial that touts the virtues of proximity payments. What's on the future agenda for wireless micropayments? Change for highway tollbooths, fares on subways and buses, and still more vending machine noshes are probably in the picture. But fantasy and reality have a wide chasm to cross before this wireless marketing wish comes true for mainstream businesses and their customers. What's your interest as a mobile marketer? Your choices for processing micropayments will dictate budget line items for your wireless marketing plan.

Why Collect Micropayments?

Tell me what you're selling, and I'll explain. If you're a wireless content publisher, you might charge by the article or story. If you offer wireless games, you might charge by the download. According to an August 2001 story in *Wireless-Review*, enabling micropayments improves customer satisfaction by increasing transaction speed, which increases purchases, which increases sales revenue. In other words, make it easier for customers to do business with you, and they'll buy from you more often.

Sure, m-wallets can take care of the regular items, but micropayments have their own unique mobile commerce issues. The proliferation of micropayments could be a hassle for everyone involved, which is why it hasn't caught on yet in the United States. As a consumer, who wants to charge such small amounts to a credit card? As a traditional payment solutions provider, who wants to track millions of tiny transactions?

From the mobile user's viewpoint, there are really only three micropayment choices: prepaid, direct debit, and billed. Prepaid requires the mobile user to pay in advance for a series of anticipated purchases, perhaps with funds deposited on account. Direct debit takes funds out of a user's checking account while a billed option requires the user to have some type of account already for post-facto payment. Sometimes a consumer's choice is driven by trust, in which case, he or she might not trust mobile commerce enough to risk paying money up front or letting a business have access to his or her bank account. If so, you're stuck with the billed approach.

One downside to the merchant is that billing means a delay in receiving payment. Checks don't always arrive on time, and credit card laws allow charge disputes. Holy cow. I hope that you have lots of Rolaids for your billing department staff, because this situation can get pretty dicey. In other words, if your m-marketing ROI includes micropayment revenue, remember that billing issues will increase the overall cost of doing business this way. Hmmm. Maybe you need a new system.

In order for a business to process a micropayment, some type of technical infrastructure must exist to handle all of those transactions, like 50 cents this day and $1 the next. Either you have this system in place or someone else does. If you create your own infrastructure, you could be months or years in the making. That's not a good choice if you're dealing in nickels and dimes. If your micropayment sales don't run any larger than pocket change, you don't need this extra task. Consider farming it out. You're trading the delay in receiving payments for someone's expertise in micropayment processing. You'll no doubt pay a fee and/or a percentage or commission for related services, but you'll save time in account verification and transaction aggregation. Do some vendor research, and add these costs to your budget.

Micropayment Solutions

Who are your possible partners in the micropayment scenario? There are a limitless number of interested parties, including telephone companies, credit card companies, e-commerce wallet companies, digital cash companies, and so on. Now, let's see who might be a good partner (or not) for your business.

If you're familiar with auction sales, you might have made a purchase or two through Paypal, a payment processing go-between for merchants like eBay auctions and online users. Paypal can handle both credit card charges and checking account debits. Using PayPal (seen in Figure 9.12) as your payment solutions provider, you could encourage mobile users to pay wirelessly as long as it is linked somehow to the actual transaction. Remember, any type of disconnect within the shopping process isn't a good idea. If you can't make payment an

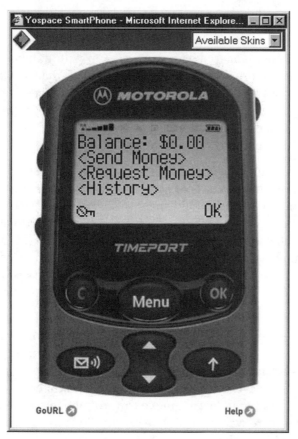

Figure 9.12 Registered PayPal users can send money from their account through a mobile telephone.(Telephone image © Motorola, Inc. SmartPhone Emulator © 1999–2001 Yospace Holdings Ltd. Used with permission. WAP Site copyright © 2002 PayPal. All rights reserved.)

integral part of checkout, you're inviting the user to *not* complete the sale. And even if such payment brokers enable simple m-commerce transactions for the wireless merchant, microtransactions aren't suited for many of these systems. Why not? Let's listen in to what the mobile user is thinking.

> "If I had to balance my checkbook after having a few dozen tiny transactions debited from the checking account I registered with this online payment service, I'd go nuts. And I'm not about to offer my credit card for micropayments. I don't want to deal with a hundred lines at 25 cents each on next month's bill."

So what's next? Credit card companies, like Visa and MasterCard, offer stored value cards. Combined with an m-wallet application, this situation could be a quick-start m-commerce solution for your mobile consumers. But again, you'd have to educate users in completing the transaction your way, so forget it.

Chalk it up to another abandoned shopping cart as your mobile customer loses interest.

Here's a thought. M-commerce merchants could sign up with eCharge (www .echarge.com)—one choice for m-businesses that have more than 1,000 transactions a month. eCharge bills digital purchases to the customer's telephone bill as well. The charge shows up as a company-specific line item on the user's phone bill. Hey—that makes sense. Telephone companies are used to this whole idea of multiple tiny amounts on an aggregated bill.

In June 2001, Cingular announced Cingular DirectBill, a wireless micropayment solution. Right now, micropurchases are enabled for rock music ringtones with the cooperation of music publishers that are licensing the songs. The music industry stands to make billions of dollars in related micropayments. But if this probably isn't your industry, who cares? Anyway, Cingular's merchant development plans will encourage many telephone companies to follow suit in the field of micropayments. Wireless telephone carriers could provide you with the simplest micropayments solution yet for your m-commerce enterprise.

Whichever micropayment solution you choose, remember the following: the industry is moving quickly. There will be plenty of financial processing and micropayment choices out there, regardless of your business scope and focus. Plug-and-play solutions could be just around the corner. One thing that will work in everyone's favor is the industry's move toward mobile payment standards. Two industry players to watch are Mobile Electronic Transactions (MeT) and the Mobile Payment Group (PayCircle).

Wireless Affiliate Marketing: Reinventing the Wheel

If you've had a Web site for a while now, you've no doubt experimented with commission-based income. I'm referring to affiliate or associate programs offered by such e-commerce players as Amazon.com. Here's a refresher. In essence, the Webmaster signs up for a sales associate account, puts specially coded links and/or banners on various Web pages, and points potential buyers to the other site. If the visitor makes a purchase through a coded link, the affiliate Webmaster or site owner is compensated for the sales referral.

Over the years, thousands of Webmasters have picked up a few dollars by incorporating relevant product links into their content. And the recipients of such product bounties aren't just small Web sites. Large portals often link content or search results to sales. As a matter of fact, when I search for the key-words "mobile," "affiliate," and "networks," Yahoo! was kind enough (err, savvy enough) to point me to a link at Barnes and Noble, just in case there were any books published on my search topic. If I happened to buy anything after click-ing through to bn.com, Yahoo!'s coffers would be a little bit fatter.

What does this information have to do with wireless marketing and sales? Well, it was only a matter of time—OK, maybe just a few short weeks—before the wireless world caught on. After all, if you can generate passive income through a wired Web site, why not do it with a wireless one? And if you're on the selling end of this proposition, you can tap into affiliate programs to generate more visitors and close more wireless sales.

Yes, the success of associate, affiliate, and bounty programs has found its way to wireless. If your wireless site has the potential to attract lots of visitors, this situation could be an excellent revenue stream for you. While there aren't many pay-for-performance choices right now for wireless Webmasters, sit tight. This opportunity is just beginning. It stands to reason that if a site has an affiliate program for its wired Web site and it develops a wireless presence, a wireless affiliate program won't be far behind.

According to United Kingdom-based Mobile Affiliates, a site touting itself as the first wireless affiliate network, Webmasters can generate revenue by plac-ing links and images on wireless sites to advertise the products and services of registered merchants. Such merchants could include a wireless portal such as a search engine, a wireless service provider, or even a manufacturer, to name a few possibilities. Mobile Affiliates acts as the go-between, introducing eager wireless Webmasters looking for ways to make a buck to merchants who are looking for sales outlets to reach wireless device users. Assuming that certain affiliate sites have the same type of visitor coveted by the merchants, it's a great arrangement for everyone involved. Depending on your needs, Mobile Affili-ates offers pay-per-click, pay-per-lead, and pay-per-sale campaigns. Someone like you can register a mobile site, as shown in Figure 9.13, and start generating income immediately without any product inventory to speak of. The two par-ties to this mobile commerce—affiliate and merchant—become partners of sorts. . . and everyone goes home happy.

This situation all sounds familiar, doesn't it? So why can't affiliates just add the special links from Web-based programs to wireless sites? Well, for one thing, such links only point to landlocked sites. Sorry, but links on a wireless site must point to another wireless site; otherwise, you're wasting your user's time. And links on WML sites viewed on WAP-enabled phones don't work when pointed to HDML or iMode sites. Oh, brother. And you thought that the difference between Microsoft Internet Explorer and Netscape Navigator was bothersome.

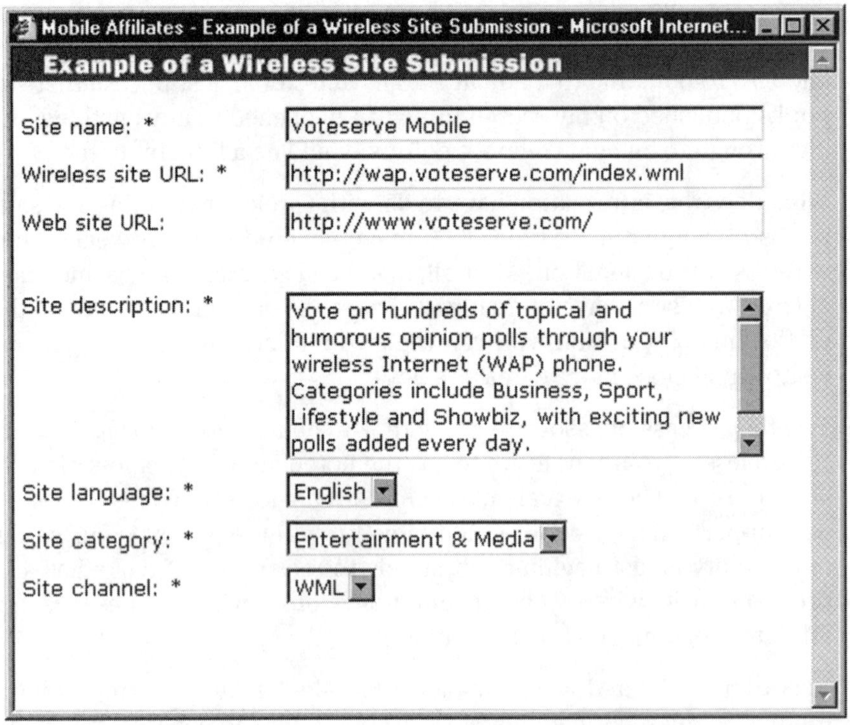

Figure 9.13 Voteserve Mobile submits its site by using Mobile Affiliate's Web interface. (© Copyright 2000–2002, Voteserve.com Limited. All Rights Reserved.)

Mobile Affiliates recognizes these differences and offers channels, links, and images to compensate for each. They have their standards act together, too. The program falls in line with standards set by the *Wireless Advertising Association* (WAA).

As a reminder, there are two sides to the "pay-for-results" story: the affiliate and the merchant. As an affiliate, you get a sales commission without having to manufacture or purchase anything or pack and ship products. If you've been a member of Amazon.com or any other Web-based affiliate program, you know what I'm talking about because you've reaped the benefits of a check or two.

Signing on as a wireless affiliate is free, which is to be expected. After all, you're a member of a sales force and should be compensated, not charged. The merchant wants you to advertise, so there shouldn't be any artificial barriers (like program sign-up fees) in place.

Are any limits to the types of merchants available through such affiliate programs? Certainly. Sites that are off the map of traditional advertising aren't accepted into the program. That would include obscene, defamatory, libelous, abusive, hate-oriented, and illegal sites, according to Mobile Affiliates. Thank goodness for their good sense. Sure, eventually someone out there will develop an affiliate sales network for such wireless sites, but I'm not interested in finding them—so don't bother me if you know of any.

How does the network make money? It charges the merchant fees that include a percentage of commissions to cover administration, setup, affiliate payment processing, network development, and management. Setup fees can be rather pricey for a small business. Mobile Affiliate's setup charge is currently $500 (USD), but it's waived if the merchant agrees to a higher transaction fee on commissions. That would be 50 percent instead of 30 percent. Put in simpler terms, for a pay-per-click program, this situation could mean 10 cents for the affiliate and five cents for the network. For a pay-per-sale program, on an item with a price tag of $100, the merchant pays $5 to the affiliate and $2.50 to the network. The merchant makes $100 minus $7.50 for a gross sales amount of. . . oh, you get the picture. Commissions vary by program, so you do the math.

Is This Right for You?

All is not rosy on the affiliate sales side. In the past, wired affiliate program participants have complained of non-paying merchants. To minimize this problem, Mobile Affiliates is one of those programs that require its merchants to have a minimum account deposit ($250 USD) to get their account in full gear. Typically, such money is held on deposit to compensate the merchant's virtual sales crew immediately. Affiliate Webmasters appreciate getting those monthly checks, and it's not nice to make them wait.

In the past, there have been other issues with affiliate marketing, such as poorly designed programs, skimpy commissions, tracking systems that don't always operate well, and so on. In spite of these, if your wireless merchant-affiliate partnership does work out, you still must recognize that the addition of links to your wireless site does not automatically translate into real income. Some affiliate program veterans have referred to such income as "pocket change" or "pin money." Program promoters claim relevance, and link positioning is everything. They say that if you've done your affiliate marketing job correctly, you'll attract repeat buyers to your virtual commission-based store, which means better sales. Then again, if wireless affiliate programs grow like their Web-based cousins—sprouting in every conceivable wireless nook and cranny—competition will be fierce.

As you might have guessed already, some of the strategies and tactics for creating and running a wired affiliate store are the same as a wireless one. Yes, you can use in-context references to selected products to help generate revenue from your free wireless content. Yes, mobile Internet users will click through and you'll make a few sales. Yes, every other wireless Webmaster will soon have links in place, too. But if you're in on the ground floor and are just launching a wireless marketing program, this method is one good way to demonstrate wireless ROI from the get-go. Be advised. Soon you'll need to devise more sophisticated techniques to make your wireless presence truly pay off.

Meanwhile, if you can't wait to make this type of money, reap the benefits of in-context Web advertising now by exploring the wonderful world of wireless product sales. It's one way to get your foot in the door of a growing market. Current programs available at LinkShare.com, an affiliate marketing service provider, include Handspring and AT&T Wireless—two companies with a strong foothold in the wireless space.

Summary: Top Five Expert Tips

1. Take control of the mobile point of sale. Consider arming your sales reps with mobile handheld devices to make life easier for everyone.

2. Get rid of those bulky sales force binders. Start distributing information in mobile-friendly format to your sales team. Updates will be quicker and less costly.

3. Talk to your wireless carrier about mobile commerce solutions. You might discover a built-in solution for your payment and shopping cart needs.

4. Investigate mobile affiliate marketing as a way to test the m-commerce waters. With experimentation, you could soon be ready for your own independent m-commerce adventure.

5. This early in the game, you should consider different ways to educate your user about mobile commerce to ease the transition. They'll appreciate your attention to detail, perceive you to be more knowledgeable, and you'll earn their trust.

CHAPTER 10

Mobilizing Customer Service

"Consider yourself at home. Consider yourself one of the family."

As sung by the Artful Dodger in the Oscar-winning musical "Oliver!"

W ireless offerings have a long way to go before users start feeling at home. When it comes to understanding the mobile world, many enterprise marketers are still in awe. So, when it comes to plain vanilla customer service, it's no wonder that these companies are still struggling. But it needn't be that way. Right now, there are at least a half dozen ideas that you can incorporate into your wireless customer service without much fuss. Some of these ideas might not have been obvious for serving your mobile users until now.

Wireless customer service is more than creating a scaled-down, mobile version of your wired Web presence (as you'll soon discover). Unfortunately, some of the biggest flaws in Web-based customer service are making their way to wireless enterprises. So, here's a bit of advice. The wireless user craves customizable, interactive, and responsive service, not a quick fix. Until enterprise marketers sing the right customer service tune, users will be far from impressed with wireless offerings. And, like the boy Oliver, they'll notice that they're being served gruel.

About This Chapter

This chapter will provide tips for enhancing customer service activities to meet current and future customers' needs. You'll read why wireless might not add anything to customer service right now. You'll ponder how processing customer e-mail has changed and why some of your current procedures won't transfer. And I'll remind you to revise your company's privacy policy to incorporate current customer needs.

Thinking about how location-based services can help your business? I'll touch on some good concepts and some bad ones related to the *Emergency 911 (E911) Federal Communications Commission* (FCC) project. Do you want to help your staff work with live and untethered mobile folks? I'll share a few thoughts and personal opinions in that regard, too. Finally, you'll get a few ideas on deploying helpful mobile applications to aid your customer in doing business with you again. Right now, wireless customer service is in its infancy, and there are still plenty of opportunities.

Enhancing Customer Service

If you have any kind of Internet presence at all, your current customers might expect to find you wirelessly sooner rather than later. It's up to you to meet these expectations by augmenting your current products and services with the value-added appeal of wireless customer service.

Notice that I said "might expect." When would you *not* initiate wireless customer service? How about when you have no reason to pursue a wireless presence yet? In fact, there are several successful Internet players who have decided to delay incorporating wireless into their marketing and sales activities. In its current state, wireless technology doesn't meet their customers' needs.

The Lands' End catalog isn't jumping on the wireless bandwagon anytime soon. Wireless devices don't contribute anything to its sales of merchandise or to its customer service activities, according to a story in the May 23, 2001 issue of *E-Commerce Times*. Catalogs and the Web are a much better combination of tools for this company's needs. If you've ever been to www.landsend.com and experienced a chat-based customer service application called Lands' End Live, you'll understand why. When I shopped there last, I asked a live customer service representative to help me locate a king-sized quilt. She pushed colorful Web pages to me so that I could see exactly what we were chatting about. The current state of mobile technology doesn't allow this function, although it might someday. When it comes to home decorating, I'm not interested in buying something without seeing it. Even if a customer service agent could push the picture of a quilt to my wireless device, the tiny screen on a handheld device wouldn't do the item justice. If you can't push useful pages to a wireless user, what can you do to bring your customer service into the wireless age?

E-Mail Management

Fortunately, connecting with wireless customers via e-mail isn't difficult at all. E-mail sent from a mobile device appears in a desktop user's inbox just like any

Figure 10.1 The author sends a test e-mail to herself by using an emulator connected to her WAP site. (SmartPhone Emulator © 1999–2001 Yospace Holdings Ltd. Used with permission. Telephone image © Nokia.)

other e-mail. Where it came from and how it got there is transparent to the recipient. With the exception of a faulty reply-to field, an e-mail sent through my WAP site, in Figure 10.1, looks the same as an e-mail sent through the contact form on any wired Web site. Want proof? Take a look at Figure 10.2 for the results of that transmission. The same holds true for any e-mail that I might send to or from a wireless Visor handheld or an Ericsson Web-enabled telephone.

How can you tell which users have e-mailed you from a mobile device? Some signs are obvious, such as "From" fields that include MaryLouUser@palm.net, missing fields that the system forgot, misspellings from fat-fingering on a mobile telephone, or even the sheer brevity of the message. Unless you look closely, you can't be sure of the user's device. And even if you *do* look closely, you *still* can't be sure of the user's device. When in doubt, err on the side of caution.

There is one way to answer the "which device" question. If your user is previously registered, your customer database might contain multiple contact fields—one for a regular e-mail account and one for a mobile device. In the beginning,

```
X-Apparently-To: kimbayne@yahoo.com via web14607.mail.yahoo.com; 22 Oct 2000
13:02:03 -0700 (PDT)
X-Track: 1: 40
Date: Mon, 22 Oct 2000 22:01:59 +0200
From: noreply@mbasics.com
To: kimbayne@yahoo.com

Sent from wapsite mgo.to/kimbayne

Reply email:
editor@marketingwirelessly.com

Message:
I'm checking this out as an example for my book.
```

Figure 10.2 E-mails from wireless devices look the same as every other incoming e-mail addressed to your company.

your user registration form asks the user this information and how he or she prefers to be contacted. Having this information will enable you to recognize how your customer is reaching you and will enable you to serve her better. You could establish customer service guidelines that tell your staff to send a short reply to MaryLouUser@wireless-account.net with a note stating, "Detailed reply mailed to MaryLouUser@landline-account.com." This approach might not be foolproof, because you'll no doubt have users contacting you through e-mail addresses that aren't familiar or listed in your database.

You could code various points of your company's presence so that your inbound customer service system could recognize the point of origination. That isn't foolproof either, because users might contact you out-of-context—not through your Web clipping application, not through your telephone carrier portal, and not through the e-mail form at your WAP site. The user can send an independent e-mail message hoping for a quick response. Armed with this information, you have two choices:

1. Launch a major investigative probe into cataloging every possible source of wireless contact, including programming your system for every conceivable wireless mail server in existence.

2. Revamp your approach to e-mail replies.

When your customer service department replies to incoming customer e-mails, you don't need to do anything different with one or two exceptions: forget about HTML-formatted e-mail and attachments. The mobile user can't see them and doesn't want them. Now that your user is wireless, you must be extra sensitive to his or her needs. After all, he or she might be paying dearly for wireless service, and every kilobyte or minute counts against his or her monthly service plan.

You might be interested in knowing how SMS text messaging fits into this scene. As a reminder, SMS refers to those text-based messages sent through various means to a mobile user's telephone, PDA, or other wireless device. For the most part, marketers are looking at SMS as a tool for mobile advertising. But there are customer service applications for SMS.

As a one-shot deal, SMS could help in a pinch as a very personalized approach to customer service. For example, a freight carrier might offer its customers the option to get a text alert when a package arrives at its destination. I remember the time that the sales person I was scheduled to meet in a trade show booth wasn't there when I arrived. I had only a few minutes before I had to make it to a seminar across the exhibit hall. I recalled those pagers that restaurants give patrons waiting for a table. Then, it struck me. Rather than risk interrupting the session with an incoming phone call, I asked a booth representative to e-mail a message to my telephone when the person returned. A few moments later, I glanced down to see a message. My contact person had returned and would be at the booth until 2:30 p.m.

Permission-Based Wireless Marketing

If your customer has been nice enough to let you have a number once, never delude yourself into believing that it's fair game for future contact. Most users don't want you to use mobile contact information—like telephone numbers and SMS addressed—for ongoing business purposes without prior permission. No matter how convenient it would be for you, don't add mobile numbers to a database unless you have specifically asked the owner for permission.

I know, I know. This point is where lines are drawn in the sand between different marketing philosophies (or, should I say, marketing ethics?). The concept of opt-in permission marketing is very important when dealing with mobile users, no matter how they communicate with you. You can disagree with me, but now you know where I stand.

Got it? Good! Now for a short quiz. What works better than opt-in activities when it comes to serving your mobile customers? Nothing.

If your Web marketing staff barely met your guidelines for following a customer's e-mail contact preferences, it's time to develop some wireless marketing self-discipline. Your mobile user might not be able to find or read your privacy policy, so it's up to you to adhere to the highest standards. For some inspiration, take a look at this poster created by online privacy advocate TRUSTe, as seen in Figure 10.3.

Figure 10.3 TRUSTe educates marketers with its "Privacy Is Good Business" poster. (Poster © 1997–2001 TRUSTe. All rights reserved.)

During the course of serving mobile customers, you'll no doubt receive transmissions from a variety of devices, accounts, and services. You'll be tempted to keep track of all of these so-called sales leads. Before you get knee-deep in user abuse, I want you to repeat this wireless mantra to yourself several times:

It's more important for the mobile customer to know how to get in touch with you than for you to know how to get in touch with the mobile customer.

Again, it's more important for the mobile customer to know how to get in touch with you than for you to know how to get in touch with the mobile customer.

One more time. . .

SMS Preference Service

The *Direct Marketing Association* (DMA) has known for a long time that getting permission is better than asking for forgiveness. You might remember the DMA for its marketing practice guidelines for direct mail, facsimile transmissions, and telephone soliciting. Back in 2000, the DMA started organizing the industry into creating standards for an SMS preference service. Finally, in September 2001, the DMA and the *Wireless Marketing Association* (WMA) teamed up to launch the service, long put on hold for funding delays.

As part of the SMS Preference Service, wireless marketing companies pay an annual fee to clean their databases by comparing it to the DMA opt-out database each month. At this book's writing, exact fees for the service hadn't been established. Keep in mind that this service is two-part and voluntary:

1. Mobile users must take the initiative to register with the service and indicate their preferences.
2. Marketers must take the initiative to pay for the service and update their databases.

Will this solution solve the problem for mobile users? There's no guarantee that interested parties will take corrective action. Only time will tell. It's really an industry effort to self-regulate before mobile spam gets out of control. This discussion leads me to the next topic: your privacy policy.

Privacy Policy Creation

Whether your company chooses to participate in the SMS Preference Service or not, you still need to update your current policy guidelines with regard to your use of personally identifying information. Do you need a good tool for creating or revising a privacy policy so that you and your mobile customers can make peace? Use this one:

DMA's Privacy Policy Generator. It enables you to complete a questionnaire to create a statement for posting at your Web site. You can read privacy policy tips on the Web at www.the-dma.org/library/privacy/creating.shtml plus use the form for creating a privacy policy.

Wireless FAQs and Tutorials

In the white paper titled "The Insider's Guide to Next-Generation Web Customer Service," by Greg Gianforte of RightNow Technologies, Inc., the author outlines three generations of online customer service:

- **First Generation:** Static Information, Web Infancy
- **Second Generation:** Delayed Answers, the E-Mail Black Hole
- **Third Generation:** Immediate Answers, What the Customer Ordered

In Gianforte's third generation, he emphasizes the need to provide the customer with precise and pertinent information and "content created by means of a customer-driven, self-learning knowledge base." Self-learning documents or FAQs are a way for customers to get what they need quickly, which translates to a positive customer service experience and repeat visits.

Your Web site probably has a document called FAQs. You might be wondering how to repurpose it for your wireless site. No doubt, your document is at least a few pages long. Will it serve your mobile customers to duplicate it? Many mobile customers don't have time to scroll through long documents. Besides, your wireless presence should be uncomplicated enough that you don't need a long explanation, either.

Here's a better idea. Many of your initial wireless users will come by way of your wired presence. Consider creating a wireless FAQ or tutorial for these people. Yahoo! Mobile offers its wired users a choice of featured tours to acquaint them with several wireless topics, including launching a mini-browser on a Web-enabled telephone, accessing Yahoo! on a Web-enabled telephone, and finding Yahoo! Yellow Pages listings on the telephone. In Figure 10.4, Yahoo! educates the Web-based visitor on accessing his or her account on a mobile telephone's mini-browser. Links to other features of Yahoo! Mobile are included, such as reading news articles—seen in Figure 10.5—and searching Yahoo! Weather by zip code or city name.

Web pages that are geared toward your wireless customer can meet several needs:

- Informing the user of the depth and breadth of your wireless presence
- Educating the user in the use of each wireless service

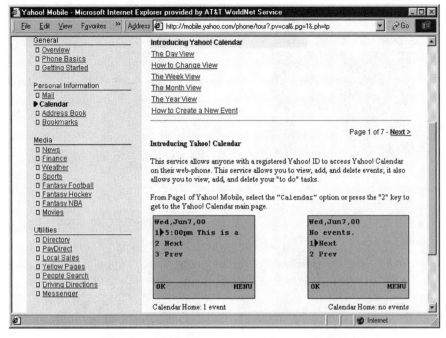

Figure 10.4 Yahoo! Calendar enables anyone with a registered Yahoo! ID to access an account on a Web-enabled telephone. (Reproduced with permission of Yahoo! Inc. © 2002 Yahoo! Inc. YAHOO! and the YAHOO! Logo are trademarks of Yahoo! Inc.)

- Illustrating ease-of-use through device-specific screen shots
- Answering questions about wireless use in a simple, step-by-step format

Wireless Tools Deployment

Your wireless presence can be jump-started immediately by building and offering useful mobile tools to your built-in market. Here are a few examples of this particular customer service approach in action.

E-mail support. In October 2000, QUALCOMM extended the use of Eudora, its popular e-mail software program, to Palm OS devices. The Eudora Wireless Messaging Suite not only enables users to send and receive e-mail with a wireless device, but it enables users to synchronize their e-mail files with their desktop by using the equally-popular HotSync program bundled with Palm devices. The Eudora Internet Suite for the Palm Computing platform, which includes a mail conduit and a browser, is available as a free download. Of course, Eudora didn't stop there. It also offered the same

My News

1. Select "News" from Page1

```
6 Weather
7▶News
8 Sports
9 Movies
  [Sign Out]
  [More]
OK             Page2
```

2. Select "My Stories"

```
Y! News
1▶My News
2 Top Stories
3 Business
4 Sports
5 World
OK             Yahoo
```

3. Select "Top Stories..."

```
My News
1▶Top Stories from
2 Top Sports Stories
3 Health from Reuters


OK                Top
```

4. Select "Syria's..."

```
Top Stories
1▶Syria's President
2 Clinton: Report Sho
3 Alabama Police May
4 Four Dead in Japan
5 Clinton Offers Bett
OK               DONE
```

Figure 10.5 Yahoo! Mobile provides illustrated, step-by-step instructions to the potential or current wireless user. (Reproduced with permission of Yahoo! Inc. © 2002 Yahoo! Inc. YAHOO! and the YAHOO! Logo are trademarks of Yahoo! Inc.)

opportunity to its affiliate sales network. Registered affiliates can download and offer Eudora's Palm version to its current base of Eudora e-mail users.

Directory assistance. 555-1212.com Inc., a provider of aggregated directory search services to Web users, signed an agreement with AvantGo to provide its solutions to the AvantGo mobile Internet community of more than two million registered users. 555-1212.com now extends its service capabilities to mobile device users, which has the added benefit of extending its brand to a previously untapped market.

Bill payment. billserv.com, an electronic bill presentment and payment service bureau, offers its consumers the ability to view and pay bills through the Palm VII handheld. Users can obtain account information from the Internet, conduct e-commerce, receive instant messages, and receive and pay bills. Talk about a great way to use downtime on the road. I'm always remembering a bill that I forgot to pay while on a business trip. The company is associated with the easy-to-remember URL www.bills.com.

Account records. In May 2001, the Saudi Telephone Company announced a new automated service for mobile telephone customers. The mobile subscriber dials 902 to access his or her account records, including the

Steal This FAQ Example!

Visitors to my Web site found the following page from September through the middle of November 2001. To make life easier, links were provided for most of the following options.

Looking for other formats of Kim Bayne's Comdex Fall 2001 Party List? You're in luck! There are several options.

1. **EMAIL LIST:** Subscribe to the email version of the Party List on Yahoo! Groups to get party announcements by email.

2. **DOCUMENT:** Download a text document of the entire Party List from a link on the mobile-friendly pages at www.kimbayne.com/comdex/.

3. **PALM QUERY APPLICATION:** Get the latest version of the Party List in a Web clipping application. Download it to your PC and install it during the next synchronization. You'll be able to carry the Party List with you and access updates wirelessly.

4. **WEB CLIPPING:** Use AvantGo's Web Clipping Channel Wizard to add the mobile-friendly URL to your PDA. Sign up for a free account then synchronize your device to grab the pages.

5. **WIRELESS BROWSING:** Download and install Digital Path's DPWeb mobile browser to your wireless PDA. The basic version of the browser is currently free. Use it to view the mobile-friendly URL for the Party List.

6. **WIRELESS BROWSING:** View the list on an Internet-ready telephone by pointing your mini-browser to www.digitalpaths.net then entering the mobile-friendly Party List URL into the browser.

7. **WIRELESS BEAMING:** If you notice someone at the show with Kim Bayne's Party List on her PDA, politely ask the user to beam it to your PDA. If you notice someone at the show who doesn't have the Party List, offer to beam it to his PDA.

amount of the current bill and the payment due date. Now, the customer can access account data without having to wait on hold to speak with a customer service representative.

Service locator. Godiva Chocolatier provides access to its directory of store addresses, telephone numbers, and maps to Palm VII owners and OmniSky subscribers. The downloadable PDA application is provided through various sites, including www.handango.com. WAP telephone users can access the same information at www.godiva.com. Various organizations have their own version of a mobile locator, including Denver's Regional Transportation District with its bus locator, Starbucks with its coffeehouse locator, and FedEx with its shipping station locator.

Shipping logistics. And speaking of shipping, here's another example. GT Nexus, a provider of global e-logistics solutions, offers its customers the convenience of wireless notification services. Previously, customers could manage global shipments with multiple carriers through the Web. Now they can receive proactive notifications about their shipments on WAP-enabled phones, pagers, and PDAs. Customers can identify shipment problems early on and take action to remain competitive.

Shopping environment. Do you think that Starbucks stopped at mobile location services? No way. Starbucks, Microsoft, and Compaq signed an agreement in 2001 to create a high-speed connected environment in Starbucks North American locations. The agreement involves installing a wireless broadband network to "enhance our customers' in-store experience," said Howard Schultz, Starbucks chairman and chief global strategist in a May 2001 company news release.

Automobile rental. As part of a promotion ending March 2001, Hertz offered its Web site visitors a downloadable, free multi-purpose city guide for their hand-held computers. The Hertz-branded version of the Port@ble Guide included a Hertz location finder, telephone number, and operating hours for each branch.

"Today, more of our customers use hand-held computers or *Personal Digital Assistants* (PDAs) and rely on information in their PDAs while traveling," said Frank Camacho, Hertz's staff vice-president of marketing, according to a company news release. The Hertz spokesperson said that the company demonstrated its leadership by providing mobile technology to improve the customer's experience.

Did you catch it? Enhance the customer experience. Improve the customer experience. That's the real focus in adding wireless to your offerings, isn't it? What's the point if your customer isn't being served better?

Is the Light on but No One's Home?

Evaluate your current online customer relationship approach. Do you rely more on technology than on human contact? Put yourself in the shoes of the online user. The next time that a customer of yours orders something on your Web site, keep track of how long it takes for each of the following to happen:

- He or she receives a detailed confirmation of his or her order by e-mail or fax.

- Customer service follows up on an item that is backordered and not available for immediate shipment.

- Customer service correctly answers the customer's detailed question about a product or service instead of replying with a link or a boilerplate document.

Insurance Claims Unplug

According to a July 2001 story in *Insurance & Technology* magazine, Selective expanded its claims management to support its field insurance adjusters' needs while out and about serving customers. Now, you might be wondering why I brought this topic up. After all, the company's new tool is designed to help its employees, right? That's half right. Apparently, having a mobile application provides insurance adjusters with more freedom, which enables them to provide better customer service. Typically, insurance adjusters spend hours making copious notes about claims cases in an effort to provide fair settlements. Often, these notes must be copied into a computer system if they hadn't been keyed in at the beginning. And there's a ton of data that's not available to these workers while "on the scene." Imagine how much that slowed down the process of settling and eventually closing a claim.

So, back in the 90s, the company decided that it had had enough. It changed from telephone-based to field-based operations. And that's where mobile technology came into play: using a wireless laptop solution.

Anyway, to make a long story short, in February 2001, Selective's *Mobile Claims System* (MCS) was introduced. Based on Windows, the system supports Microsoft Exchange and can be accessed from a laptop.

Now, this isn't an application that a customer would have access to, but one that a customer service person, like an insurance adjuster, would use in the field to speed the processing of what would have been tons of paperwork. Imagine a dazed driver at the scene of a car crash, and then imagine how quickly the insurance agent can give him the support that he needs to feel that at the very least, his liability worries are under control.

But my story gets even better. About that same time, HUON Corporation, Perot Systems, and Emrys Technologies all got together to spearhead the development of a PDA solution for claims adjusters. Now, an adjuster can use a small, handheld device to collect and enter data from the field and to follow the claim through to settlement. This function enables the insurance adjuster to process the claim right in front of the insured individual, also minimizing concerns about how long it will take to settle the claim. Policyholder information can be accessed from the PDA, which also lends itself to improving claims efficiency.

If your customers aren't happy with your Web-based customer service, they won't be happy with your wireless customer service, either. Before you extend your presence to mobile users, clean up your customer service act, please.

Flying Without Wires

Travelers are spending more time waiting in lines at airports these days. What better way to pass the time productively than to have access to the Internet? Travelers with wireless laptops and wireless handheld devices are visible everywhere you look. Noticing this trend were the presidents of many technology companies and the managers of many U.S. airports, all interested in better serving a very large and lucrative market of business travelers. Everyone decided that independent user access wasn't enough. They wanted to play, too.

In 2001, adAlive, a provider of Internet access points for PDA users, decided to do something about all that unused space found on airport billboards. They attached a gizmo to many of them that enabled PDA users to point the infrared port of their devices and access e-mail accounts and other content. Travelers at John F. Kennedy International Airport could soon obtain local city guides like 10Best and Vindigo. The content and services are free, which makes customers very happy.

iPass, a provider of remote access services, decided to provide business travelers with wireless broadband access to the Internet and corporate servers. Wayport, a provider of high-speed Wi-Fi wireless and wired Internet access, became responsible for deployment of the infrastructure. At 420 U.S. airports, travelers will be able to gain access to about 700 ISPs through the wireless LAN system. The short list of initial airports includes JFK, Newark, LaGuardia, Minneapolis/St. Paul, and the Wayne County Metropolitan Airport in Detroit. In order to use the system, the traveler must have the proper Wi-Fi hardware. Users of wireless laptops, PDAs, and PocketPCs will be able to use the service.

How else can wireless technology be used to improve the air traveler's experience?

- *Radio frequency identification* (RFID) tags can be placed on luggage and scanned to improve tracking and minimize loss.

- Baggage handlers can tell a customer upon check-in that a flight has changed gates.

- Ticket agents can walk out from behind the counter to check in waiting passengers.

With so many wireless devices and travel-related services emerging, airport managers organized into the Wireless Airport Association at www.wirelessairport.org. Formed an organization? The idea must be bigger than we thought.

Customizing The User's Experience

Another way to deliver excellent wireless customer service is to make technology easier. You already know how Web sites can make simple decisions on a user's behalf or let the user take charge. Web clipping applications can have many of these same features that can be used to customize the individual user's mobile experience.

Location Tracking

Location tracking technology should make it easier to find a mobile subscriber within a few blocks. Say, how is that possible? The technology can either be built into a mobile telephone handset or it can be built into a mobile telephone network. A few wireless carriers are backing the latter approach—I'm assuming because it's practically impossible to retroactively fit the millions of handsets in use today. Eventually, that argument won't hold water. Just wait a few years, and everyone will have new equipment anyway. I'll tell you more about location technology and the FCC's directive later.

If you're not a wireless carrier, you might still want to know how to tap into this little technology gem. Your wireless design firm can tell you about tools for pinpointing a mobile user's position if it's your intent to provide location-specific service. For example, your user might be looking for a nearby gas station, in which case knowing his zip code will help you provide the exact information and nothing more. When designing a Palm OS wireless application, the programmer can include the value %ZIPCODE—as one example—to help provide answers to such questions. You might also wish to allow the user the option of requesting information in a different zip code, which would be useful if he or she is going on a trip and wants to do some preplanning.

Compare these two examples for providing location-specific information. In the Real Cities example seen in Figure 10.6, the user has the choice of selecting a state, entering a zip code, or selecting a newspaper name to obtain local news. In the BrandFinder example shown in Figure 10.7, the Web clipping source code includes a tag for obtaining location-specific information relative to the nearby wireless base station. The system then compares this information to the company's database to select the correct data for delivery.

Such location information doesn't identify the user, but it does have the potential. Each wireless device has a unique identification code that could be used to track individual users. For privacy purposes, I'm not a big fan of tracking an individual user's device ID and then logging his or her location-specific requests for database mining purposes. You make the call on this one. The hair on the back of my head stands up when I start daydreaming about the potential abuse.

Figure 10.6 Real Cities provides local news to mobile users through a downloadable Web clipping application for Palm OS® software users. (Web clipping application Copyright © 2000 RealCities.com.)

By the way, the user does have some control when using certain mobile devices, as seen in Figure 10.8. When the customer uses an application to request location-specific information, the Palm user can elect to receive a

Figure 10.7 Vicinity's Brandfinder application offers users the option to locate the closest business by manual address input or automatically. (Web clipping application © 2000 Vicinity Corporation, GDT Inc., NavTech, InfoUSA.com.)

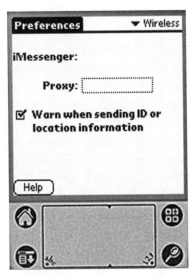

Figure 10.8 Palm™ handheld devices enable users to be notified when sending ID or location information.

warning shown in Figure 10.9. Obviously, if the user cancels the transaction, he or she won't be able to use the application's "autofind" feature.

E911, Carriers, and the FCC

Beginning October 1, 2001, all wireless carriers were required to provide *Automatic Location Identification* (ALI) services as part of the second phase of E911 implementation. As of September 2001, most wireless carriers were begging for more time from the FCC because it's just not soup yet—advanced mobile location detection technology, that is.

Just so you know, the FCC's wireless 911 rules for mobile telephone carriers were designed for public safety issues, not wireless marketing issues. Advocates say that it will "improve the reliability of wireless 911 services and provide enhanced features generally available for wireline calls," according to the FCC's Web site at www.fcc.gov/e911/.

Of course, once everything *is* working, the games will begin. Location-based customer service has its upside and its downside.

The Upside of Location-Based Customer Service

Here are three good ideas for location-based customer service. Can you think of a few more?

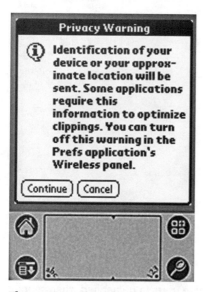

Figure 10.9 To maintain privacy, the user can stop his or her handheld from sending certain information to a company.

- Location-specific services, such as m-coupons for local businesses and other relevant data, can be targeted to opt-in mobile customers more accurately. Marketers can take advantage of the immediacy of a user's location to provide relevant shopping discounts based on an opt-in marketing profile and user contact preferences. You might think of this example as more fitting to mobile advertising than customer service. That depends. Who started the dialogue... the customer or you? If the customer asks for local merchant coupons while driving around town, then it's good customer service to deliver them.

- Companies in the emergency services field can provide immediate assistance to a mobile user who is stranded, lost, or injured. Such companies might include the AAA Automobile Club, which offers its members roadside assistance. E911 services could be used to provide help to a member and his disabled car when the user is unable to tell the tow truck driver his location in an unfamiliar area of town.

- Road travelers can use a location-specific suggestion or two on where to stay for the night when the kids are screaming in the back seat and the driver has just missed the last exit off the interstate. Rather than risk an accident while thumbing through a menu, the mobile user could use one-touch dialing to toggle the number of a business finder service, such as BeVocal at 1-800-4BVOCAL, and then use voice-activated menus based on speech-to-text technology to get directions to the nearest hotel. Frequently used cities can be included on a Web-based form when the mobile user sets up his or her account preferences. His or her favorite locations will display on the telephone when he or she gives the appropriate voice command.

The Downside of Location-Based Customer Service

Here are three bad ideas for location-based customer service (warning: don't do these!):

- Location-specific services, such as m-coupons and SMS advertisements, can be delivered anytime you want to your roaming customer. Marketers can take advantage of the customer's good will to keep tabs on his daily location while simultaneously trying to steer him away from or toward a particular business. Eventually, the user will shut off his device, upgrade to a new device, or sign up for a new carrier—leaving your company and its intrusive marketing practices behind (warning: don't do this).

- Those involved in direct marketing might wish to sell mobile telephone numbers, device ID numbers, and location-specific customer logs to partners, list brokers, and other companies just to turn a fast buck. Such companies might include disreputable telemarketing firms that wish to leverage the opportunity to call mobile users anytime, anywhere to bug them about a new product or service (warning: don't do this).

- Marketers involved in corporate espionage might tap into mobile user information to keep track of a few senior executives from competing firms. Using a combination of device IDs and location-specific information, jokesters could post a daily log of a person's whereabouts on the Web, complete with fictitious commentary on what he's really doing in New York at this year's PC Expo (warning: don't do this).

In summary, you never know what wonderful ideas you'll come up with for providing location-specific services to your mobile customers. Likewise, keep your eyes open for those stinky ideas that don't have the best interests of your customer in mind. Avoid implementing those stinky ideas. If you lack self-control and succumb to the temptations of marketing, I guarantee that your wireless marketing presence won't come out smelling like a rose.

Helping Your Staff Work with Wireless Users

Wireless customer service includes many of the same elements of a Web-based customer service program. Here's a checklist of areas to investigate:

- Your call center environment needs a method for managing wireless traffic seamlessly so that incoming requests are routed and handled in a timely and appropriate manner.

- Your telephone, Web-based, and wireless sessions must be integrated so that waiting customers are treated fairly. Your goal is to make sure that your customer believes that your wireless service is as good as, if not better than, other methods of communication.

- For quality assurance purposes, you need a way to monitor communications between your staff and wireless customers. Use this data to troubleshoot poor customer service and improve training for everyone.

- Your system must be able to log and follow up on incoming queries, such as sending transcripts of sessions to the wireless customer's landline account if the user elects it.

- The biggest problem with wireless customer service is the lack of follow-up. Another big problem with wireless customer service is too much follow-up. Are you confused yet? Well, you need to walk a fine line.

Real-Time Interaction

One of the biggest criticisms about the early days of the wired Web was the lack of real-time customer interaction. Customer e-mails went into what appeared to be a black hole. Even today, some companies still show turn-around times of up to 72 hours before you receive any confirmation that you have even submitted a request for help.

OK, so you're in tune and on time with customer e-mails and other inquiries. That's good. Don't pat yourself on the back just yet. Have you thought of a way to communicate with your customer while he or she is on his or her wireless device, assuming that he or she wants to be contacted?

Low- to no-cost options for real-time wireless customer interaction exist now. One of them is called the telephone. OK, you knew that. But if you're having a bad voice day or you really, really want to appeal to gadget gurus, you need a way to chat with or message them in real time. Did you know that one in five users has instant messaging capabilities, most of it on the desktop?

Many business professionals use commercial *instant messaging* (IM) services. IM could be a short-term customer service solution. These services don't cost anything, and you can claim that your company agents are now reachable by wireless devices. For reliable business use, however, free services aren't the best choice. There are security issues, which means that every time you conduct company communications over a public non-secure channel, you are risking the leak of company secrets. But one real advantage to using IM services is that most online users are already familiar with such platforms. GartnerGroup estimates that "seventy percent of enterprises will have workers using such services" by 2003. America Online, MSN, and Yahoo! are a few companies that provide registered users with free IM tools. Your company could work with one or more of these companies to adapt existing software to your unique customer service needs while addressing reliability and security issues head on.

But which service do you choose? Some IM providers enable the Web-based user to organize contact lists from other services, as seen in Figure 10.10. This feature enables your company to extend its reach to more customers instead of having to narrow down your selection to one particular IM service.

I don't want you to get too excited about IM yet. Let me be a little blunt about what works and what doesn't work for professional business use.

The Trouble with Free IM

Consumer-based instant messaging systems have several well-publicized problems. There's no guarantee that you'll have access to your wireless customers when you need it. You might be trying to reach each other at a high-traffic time without success. Maybe the wireless network is blocked by the fact that your user is inside a building.

Here are reasons why you shouldn't rely on free IM for your company's wireless customer service:

Compatibility issues. Not every free IM service is available for every flavor of mobile device. Macintosh users, Palm VIIx handheld users, or Web phone users could be out of luck, depending on which Web-based IM service you choose for your customer service standard.

System errors. Systems have been known to lose records requiring users to enter friends lists all over again. Services don't always recognize when a user—like your customer service representative—is online, so the user might think that you're not available when you are.

Transmission lags. Network delays in text transmission frustrate and alienate customers. If the message doesn't get to its intended recipient during the session, it might show up as a stored message at a later time, begging the question, "What's this about?"

Password amnesia. On most major IM services, users must enter a password to chat with you, slowing down the immediacy of good customer service. Free IM systems might claim that you're not logged in when you *just* logged in. The system will say that's not your password. Your wireless customers could be screaming, "Hey, can I get some help over here?"

Figure 10.10 AT&T IM Anywhere offers Web-based users the ability to consolidate other IM contact lists, including AOL and MSN. (Copyright 2002 AT&T. All Rights Reserved.)

No audits or archives. Unless your system has a method for storing the text of IM communications, your customer service staff might never improve. How can you follow up on sessions to make sure that your people are doing their best? And what if a customer claims something that you can't disprove?

Nosy competitors. Your competitor can reach you at any time to pick your brain, but registered site users might be less likely to sleuth at your expense. Say, who are you really "IM'ing" with that information, anyway?

OK, I hear you. Competitors will always try to find a way to get you, so using free IM isn't the only problem.

Unsolicited contact. Spam is a growing problem on IM systems that allow keyword searches of user profiles. Do you want your customer service department associated with a system that harbors spam-meisters?

Destructive viruses. Have you ever received a virus by instant message? If you ever do, how will your computer system handle it, if at all? Now, this situation doesn't appear to be a common and frequent threat, not like viruses in e-mail attachments, but it's one that you should be aware of.

System outages. What's your backup plan if your free service provider is having down time or system upgrades? You get what you pay for.

Security breaches. Do you write your company secrets on the bathroom wall? Then I've got a joke for you. This Internet CEO walks into a bar and he says. . . oh, you've heard it? Yeah, so did everybody else. A March 2001 story at CNET News.com revealed that so-called confidential ICQ instant messages between Sam Jain, CEO of eFront, and executives were posted on the Web and then mirrored to, discussed, and satirized on several different sites including Slash.org, RetardMagnet.com, IBlameTim.com, and overclocked.org. I hope that your employees didn't tell any bad jokes the last time they used free IM for company business, or you could be the subject of a scathing and widely publicized Web parody or two.

Not for Commercial Use

Perhaps by the time you read this book, many of the problems with free IM will have been solved. I am confident that the companies mentioned herein are working on the problems as we speak. In fact, I know they are. Meanwhile, here are some real examples of what individual users might experience if you choose to rely on free IM services for your company's live wireless customer service.

AT&T IM Anywhere^{SM}. This service offers the Windows-based desktop user seamless integration of more than one instant messaging service, including AOL, MSN, and Yahoo! Messenger. As a clarification, AT&T IM Anywhere is a member perk that I discovered while using my AT&T WorldNet service account. Messaging with mobile devices is available. AT&T tells its Web visitors that they can use a cell phone, pager, or PDA to extend the IM service's capabilities. At the time of this book's writing, the service relied on two-way SMS.

How does the user use this service? According to AT&T WorldNet's Web site, he or she addresses an e-mail message to im.mobilepassword@im.att.net, where mobilepassword is the user's mobile password. The message subject line contains im username—and, well, you get the picture. I don't think that this process is what you had in mind for *live* customer service. The good news is that the software allows users to know when you're logged on to a pager, PDA, or mobile telephone.

AOL Instant Messenger. This service has an intuitive menu-based interface. For example, the screen on a Palm handheld device is easy to use, as seen in Figure 10.11. Both Macintosh and Windows users are supported. The application is downloaded and installed like any other handheld application. I really liked the idea of using AOL Instant Messenger until I discovered that my Palm.Net service wasn't supported at the time. Whoops. How are you going to reach me, then?

Yahoo! Messenger. Figure 10.12 shows the simplicity of the Yahoo! IM interface. Once logged on, I could see all my Buddy List names—in Figure 10.13—and the application was fairly easy to use. I noticed that one of my contact names was outdated. As proof of the lesser functionality found in wireless versions of popular software, Messenger said, "On the Palm VII, you must add friends using the desktop version of Yahoo! Messenger."

I tried testing the service by using my significant other as a Guinea pig. His desktop version didn't reveal that I was online, which was strange because I had made sure that my user preferences allowed him to see me, but then again, I could be wrong. No doubt due to network delays, my handheld took a while to

Figure 10.11 AOL IM uses a simple menu and forms-driven interface for setup, password entry, and so on. (© Copyright 2002 America Online, Inc. All Rights Reserved.)

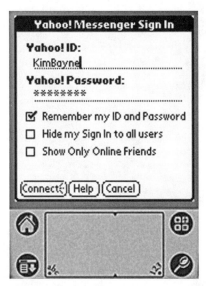

Figure 10.12 Yahoo! Messenger sign-in is very straightforward on a Palm™ handheld device. (Reproduced with permission of Yahoo! Inc. © 2002 Yahoo! Inc. YAHOO! and the YAHOO! Logo are trademarks of Yahoo! Inc.)

update my online friends list. When it finally updated, the IM software didn't recognize that my better half was online. Eventually, Bruce's desktop version

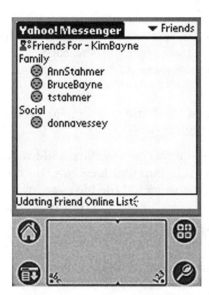

Figure 10.13 A Palm™ handheld user can use Yahoo! Messenger to view his or her Friends Online list. (Reproduced with permission of Yahoo! Inc. © 2002 Yahoo! Inc. YAHOO! and the YAHOO! Logo are trademarks of Yahoo! Inc.)

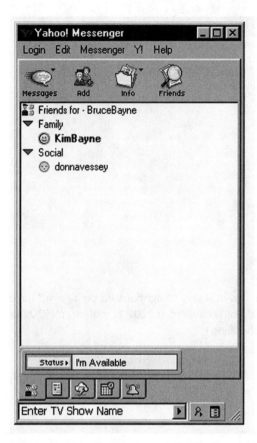

Figure 10.14 A smiley face in the desktop version of Yahoo! Messenger shows that Kim Bayne is connected to the service. (Reproduced with permission of Yahoo! Inc. © 2002 Yahoo! Inc. YAHOO! and the YAHOO! Logo are trademarks of Yahoo! Inc.)

showed my true status, as demonstrated by Figure 10.14. (Don't be confused about whose screen you're seeing. We both know Donna!)

Bruce and I were talking on the phone—he was on a landline and I was on my mobile—while we tested out the service in different locations. He claims to have sent me an instant message, but I didn't get it. I tried to reset my message alert options, as seen in Figure 10.15, while wondering if this option was the right one to reset. I should have read the documentation beforehand, but I can't help thinking that mobile applications should be more intuitive.

Anyway, during our telephone conversation, Bruce's desktop version of Yahoo! Messenger indicated that I wasn't online anymore, even though I hadn't disconnected. Go figure. Before I forget, news reports say that the next desktop version of Yahoo! Messenger will include cool cartoon animations. Okay, I guess I'll figure out a customer service use for that eventually.

Figure 10.15 Kim discovers that message alerts aren't available on her device. Who knew? (Reproduced with permission of Yahoo! Inc. © 2002 Yahoo! Inc. YAHOO! and the YAHOO! Logo are trademarks of Yahoo! Inc.)

There are plenty of less-than-optimal choices for business IM. I could go on evaluating the faults of free IM services for wireless customer service, but I won't because most individual users aren't concerned that much. Most of the kinks in these systems are disappearing on a daily basis. Hey, I don't mean to bash these services. As an end user, I've used each on the desktop and they are pretty good for casual personal use. But if you plan to use free services for business purposes, have a backup in place. It would be a shame to have your wireless customer service presence make you seem like an amateur.

AVT Video Instant Messenger. These guys say that instant messaging has more than 130 million users worldwide, which is why they saw an opportunity for a business application or two and went for it. *Alpha Vision Tech* (AVT) offers an instant messaging service that enables enterprises to host a private messaging service of their own. That could be very useful if you decide that IM services are essential to your customer service department. Quite nicely, the service supports video, audio, text, or any combination thereof. Its sister product, the AVT Video Conferencing Solution, works for online meetings that can connect up to 12 users anywhere in the world, providing features such as data collaboration and streaming content. Think about the customer service possibilities.

Now, you might be wondering whether this wonderful business application has a wireless component. Not when I wrote this book, but AVT's next version of its video IM *will* integrate SMS text messaging capabilities. Yes, I know. SMS delivery is at the discretion of the wireless network traffic, so this function is still not an optimal solution for real-time customer service.

But all is not lost. All sorts of application developers and service providers are looming on the horizon with business-oriented, wireless messaging solutions. Keep your eyes peeled. Real customer service solutions should be in place by the time you finish this page.

In Search of Live Customer Service

Still in search of a live wireless customer service solution, I came across a Web clipping application called Palm Answer, powered by May We Help? The company uses one-to-one text chat technology to provide users with event information, flight information, driving directions, roadside assistance, and technical support. As of January 2001, MayWeHelp.com's wireless PalmAnswer product exceeded 16,000 downloads from the Palm.net service, making it the 6th most downloaded wireless Palm application on the Internet. The application promises to have a real, live person available. Oh, boy. I couldn't wait to try this service out, as shown in Figure 10.16. At the time of this book's manuscript submission, the service was in its final beta stage.

Figure 10.16 PalmAnswer makes the Internet personal with live agents standing by. (PalmAnswer is a product from MayWeHelp.com. © 2000. All rights reserved.)

Connecting to Trade Shows

Looking for more ways to improve mobile customer service? Take trade shows, for one example.

Attendees at Oracle AppsWorld in Paris, France in 2001 were able to forget about carting around the paper show guide that normally accompanies such conferences. Web-enabled telephones became the tool of choice for conference attendees interested in accessing show schedules.

Registrants for Planet PDA: The Global Summit on Handheld Productivity, held December 2001 in Las Vegas, Nevada, were e-mailed an offer to sign up for Planet PDA Wireless Notifications. Sponsored by Air2Web, the service delivered show news to a user's mobile telephone or wireless PDA. Reminders about keynote sessions and other news were sent throughout the show.

At Handango, I found references to trade show exhibit guides put in place by various companies. There's no limit to the ways that mobile handheld devices and their applications can be applied to enhance the attendee experience.

One last thought—by creating a network-enabled data access point for mobile users, your trade show efforts can speed requests for literature, RFQs, and so on. A device user can simply beam over his or her contact information, saving data entry and minimizing transcribing errors from reading smudged paperwork. Selected mobile wallet information, such as name, title, address, phone number, and e-mail, can be beamed to a device in the exhibit booth, saving everyone time and energy. In fact, if you haven't used that idea yet, go to the chapter about public relations for a neat example.

Improving M-Customer Service

When revamping your customer service efforts to include mobile customers, consider the following. Customers want to be able to contact you and your company through multiple means, including over the Web, through wireless devices, and by mobile telephone. Mobile customers want access to their accounts and the ability to update information. Eliminating one avenue of customer contact in favor of wireless access is not a solution. Finally, your customer service activities will improve immensely when you provide real-time access and processing to both mobile customers and in-the-field customer service representatives.

Effective mobile customer service entails the following:

- Empowering the customer by offering him or her a wireless extension of your current presence

- Enabling customer convenience by streamlining and making portable typical business processes

- Creating easy-to-use mobile tools that meet a customer's immediate personal needs

- Providing the customer with a mobile "destination" for conducting future business

Summary: Top Five Expert Tips

1. Wireless communications have the implication of immediacy, which means that your customer service staff should be trained to respond accordingly.

2. Expand your e-mail guidelines to address the processing of wireless-originated mail. Consider that such users might not want further contact with you through this channel.

3. Free, commercially available instant messaging services are not the best solution for customer service. Sit tight until a business-oriented answer emerges to meet your professional needs.

4. Find wireless ways to make attendance and exhibiting at trade shows easier. Your booth visitors and staff will thank you for it.

5. Avoid succumbing to the marketing pitfalls within location-based technology. User privacy will rear its ugly head if you abuse your power.

CHAPTER 11

Measuring Wireless Marketing Results

"'Cause when you worry your face will frown, and that will bring everybody down. Don't worry, be happy."

As sung by whimsical jazz singer and a cappella vocalizer Bobby McFerrin

I f you, like singer Bobby McFerrin, believe that humor helps people cope better, then you're on the right track. But if you put on a happy face to avoid the truth about your mobile marketing program, here's a quick quiz. Which department is routinely downsized when business plans begin to flutter? Marketing. Avoiding the truth does not ensure job security.

Your wireless marketing program requires that you produce and report corroborating metrics on a regular basis. Gauging the performance of any new marketing program is essential to demonstrating its continued relevance to your overall business goals. Without a detailed initiative that tracks results, it's fairly hard to ascertain how to allocate budgets. Without a proactive attitude toward updating, upgrading, and uprooting nonfunctional or mediocre activities, your wireless marketing program will degrade and eventually go away.

So don't worry. Make everybody happy. Measure the goals of your wireless marketing program against the results. There'll be a lot less frowning come review time.

About This Chapter

The purpose of this chapter is to get you thinking about reporting the value of your mobile marketing program to management. What are they looking for? Do they want exact ROI numbers, an overview of your general successes, or a combination of both? This chapter will touch on a handful of factors that can be used to measure and/or justify your ongoing mobile marketing program.

It's no surprise that many metrics apply regardless of the media. In fact, many mobile e-metrics are similar in form and function to wired Web e-metrics. Your ability to gather numbers might rely heavily on your mobile marketing infrastructure, which includes the reporting capabilities of your mobile application service provider or wireless ad network. No matter what your situation, this chapter will help you decide on a few basic measurements to start, with the understanding that measurement capabilities will evolve as mobile technology matures. At the very least, you'll come away with an understanding that mobile marketing has the potential to pay off in both hard and soft terms, just like any other form of marketing.

What Drives Mobile ROI?

Compared to all other marketing activities, ROI gets the most lip service with the least amount of commitment. But it's really not that hard to embrace an ROI frame of mind. Throughout this book, you've thought about your objectives for various functional marketing areas and how mobile devices could improve your chances of attaining these goals. As a general review, here are a few of the typical goals that you might have identified:

- Building brand penetration and equity through mobile access
- Improving communications between marketing and sales crews
- Improving customer service functions with the addition of mobile access
- Increasing reach into the mobile user market
- Increasing the number of qualified sales leads among mobile users
- Lowering field sales support costs through the deployment of mobile tools
- Reducing traditional or Web-based selected marketing expenditures
- Shortening order processing and fulfillment timeframes

As you've noticed, the quest for marketing ROI is often built around decreasing expenses and increasing income, but there are always other measurements to pursue. Some factors produce rock-solid evidence while others produce feel-good results. Depending on your goals and methodology, you could crunch numbers in many different ways. Ask yourself this question: What do you want to know about your mobile marketing program?

Ask the Right Questions

To demonstrate that you've achieved mobile marketing goals, I offer a few suggestions on not only quantifying ROI, but also showing other helpful results.

How Much Money Does Your Wireless Presence Save?

One of your goals in reaching and serving the mobile user could be to lower the costs of an established program. You might wish to minimize data entry errors by your customers or personnel, because correcting errors drains time and resources away from more productive activities.

Mobile applications provider Mobyz helps medical practices reap savings from capturing billing data more quickly, according to "Achieving Return on Investment in Mobile and Wireless Business Applications," an August 2001 white paper by consulting firm Summit Strategies. Through the use of the Mobyz Healthcare application, a medical business can use wireless devices to capture data related to charges and prescriptions. After paying around $60,000 USD for an in-house installation, Mobyz claims that a small practice could possibly save $30,000 to $50,000 in one year. In other words, wireless support would pay for itself in 12 months—and savings thereafter would be icing on the cake.

What Did Your Wireless Presence Cost to Launch, and What Does It Cost to Maintain?

If you've kept excellent track of all of the big and little amounts, you could extrapolate ROI based on overall and monthly sales made by mobile handheld device users. If your mobile presence is not m-commerce enabled, you might have to apply this data to less-measurable marketing goals.

How Productive Is Your Mobile Advertising?

Track whether or not mobile clickthrough or response rate is better than, worse than, or at par with other forms of advertising. Be honest in deciding whether these results are a factor of different ad creative, placement, or the actual media—that is, mobile access.

Some measurements are easier to come by than others. Here's one such scenario. Imagine running a targeted advertising campaign that delivers discount coupons to opt-in wireless users. You can compare coupon redemption levels for offers delivered to different segments of the mobile user population. You'd then use this data to decide which offer performed better or which mobile population segment was more lucrative.

If you're into showing how well mobile advertising has increased revenue, here's another approach. Calculate the cost of the campaign, review the number of wireless coupons redeemed, and compute net sales to determine how the program performed. But no matter how you compute your mobile marketing payoff, remember that sometimes mobile ROI isn't always about expenses versus sales.

How Many Users Access Your Mobile Services, and Who Are They?

In a September 24, 2001, *Computerworld* ROI magazine article titled, "Leading the Way on Wireless," writer Alan Radding reports that one-third of Fidelity Anywhere's registered users represent new accounts for the stock brokerage. Fifteen percent of the visitors to the wireless section of Thrifty Car Rental's Web site downloaded the company's interactive mobile application for their Palm handheld devices, according to *Computerworld*. Thrifty executives believe that most of its wireless users are already current customers. That could mean that the mobile customer's perceptions of these mobile enterprises have strengthened along with each company's brand value.

If you've used a wireless application portal to promote your wireless application, you might have access to simple numbers (like how many people downloaded the software), as seen in Figure 11.1. But without registration or login prior to download, you might not be able to compare these users to those already frequenting your Web site, which will limit your ability to show ROI. That's the trade off for the added visibility that you will gain from associating with a popular repository.

How Does Your Mobile Presence Compare?

It would be helpful to know, if you can gather this data, whether your mobile presence attracts a different customer demographic than your wired Web presence. Overall, do you know whether your mobile customers are younger, more affluent, or have a higher education? Industry statistics might point to these trends, but a mobile user survey can help you conclude that such trends apply to your company as well. If one of your goals is to court these coveted users, you might have some positive results to convey to management.

Now, determine whether or not it costs less to acquire a new customer wirelessly when compared to traditional or wired Web means. Determine whether or not it costs less to process an order wirelessly when compared to traditional or wired Web means. But keep in mind that sometimes the ROI truth hurts. Giga Research reports that mobile user support can be as high as three times more costly than wired Web user support, according to a June 22, 2001, report titled "Mobile vs. Tethered Support Costs." One of the biggest complaints

Figure 11.1 Handango lists StockBoss Interactive as one of the most popular downloads for RIM handheld devices. (Copyright © 2002 Handango, Inc. All rights reserved. Handango is a trademark of Handango, Inc.)

among call center employees is multiple and incompatible applications for serving customers. Imagine having to answer the telephone, disengage, call up a browser window, disengage, check the fax machine, disengage, and so on. This particular cost comparison might no longer be an issue once fully integrated customer service becomes the norm.

How Much Have Your Order Processing or Sales Solicitation Functions Improved?

The *Atlanta Journal-Constitution* reported a 30 percent increase in "solicitor subscription productivity" after it outfitted its door-to-door sales force with handheld computers, according to an August 23, 2001, news release. Previously, the daily newspaper's sales team would suffer through cold calls made door-to-door based on little or no prospect information. Now, handheld devices reveal a resident's subscriber history and recommend custom offers to help encourage more subscriptions.

Another measurement could include a time and accuracy comparative study of automated order processing on your telephone system, on the Web, and via mobile handheld devices. Automated orders aside, some aspects of customer service shouldn't be measured in these terms, so I ignored them purposely. For example, don't pit automated mobile order processing against live order processing, as in when a customer service representative talks to a person on the telephone to take his order. Comparing the two might put you on the wrong path. There is no benefit in seeing how fast your staff can hang up. The customer might beat you to the punch and utter, "You are the weakest link. Goodbye!" But let's get back to the focus of this chapter.

How Much Traffic Does Your Mobile Site Generate, and How Often Do These Visitors Return?

Sometimes an increase in wireless site traffic can imply that a related PR campaign paid off—that is, generated appropriate interest (as seen in Figure 11.2).

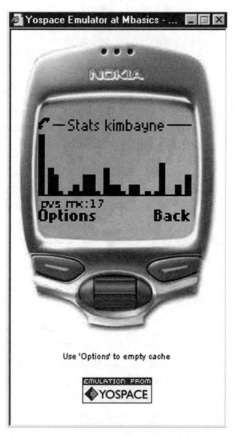

Figure 11.2 Statistics for Kim Bayne's WAP site show a spike in interest just before her presentation at a major trade show. (WAP Site hosting courtesy of Mbasics. All rights reserved. SmartPhone Emulator © 1999–2001 Yospace Holdings Ltd. Used with permission. Telephone image © Nokia.)

In the example, my e-mail and Web-based promotional activities, conducted a few weeks before a scheduled seminar, appear to have encouraged Web-enabled telephone users to drop by. This data can be extrapolated to infer that certain marketing activities might be more effective than other marketing activities for attracting mobile traffic. But unless your wireless site has sophisticated tracking capabilities, you might not be able to apply such numbers to demonstrate true ROI. From such rudimentary statistics, I couldn't possibly tell you whether an increase in mobile site traffic resulted in increased sales of my books, mainly because there's no conduit for m-commerce through my mobile site yet.

A computation of visitor return rates can demonstrate the effectiveness of selected mobile offerings but might not produce the hard numbers that your management needs. For example, you can begin to form a picture of how "sticky" your wireless site is or can become. And while this results-oriented data can help you pinpoint lapses in content or features, it can't be readily applied to demonstrate cost savings or sales.

Can ROI Be Realized?

Not all aspects of a mobile marketing program can be measured, although you're certainly invited to try. For example, customer convenience is a term that often defies real computation, but you can still deploy wireless capabilities for your customers anyway—just because you're such a nice person.

If you were concerned about achieving an ROI on your mobile investment at all, a few outside opinions wouldn't hurt before you got started. At Palm.com (www.palm.com/enterprise/), a visitor can take a quick quiz, as shown in Figure 11.3, to determine the readiness of his or her enterprise for mobile deployment. After calculating the score, your results could lean toward outfitting your sales force with mobile devices—as seen in the sample results shown in Figure 11.4—but your ROI realization might not be as great as you had hoped. To be honest, this business justification quiz is not restricted to mobile marketing needs. And I admit, if you're this far along in the book, you're probably already committed to a mobile project of some sort (predictable ROI or not).

The Problem with ROI Thinking

In June 2001, Jupiter Media Metrix released a report about online advertising that challenged the typical thinking behind ROI computations. JMM determined that ROI is much higher—nearly 35 percent higher—than most marketers believe. Many marketers use measurements related to clickthrough

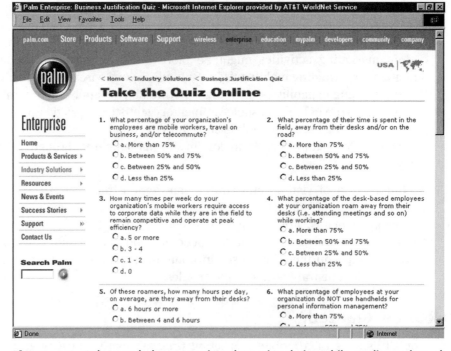

Figure 11.3 Palm.com helps enterprises determine their mobile readiness through a Web-based questionnaire.

behavior, a Web advertising standard that has been debated furiously in several e-discussion groups. Instead, JMM emphasized the value of branding as a factor in determining true ROI. JMM analysts also pointed out how integrated marketing campaigns across several channels contribute to buying behavior and that not all such data is easily tracked. Now, if this analysis holds true for mobile marketing, accurate ROI metrics might elude us once again.

So Much for Traditional Measurements

In the white paper "E-Metrics: Business Metrics for the New Economy" by Matt Cutler and Jim Sterne, the authors outline five core measurements used by most e-businesses: hits, impressions, page views, unique visits, and unique users. The most telling comment was the paper's statement that "analysis is about understanding customers, not page views or hits." To apply this improved focus to mobile e-metrics, certain technical capabilities must be in place beforehand. For a clue, can you say, "Got milk?"

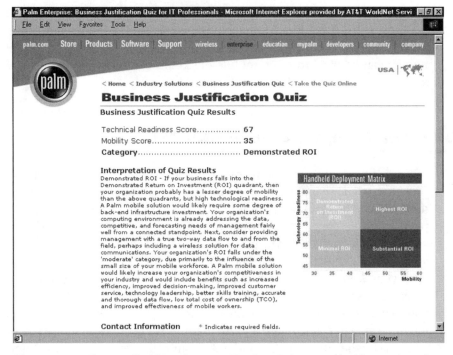

Figure 11.4 The Handheld Deployment Matrix at Palm.com says that my imaginary business would experience a moderate ROI due to the small size of its mobile workforce.

Wireless Cookies and User Behavior

In order to understand your mobile customer's behavior, you must be able to track it. The most obvious technique, and sometimes the most controversial, is the use of cookies. If you need a quick review, here it is. A cookie is a text string that the server sends to a user's personal computer, computing device, or mobile gateway. Cookies can last for just one session, or they can last for a while depending on the expiration date. Cookies can offer marketers varying abilities in logging customer behavior, either individually or by aggregate. For example, cookie tracking can report the clickstream or path taken by a mobile visitor through your wireless site.

Sans the cookie crumbs, rough behavior modeling can be applied to determine time delays between the receipt of a requested wireless coupon and its redemption. By tracking user behavior after mobile contact, you might uncover a definable pattern to help you determine what your mobile user really wants. While this information isn't directly related to ROI, you'll want this information on which to base program revisions. This process, in turn, will increase the chances that you'll achieve ROI much sooner.

Please understand that this brief discussion is not an endorsement of the use of cookies or intrusive behavior-tracking practices. These ideas are here purely for informational purposes. If you're interested in how cookies and other technology can be used to track mobile customer behavior, contact your wireless service provider for additional information.

You Mean I Can't Measure That Yet?

After you start exploring the world of wireless metrics, don't be surprised if you find that not all capabilities are available on all platforms or with all mobile device types. I might have mentioned a capability that is unavailable to you, simply because you're courting mobile telephone users rather than PDA users. Your service provider might not be up-to-speed yet, but they're working on it. For now, you might be able to compute the number of wireless applications downloaded from your Web site, but you might not be able to track how they found out about your wireless access. You might be able to track a spike in WAP site traffic, but you might not be able to pinpoint who referred these people to your site. You might be able to track where a particular mobile user is standing at the moment when he or she pulls in data wirelessly from your site, but you might not be able to track application usage before that person logs on. Perhaps with enough demand for more accurate mobile metrics and more synergy between various media, the wireless industry could meet many of these tracking needs in no time.

Summary: Top Five Expert Tips

1. Avoid simplistic bean counting or tracking results that lack credibility. Tie measurement to real goals.

2. Some metrics are more elusive than others. Remember the importance of branding and other marketing activities in computing your ROI.

3. Solid numbers aren't always available. Many intangible aspects of your mobile marketing program, such as improving customer convenience, might be difficult to quantify but should be observed and reported nonetheless.

4. Raw numbers aren't as useful as the big picture. Tracking user behavior and applying it to user needs can put you closer to serving your customers for life.

5. Keep an ongoing record of your mobile marketing ROI so that you can report the status of your program at any time. Don't wait until the end of a campaign to tally the numbers, or you'll have no room to regroup.

CHAPTER 12

Budgeting for a Wireless Future

"Buddy, can you spare a dime?"

From the 1930's Depression-era song of the same name, as sung by crooner Bing Crosby

In case you're wondering, I promise not to repeat a well-known line from the movie "Jerry Maguire." Fans of actor Tom Cruise know what I mean. But I will tell you something—if you don't have a clear view of your wireless marketing budget, you're not alone. About 19 percent of United Kingdom companies do not have a defined budget for m-commerce, according to a survey completed jointly by the e-business Expo Trade Show, Compaq, and *Computer Weekly* magazine. That study, which included 500 companies, was conducted in the fall of 2000. A few marketers in the United States have admitted to me that they don't have actual budgets for wireless marketing, either. They just figure it out as they go along. Well, I wish them luck. How applicable is this information? Without a defined budget, your mobile marketing program starts out in its weakest position for enterprise-wide buy-in.

In a more recent report, budget expenditures for wireless initiatives still accounted for a low percentage of IT budgets, according to META Group, Inc. If the same attitude about the value of wireless holds true in your organization, you could have an interesting wait in your quest to launch a decent m-presence. The September 2001 report surveyed 351 professionals in 10 different industries around the world, so you can't claim that these results are limited to one type of enterprise. Titled "Wireless Adoption, Trends, and Issues," the report from research firm META Group concluded that wireless planning is fairly common. I guess that it doesn't hurt to be prepared even if you haven't attracted those supporting dollars yet.

Want some good news? Most marketers say that the recent economic downturn has had minimal-to-no impact on marketing budgets, says an October 2001 article in Crain Communications' *BtoB Magazine*. So maybe you're thinking that you've got a little play in your budget and can reallocate funds. Be forewarned. Some folks claim that wireless money is being wasted. Forrester Research analyst Jordan Kendall says that companies don't take wireless seriously because they treat it like a toy. In a 2001 conference presentation, Kendall advised companies to pursue real business applications rather than the novelty of wireless. He said that high-impact applications are a good buy for enterprises. Deploying wireless so everybody can check e-mail in the airport isn't nearly as valuable as enabling the shipping department to check inventory and fill orders wirelessly. If you approach your wireless marketing plan from the perspective that you offer value rather than technology, you won't have to beg management for a handout.

About This Chapter

Most line items for a detailed marketing budget are mentioned throughout this book, even if their associated costs aren't. In this final chapter, I've included a few more items you should look into with a few insights on how to approach them.

I won't lie to you. This chapter is not a plug-and-play blueprint for your wireless marketing spreadsheet. Yeah, I know you're disappointed. It's not that cost data doesn't exist, but it's too general to be of any use to individual marketers—and I couldn't possibly fit every scenario into these pages. As the author, I've found that any attempt to estimate what it costs exactly to build a wireless marketing presence would make this book dated faster than a Vaudeville comedian's jokes. Ancestors of mine aside, this chapter is not the end. It's the beginning. After finishing this book, you'll still need to get a grip on your company's m-marketing requirements. Once you do, you can start the process of researching legitimate estimates to meet your budgeting needs.

You Know the Drill

The act of nailing down representative costs for a wireless presence was like shooting at a moving target for this first edition of *Marketing without Wires*. There are several reasons. For one, whenever I managed to get my hands on a few numbers, they changed. Every week, one or more companies make a wireless-related announcement that alters the landscape. Just when someone claims that he is the only mobile ASP providing a certain solution, someone else comes along. After several attempts to pull together a realistic budget, I decided that it was your job anyway. So here's my advice. Include cost *ranges* in your budget rather than exact numbers, even if you know them. In this fast-moving market, you need room to adjust.

Now for the fun part, which includes peeking into marketers' wallets. My requests for sample budget data from enterprise marketers were met with raised eyebrows, one quite snippy "I'm not gonna tell you that" statement—*you know who you are*—and lots of stonewalling. Most marketing managers were pretty cool about it, saying that they preferred to not release such information (or, in a poker-faced manner, they politely told me that the final numbers weren't in).

Actual dollar amounts were just as hard to obtain from service providers, agencies, and other outside vendors. A typical, useless response was either "It depends" or "How big is your budget?" My retort should have been, "How about a dime?" One site provided ample information about its suite of mobile enterprise solutions for marketers, stopping dead short of actually telling you what it costs. Words like "tailored to your needs" were pretty common, along with a mail form so that someone could call you back. Everyone's jockeying for position now, so no one wants to be pinned down—at least not in a printed book with a shelf life. To get real answers, I should have claimed that I was calling from the Internal Revenue Service. As a customer, you can just give your real program specifications to vendors and ask them to spell it out for you.

Yes, some consistencies in pricing do exist, like the costs for off-the-shelf software or PDA network access, which are priced for the mass market. Those appear to be fairly predictable right now. Still, this whole experience reminded me of the early days of the commercial Web. Early mobile marketers are reticent to admit their successes, mainly due to fear of discovery by the competition. That's understandable. But vendors should be more forthcoming with information, so what's their excuse?

People with cutting-edge knowledge can often call the shots, that's for sure. So here's my prediction. When activities associated with mobile marketing deployment become more mainstream or perhaps more *commoditized*, I believe that the world of wireless enterprise marketing will become a marketer's dream. The coming shakeout in the market should make pricing a bit more stable. Meanwhile, get lots of bids and ask lots of questions.

While you're doing your job as a marketer, I'm going to keep doing mine as a busybody. If you want to keep up on my progress as a marketing budget spy, subscribe to my e-mail newsletter "Marketing Wirelessly." Go to www .marketingwirelessly .com for more information. I'm sure that someone is bound to crack sooner or later.

Budget Cost Centers

This book mentions several areas that will impact your wireless marketing budget. Some are directly related to core marketing functions, like advertising placement and public relations, while others are peripheral to the cause. For individual projects and ideas for budget line items, review the chapters in this book. At the same time, here are a few more areas to consider.

Wireless Marketing Team

If you're thinking of doing much of your wireless deployment in-house, you'll need to add a few line items for wireless programmers and other personnel. Currently, all types of wireless talent are in demand—so expect to pay more. Programming personnel with an entry-level skill set can earn at least $45,000 USD per year—probably more. Check out the various job sites to see current salaries associated with open positions. Then, talk to your IT department to see whose budget takes the hit on this one.

If such salary levels are too rich for your marketing budget, outsource as much as possible—a cost-cutting measure that will work to your project management advantage. You can pick and choose which projects to farm out to individuals or firms that have the best expertise, making your project quality higher and your startup costs lower.

High-tech job site Dice.com offers three calculators for estimating marketing team expenditures. At www.marketing.dice.com/rateresults/, you can conduct a full-time salary query (seen in Figure 12.1), a contractor salary query, and a contractor hourly rate query. For more examples of rates, look at Chapter 4, "Chartering Your Wireless Marketing Team."

Mobile Handheld Devices

Need a good resource to plug preliminary numbers into your spreadsheet for outfitting your wireless marketing team? LetsTalk.com is one Web site that can offer you some costs for cell phones, PDAs, and pagers. It looks like most brands and services are offered here (see Figure 12.2). You might know of other favorite sites with similar pricing information. Remember to take into account mail-in rebates or service plan discounts that might come with a purchase.

Wireless Access

If your wireless staff relies on PDAs and you know that they will be online frequently, consider an all-you-can-eat plan. Many PDA network service providers offer monthly plans with unlimited kilobytes. For enterprises operating their own wireless servers and networks, costs are more elusive. If so, sit down with your IT people to hammer out this part of your budget.

If you're taken with the idea of providing mobile fax capabilities, eFax Plus offers a downloadable application for PDA users. eFax Plus costs $9.95 USD

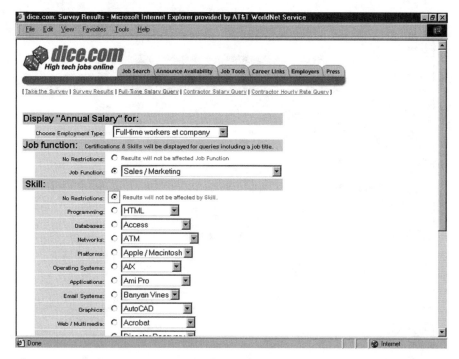

Figure 12.1 Dice.com can project salary estimates for workers with different skills to help you budget for new marketing hires.

per month plus $10 USD setup. These fees could change, so check their site for updates. And that's just the basics. The actual sending and receiving of faxes can mount up, too. Sure, prices like these are always subject to change, but at least you know that there's more to wireless access than kilobytes (and you can plan accordingly).

Mobile Applications

Off-the-shelf applications or providers that offer rent-an-application plans can put a lid on costs when compared to developing custom applications. No matter what, decide to standardize the mobile software used by your marketing department. Standardization will enable you to reduce IT support costs. Is this result a good bet? Look into mobile applications associated with desktop software currently in use. Users will come up to mobile speed quicker, and you'll avoid incompatibility problems with documents created in the field.

M-Commerce Deployment

Here's a tool for you. Check out Network World's Buyer's Guide, as captured in Figure 12.3. An Excel spreadsheet of the guide is available at www.nwfusion

Figure 12.2 LetsTalk.com is one of hundreds of Web-based malls where users can buy mainstream mobile devices.

.com/ecomm2001/ecomm0226.jsp for download. Because you've been so patient, here are a few costs that I pulled together based on Network World and a few other resources.

Dedicated M-Commerce Server

Low Estimate: $20 to $2,999 per month plus setup fees

Medium: $3,000 to $9,999 per month plus setup fees

High: $10,000 to $100,000 per month plus setup fees

Sample Related Services to Include

- Product catalog creation and content management
- Sales order database development and integration
- Site traffic statistics reports
- Source code conversion, as in HTML to WML translation
- Staff training

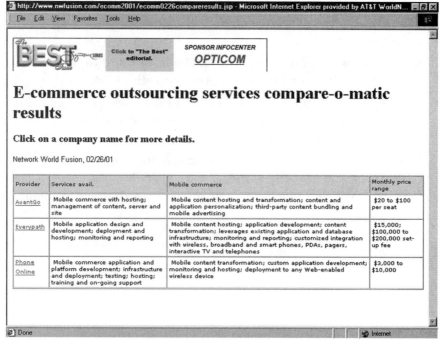

Figure 12.3 Network World Fusion's compare-o-matic helps users compare two or more e-commerce outsourcing services.

- Wireless marketing communications applications
- Wireless site design

Mobile Advertising

If you're concerned that delivering ads to mobile handheld users will be too expensive, do a quick comparison. Ask a wireless advertising network its *cost per thousand* (CPM) for a certain ad campaign, then compare it to a wired Web placement. Visit Internet.com's Ad Resource at www.adres.internet.com/adrates/ for a sample rate guide with more information.

Summary: Top Five Expert Tips

1. Avoid getting talked into programs and placements that you don't need or want. Establish the goals and needs of your wireless marketing program before you ask vendors for price quotes.

2. Prioritize your budget to ensure that high-impact applications get the most attention. You will achieve an ROI on your wireless marketing program more quickly.

3. If at all possible, minimize costs and improve workflow by standardizing mobile applications for your wireless marketing team.

4. Compare and contrast the advantages of in-house versus outsourced deployment, then budget individual projects accordingly. Marketing is not an "all or nothing" proposition.

5. As wireless enterprise services become more commonplace, prices will fluctuate. Remember to ask for service upgrades, plan reviews, and better pricing every few months as your wireless marketing program progresses.

Glossary

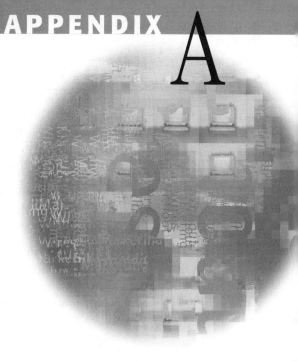

The following definitions are based on how I use or refer to them throughout this book. You might think of other definitions depending on your industry focus or personal experience. This appendix is organized in alphabetical order. As a quick reference, it contains only a brief sampling of definitions related to the wireless world. Visit www.marketingwithoutwires.com for links to more current and comprehensive information.

A

Access   As a verb, access is the act of a mobile handheld device gaining admittance to the Internet. As a noun, access refers to the actual admittance of a mobile device into a network or Web site.

Access fee   A special charge assessed to the mobile user for connecting to wireless content or services. Charges can be based on fixed monthly or hourly rates or per kilobyte retrieved or received.

Activation or setup   The initial fee charged to the user for creating a new subscriber or service account.

Air time   Time spent using a mobile telephone. Airtime minutes are logged and charged against a user's service plan.

Alphanumeric   Containing both letters from the alphabet and numbers.

B

Bandwidth   Bandwidth affects the amount of data or information that a system can handle and transmit over a wireless network. The greater the bandwidth, the better the transmission. Sometimes bandwidth is called the "pipe." The author often compares a lack of bandwidth to "sucking ketchup through a straw."

Broadband   Related to bandwidth, broadband or wide bandwidth enables the transmission of more than just voice and data. Rich media or video services can be handled by broadband services.

Bundling   Service providers often combine services in an attempt to attract subscribers. For example, telephone carriers might bundle voice mail, caller ID, and SMS services in one monthly mobile service plan. The subscriber saves on bundled services when compared to à la carte pricing plans.

C

Carrier   See Operator.

Carrier barrier   See Walled Garden.

Co-branding   When two or more company names or trademarks are used in association with a marketing activity. Presumably, the act of co-branding enables partners to leverage the strengths of the other partners. Mobile telephones and other devices can carry the name of more than one company.

Content   Text-based information on a Web site, in a data transmission, or in a mobile application. Such content can include news, sports, weather, company or product information, and more.

Customer acquisition cost   The average computed cost of advertising and marketing to attract and close a sale with a buyer or user.

D–G

Dial-up connection   Access to a network can be achieved when a mobile handheld device dials a local telephone number and connects to a computer or telephone network.

E-911   An emergency service that has been enhanced to send subscriber location information to the emergency operator.

Encryption   A way to scramble information so that thieves and other unscrupulous individuals can't decipher it. Encryption is used to make credit card numbers and PINs unreadable when transmitted over wireless networks.

FCC (Federal Communications Commission)   A United States government organization in charge of telecommunications.

GSM (Global System for Mobile Communications)   One of the world's most popular standards, it is used for mobile telephone systems in Asia, Australia, Europe, Latin America, and North America.

Gateway   The link that enables mobile handheld devices to connect to service networks.

H

HDML (Handheld Markup Language)   An offshoot of *Hypertext Markup Language* (HTML), this computer code or language enables programmers or Web masters to create pages that are readable by selected handheld devices.

HTML (Hypertext Markup Language)   This computer code or language is used to format Web pages for reading in a desktop application known as a browser. HTML enables programmers or Web masters to create pages that are readable in a browser. HTML is used to link words on pages to other pages so that users can jump from page to page with just a mouse click.

Handheld device   A palmtop computing device that, when outfitted with a wireless modem, can be used to access and send e-mail, Web pages, files, or other communications.

I

IP (Internet Protocol)   A technical standard for communicating between standalone devices or computers and servers. IP is used to communicate between all systems and servers on the Internet.

ISP (Internet Service Provider)   A business that provides Internet services, like e-mail or Web access, to companies or individuals.

Intranet   A computer network restricted to a single organization. Mobile users might wish to have wireless access to a company intranet to gain access to data or databases stored on selected servers.

J–L

KB (Kilobyte)   A kilobyte equals 1,000 bytes of data. PDA networks charge users by kilobyte received.

Landline   Compared to wireless systems, a landline is a wireline or cable connection to traditional telephone systems and Internet gateways.

M

Microbrowser   A scaled-down version of Internet software that enables mobile device users to view content and sometimes graphics on a mobile-friendly Web site or a site residing on a wireless server.

Modem   A peripheral or built-in computer device that enables users to dial local telephone numbers for access to the Internet. Modems convert data for transmission purposes.

Multimedia messaging   This service makes it possible for users to receive text, color images, audio clips in one message on their mobile telephones. Compare this to SMS, which only allows the transmission and receipt of simple text.

N–O

Operator   A company that manages a telephone network and sells access to that network to subscribers or users. Examples of operators are AT&T, Verizon, and Sprint. Also known as Carrier.

P

PDA (Personal Digital Assistant)   PDAs are personal organizers that help a user keep track of appointments, names and addresses, and other personal information. Many PDAs are now wireless, which enables them to access data on the Internet.

Paging   Paging refers to the act of either a user or a system sending a text message to the screen of a mobile handheld device. Such messages might cause an audible alarm. Messages can be sent either by telephone dial-up, a Web-based form, or by e-mail.

PIN (Personal Identification Number)   A short series of numbers used as a security code to establish identity. The user enters the PIN to authorize entry into a secure system, such as a mobile financial system that might contain bank account information.

Q–R

Rich media   A combination of media types that includes high-quality and streaming audio, video, and graphics. The capability of a wireless network to handle rich media will enable advances in wireless entertainment and communications.

Roaming   When you are not within your calling area (that is, the area where you normally make mobile telephone calls), your mobile handset will initiate this activity in order to locate the nearest compatible telephone system. Most mobile telephone carriers assess a roaming fee to out-of-area users, depending on the service plan selected.

S

SMS (Short Message Service)   A service available on most digital telephone networks that enables users to send and receive text messages up to 160 characters each.

Service plan   An agreement stipulating how many minutes or how much data the user can use or access in one billing period. Service plans often carry a set fee that the user pays to the carrier. Additional time charged to the user is more expensive than individual units allowed in the plan.

Service provider   A business that sells or rents applications, services, or access to mobile telephone, wireless PDA, pager, and Internet users.

T–V

Trimode   Mobile telephones with trimode capabilities can access three modes of mobile telephone networks to allow interoperability while traveling.

URL (Uniform Resource Locator)   A text-based combination of alphanumeric characters that tells the Internet which pages to view. For example, users who enter www.marketingwirelessly.com will be directed to the author's Web site for her e-mail newsletter for enterprise marketers.

Voice recognition   Technology that recognizes phrases and words spoken by the user. Voice recognition is used to gain access to menu options via the telephone. The user speaks his or her command or request clearly to access selected information.

W

WAP (Wireless Application Protocol)   WAP is one of the widely accepted protocols in use today for wireless communications. WAP enables mobile telephones to access Web pages through telecommunications systems.

Walled Garden   Users on different wireless networks may not be able to access or view content on other networks. This concept is called "the walled garden" because such restrictions mean that not everyone can enjoy the same "view" of the wireless world. In the case of two-way text messaging, wireless carriers are beginning to enable interoperability between systems.

Wireless   An adjective used to describe how a mobile handheld device transmits and receives voice or data without a wireline or cable connection.

Mobile Handheld Devices

This appendix is organized in alphabetical order. As a quick reference, it contains only a brief sampling of companies that offer mobile handheld devices. Visit www.marketingwithoutwires.com for links to more current and comprehensive information.

Alcatel

URL: www.alcatel.com/consumer/mobilephone/

Notes: Mobile telephone manufacturer

Audiovox

URL: www.audiovox.com

Notes: PDA and mobile telephone manufacturer/distributor; notable product line—Maestro; operating systems—Microsoft Windows for Pocket PC

Casio

URL: www.casio.com

Notes: PDA manufacturer/distributor; notable product line—Cassiopeia, palm-sized PC, Pocket Viewers, wrist PDA; operating systems—Casio OS, Microsoft Windows CE, and Microsoft Windows for Pocket PC

Compaq

URL: www.compaq.com

Notes: PDA manufacturer/distributor; notable product line—iPAQ, iPAQ Blackberry; operating systems—Microsoft Windows CE, Microsoft Windows for Pocket PC, and Proprietary OS for Blackberry

Cybiko

URL: www.cybiko.com

Notes: PDA manufacturer/distributor; notable product line—Cybiko Inter-Tainment (PDA with MP3 player); operating systems—CyOS

Denso

URL: www.denso.com

Notes: Mobile telephone manufacturer; notable product line—Touchpoint

Fossil

URL: www.fossil.com

Notes: Manufacturer/distributor/retailer of Wrist PDA for the Palm and Pocket PC user

Franklin

URL: www.franklin.com

Notes: PDA distributor/retailer; notable product line—Franklin Bookman, eBookMan, Rolodex Personal Organizers, Datapage Organizer; operating systems—eBookMan OS, Palm OS, and Microsoft Windows CE

HandEra

URL: www.handera.com

Notes: PDA manufacturer/distributor; notable product line—HandEra TRGPro, HandEra 330; operating systems—Palm OS

Handspring

URL: www.handspring.com

Notes: PDA manufacturer/distributor; notable product line—Trèo (PDA with telephone); Visor, Visor Deluxe, Visor Edge, Visor Neo, Visor Platinum, Visor Prism, Visor Pro, and so on; operating systems—Palm OS

Hewlett-Packard

URL: www.hp.com

Notes: PDA manufacturer/distributor; notable product line—HP Palmtop, Jornada; operating systems—Microsoft Windows CE, Microsoft Windows for Pocket PC

IBM

URL: www.ibm.com

Notes: PDA manufacturer/distributor; notable product line—WorkPad; operating systems—Palm OS

Kyocera

URL: www.kyocera-wireless.com

Notes: Mobile telephone manufacturer; notable product line—Q phones, QCP series, SmartPhone (mobile phone with PDA manufacturer/distributor/retailer using Palm OS)

Levi Strauss & Co.

URL: www.dockers.com

Notes: OK, so it's not a device, but it is part of a trend. The Dockers Mobile Pant has hidden seam pockets for carrying all of your mobile gear. It looked so cool that I had to get a pair for Bruce, my husband. The PR guy said that he'd let me know when the company starts making them for women. I can hardly wait to ditch that fanny pack.

Matsucom

URL: www.onhandpc.com

Notes: Notable product line—OnHand PC (PDA wristwatch); proprietary operating system

Mitsubishi

URL: www.mitsubishi.co.jp

Notes: Mobile telephone manufacturer

Motorola

URL: www.motorola.com

Notes: Mobile telephone and pager manufacturer; notable product line—StarTAC, V Series 60 Phone, Timeport Series Phones; V200 Personal Communicator (combination wireless phone, speakerphone, PC-like keyboard, for two-way text messaging, WAP browser)

National Semiconductor Corporation

URL: www.national.com

Notes: manufacturer/distributor of WebPAD appliance (touchpad/monitor) for wireless Internet access and e-mail

NEC

URL: www.neccomp.com or www.nec-global.com

Notes: Mobile telephone and PDA manufacturer/distributor; notable product line—MobilePro; operating systems—Microsoft Windows CE, Microsoft Pocket PC

Nokia

URL: www.nokia.com

Notes: Mobile telephone manufacturer; notable product line—Nokia 5210, Nokia 7650, and Nokia 6510

Palm

URL: www.palm.com

Notes: PDA manufacturer/distributor; notable product line—Palm IIIc, IIIxe, V, Vx, VII, VIIx, m100, m125, m500, m505, and so on. Operating systems—Palm OS, of course.

Panasonic

URL: www.panasonic.com

Notes: Mobile telephone manufacturer; notable product line—Allure, Duramax, ProMax, and Versio

Psion

URL: www.psion.com

Notes: PDA manufacturer/distributor; notable product line—Series 5MX Palmtop, Revo, marRevo, Series 7; operating systems—EPOC

RIM (Research in Motion)

URL: www.rim.net

Notes: PDA manufacturer/distributor; notable product line—RIM Blackberry wireless handhelds; operating systems—Proprietary OS

Samsung

URL: www.samsungelectronics.com

Notes: Mobile telephone manufacturer

Sanyo

URL: www.sanyo.com

Notes: Mobile telephone manufacturer; notable product line—SCP-5000, SCP-6000

Scott eVEST

URL: www.scottevest.com

Notes: This company is another one that sells apparel for the mobile handheld user. With a bunch of pockets for carrying PDAs, digital cameras, mobile telephones, and other geeky stuff, the vest has conduits for headphones and wires. Just remember to take it off and run it through the X-ray machine at the airport.

Seiko

URL: www.seiko.com

Notes: Notable product line—Smartpad for Windows (Notepad uses infrared technology to transfer handwritten text to the PDA); operating systems— Palm OS

Sharp

URL: www.sharpelectronics.com

Notes: Organizers and handheld PCs; notable product line—SE 500, Wizard, YO, Mobilon, Zaurus; operating systems—Proprietary OS, Microsoft Windows CE

Siemens

URL: www.my-siemens.com

Notes: manufacturer/distributor of mobile telephones and WebPAD appliance (touchpad/monitor) for wireless Internet access; notable product line—SIM-pad SL4

Sony

URL: www.sonystyle.com

Notes: PDA manufacturer/distributor; notable product line—CLI...; operating systems—Palm OS

Sony Ericsson

URL: www.ericsson.com

Notes: Mobile telephone manufacturer; notable product line—T68, R380 Smartphone

Symbol

URL: www.symbol.com

Notes: PDA manufacturer/distributor; notable product line—SPT, PPT PocketPC; operating systems—Palm OS, Microsoft Windows CE

Timex

URL: mobile.timex.com

Notes: Notable product line—Digital Compass

Description: Wrist PDA manufacturer/distributor

Xybernaut

URL: www.xybernaut.com

Notes: Wearable and mobile computer manufacturer; notable product line—Xybernaut Mobile Assistant Series

Wireless Carriers, Network Operators, and Related Service Providers

This appendix is organized in alphabetical order. As a quick reference, it contains only a brief sampling of telecommunications companies that provide wireless paging and Internet access services for users of mobile handheld devices. Visit www.marketingwithoutwires.com for links to more current and comprehensive information.

2Roam, Inc.

URL: www.2roam.com

Notes: Wireless Internet access services; supports mobile telephones and PDAs

AT&T Wireless Services, Inc.

URL: www.attwireless.com or www.attws.com

Notes: Mobile telephone carrier; supports TDMA, GSM, GPRS, and has plans for EDGE and WCDMA

Airtel Mûvil

URL: www.airtel.es

Notes: Mobile telephone carrier; headquartered in Madrid; supports GSM and has plans for UTMS; also offers Internet access services

Alltel

URL: www.alltel.com

Notes: Mobile telephone carrier

BT Cellnet

URL: www.btcellnet.co.uk

Notes: Mobile telephone carrier; headquartered in the United Kingdom

China Mobile Communications Corporation

URL: www.chinamobile.com

Notes: Mobile telephone carrier; headquartered in Bejing

China Netcom Corporation

URL: www.cnc.net.cn

Notes: Mobile telephone carrier; headquartered in Bejing

China Telecom

URL: www.chinatelecom.com.cn

Notes: Mobile telephone carrier

Cingular Wireless

URL: www.cingular.com

Notes: Mobile telephone carrier; supports TDMA, GSM, GPRS, and has plans for WCDMA

GoAmerica

URL: www.goamerica.net

Notes: Wireless Internet access provider; supports mobile telephones, pagers, and PDAs

Jordan Mobile Telephone Services

URL: www.jmts-fastlink.com

Notes: Mobile telephone carrier; headquartered in Amman, Jordan

Latvian Mobile Telephone

URL: www.lmt.lv

Notes: Mobile telephone carrier; headquartered in Latvia; supports GSM

MCI

URL: www.mci.com

Notes: Mobile telephone carrier; offers two-way wireless messaging through SkyTel; Internet service

Metrocall, Inc.

URL: storefront.metrocall.com

Notes: Paging provider; supports advanced messaging, alphanumeric display messaging, digital broadband, and PCS

MobileCom

URL: www.mobilecom.jo

Notes: Mobile telephone carrier; headquartered in Jordan

MobilCom AG

URL: www.mobilcom.de

Notes: Mobile telephone carrier; headquartered in Germany

Mobile Telephone Networks

URL: www.mtn.co.za

Notes: Mobile telephone carrier; headquartered in South Africa

Motient

URL: www.motient.com

Notes: Wireless Internet access services for PDA users, offers eLink wireless e-mail service; also a manufacturer/distributor for external PDA modem

Mylo Wireless Service

URL: www.mylo.com

Notes: Wireless Internet access service for Sony CLI…PDA users

NTT DoCoMo

URL: www.nttdocomo.co.jp/english

Notes: Mobile telephone carrier; headquartered in Japan, developers of iMode protocol

Nextel Communications

URL: www.nextel.com

Notes: Mobile telephone carrier; supports iDEN/TDMA, has plans for CDMA2000

Palm.net

URL: www.palm.net

Notes: Wireless Internet access for PDA users plus a Web-based portal with downloadable applications

SkyTel Communications

URL: www.skytel.com

Notes: Paging provider; supports one-way e-mail and voice messaging, two-way alphanumeric paging

Smart Communications

URL: www.smart.com.ph

Notes: Mobile telephone carrier; cellular mobile telephone network provider, paging network

Southern LINC

URL: www.southernlinc.com

Notes: Mobile telephone carrier, text and numeric paging, wireless Internet access

Qwest Communications

URL: www.qwestwireless.com

Notes: Mobile telephone carrier; offers DSL, wireless, and Internet services to individuals and businesses

Retevisiûn S.A.

URL: www.retevision.es

Notes: Mobile telephone carrier; headquartered in Barcelona; voice, data, and Internet access services

Sprint PCS

URL: www.sprintpcs.com

Notes: Mobile telephone carrier; supports CDMA and has plans for CDMA2000

Telefûnica

URL: www.telefonica.es

Notes: Mobile telephone carrier; headquartered in Madrid; serves a large population of Spanish and Portuguese-speaking users

Verizon Wireless

URL: www.verizonwireless.com

Notes: Mobile telephone carrier; supports CDMA and has plans for CDMA2000

Vodafone

URL: www.vodafone.com

Notes: Worldwide mobile telecommunications network; mobile operations in 28 countries across five continents

VoiceStream Wireless

URL: www.voicestream.com

Notes: Mobile telephone carrier; supports GSM and GPRS

Solution Providers

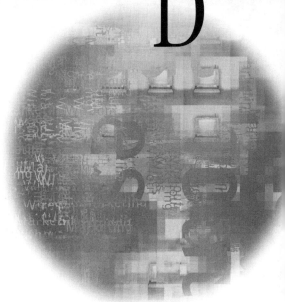

This appendix is organized in alphabetical order. As a quick reference, it contains only a brief sampling of companies that provide solutions for wireless marketing initiatives. Visit www.marketingwithoutwires.com for links to more current and comprehensive information.

AdForce

URL: www.adforce.com

Notes: Wireless advertising solution provider

Advertising.com

URL: www.advertising.com

Notes: An advertising network that can reach all online media, including e-mail, the Web, and wireless

Aerie Networks

URL: www.aerienetworks.com

Notes: Managed wireless network services

Aether Systems

URL: www.aethersystems.com

Notes: Wireless information, software, and transaction services for mobile device users and systems engineering

Air2Web

URL: www.air2web.com

Notes: mobile Internet platform and business solutions provider; offers wireless solutions for enterprise applications; enables enterprises to create, deploy, and deliver branded applications to users of Web-enabled mobile telephones, pagers, and PDAs

Airvertise

URL: www.airvertise.com

Notes: Wireless advertising solutions provider; supports WAP

ALT Mobile

URL: www.altmobile.com

Notes: Developer of the Wireless Ad Server and the Wireless Messaging Server; supports WAP and SMS carriers

AlterEgo

URL: www.alterego.com

Notes: Seller of mobile Web server platforms; assists enterprises with distributing content to mobile users

AvantGo

URL: www.avantgo.com

Notes: Wireless advertising solution provider, enterprise-class mobile solutions provider for individual users and businesses, includes mobile marketing and m-commerce solutions, workforce solutions, mobile Internet service; enables users to select and specify URLs for Web clipping and content synchronization to PDAs

Bluefish

URL: www.bluefish.com

Notes: Bundled solution for on-the-spot wireless data transmission to mobile telephone and PDA users; useful for transmitting documents to trade show attendees

DiscoPro

URL: www.discopro.com

Notes: Delivers discounts and promotions to wireless users

DoubleClick

URL: www.doubleclick.com

Notes: Wireless advertising solutions provider

GeePS

URL: www.geeps.com

Notes: Wireless advertising solutions provider

GoZing

URL: www.gozing.com

Notes: Distributes wireless promotions and coupons

Handspring

URL: www.handspring.com

Notes: Solutions training, education, and solutions provider to enterprises that are interested in deploying mobile devices; works with Extended Systems to offer mobile data and device management software

JP Mobile

URL: www.jpmobile.com

Notes: Software and applications solution provider that enables enterprises to offer wireless connectivity to users and employees

Mobile Affiliates

URL: www.mobileaffiliates.com

Notes: An affiliate network for wireless sites; connects e-retailers with wireless Web masters

NetMorf

URL: www.netmorf.com

Notes: Mobile business platform provider; offers wireless applications that give service professionals mobile access to project information

Openwave Systems

URL: www.openwave.com

Notes: Software and service provider for wireless corporate Internet/intranet access; offers instant messaging

Profilium

URL: www.profilium.com

Notes: Wireless advertising solutions provider

SkyGo

URL: www.skygo.com

Notes: Wireless marketing solutions and technology provider that creates and delivers advertising to mobile handheld device users; aggregator of wireless advertising inventory

Synchrologic

URL: www.synchrologic.com

Notes: Mobile and wireless infrastructure solution provider for the enterprise

TellShare

URL: www.tellshare.com

Notes: Distributes wireless promotions and coupons

Vicinity Corporation

URL: www.vicinity.com

Notes: Internet and wireless marketing infrastructure solutions provider

WindWire

URL: www.windwire.com

Notes: Wireless advertising solutions provider

Wireless Opinion

URL: www.wirelessopinion.com/en/

Notes: Conducts market and opinion research via wireless devices

Zagme

URL: www.zagme.com

Notes: Wireless advertising solutions provider

Index

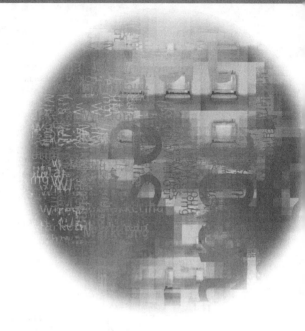